The Hidden Face of Eve

Nawal El Saadawi

Dedicated to Zeinab Shoukry, the great woman who
lived and died without giving me her name –
my mother.

Other Zed Books by Nawal El Saadawi
Woman at Point Zero
God Dies by the Nile
The Circling Song

The Hidden Face of Eve
Women in the Arab World

Nawal El Saadawi

Translated and edited by
Dr. Sherif Hetata

Zed Books Ltd

The Hidden Face of Eve was first published in Arabic.
It was first published in English by Zed Books Ltd,
7 Cynthia Street, London N1 9JF, UK and
165 First Avenue, Atlantic Highlands,
New Jersey 07716, USA, in 1980.

Cover designed by Andrew Corbett.
Cover illustration by Phyllis Mahon.
Typeset by Lyn Caldwell.
Printed and bound in the United Kingdom
by Redwood Books, Trowbridge.

Ninth impression, 1995.

ISBN 0 905762 50 9 Cased
ISBN 0 905762 51 7 Limp

Contents

Preface to the English Edition

The oppression of women, the exploitation and social pressures to which they are exposed, are not characteristic of Arab or Middle Eastern societies, or countries of the 'Third World' alone. They constitute an integral part of the political, economic and cultural system, preponderant in most of the world — whether that system is backward and feudal in nature, or a modern industrial society that has been submitted to the far reaching influence of a scientific and technological revolution.

The situation and problems of women in contemporary human society are born of developments in history that made one class rule over another, and men dominate over women. They are the product of class and sex.

But there are still many thinkers — men of science, writers, and social or political leaders — who close their eyes to this fact. They wish to separate the arduous struggles of women for self-emancipation from the revolt of people everywhere, men and women, against the present structure of society. Yet it is only this radical change that can end foreign and national class exploitation for all time *and* abolish the ascendancy of men over women not only in society, but also within the family unit which constitutes the core of patriarchal class relations. This core of relations remains the origin of the values and sanctified beliefs which throughout the ages have cemented, reinforced and perpetuated a system of class and patriarchal oppression, despite all the changes which society has known since the first human communities were constituted on earth.

Influential circles, particularly in the Western imperialist world, depict the problems of Arab women as stemming from the substance and values of Islam, and simultaneously depict the retarded development of Arab countries in many important areas as largely the result of religious and cultural factors, or even inherent characteristics in the mental and psychic constitution of the Arab peoples. For tnem underdevelopment is not related to economic and political factors, at the root of which lies foreign exploitation of resources, and the plunder to which national riches are exposed. For them there is no link between political and economic emancipation and the processes related to growth, development, and progress.

Development in such circles is visualized as a process of cultural change, of modernization along the lines of Western life, of technological advance which would permit better utilization of the resources, quicker and bigger profits, and more effective and efficient ways of pumping out oil from under the shifting desert sands or the depths of ocean beds. All this under one condition, and one condition only: such resources must continue to serve the interests of international capitalism and the multinational giants that still rule over a large part of the world. It must be submitted to the laws of unequal exchange and ruthless exploitation.

Some Arab and Islamic countries have been the theatre of such modernization processes at the hands of national governments and rulers largely controlled by Western interests. The result has been nothing more than a form of pseudo-development, a dual system composed of a small modern sector linked to the interests of multinationals and a large traditional agricultural sector producing for export, a population where a restricted minority shares in some of the gains while the vast majority sink from poverty to ever deeper destitution, a ruling class fed on opulence and wealth and the masses fed on deprivation and a loaf of bread or a bowl of rice. The income and profits generated from this form of development stream into the strongrooms of Western banks and the coffers of international corporations, while the gap between the 'developed' and the 'developing' grows ever wider and deeper. In the United States of America, the 360 billion dollar a year oil industry's 'official' profits for the five sister oil corporations increased in 1978 by as much as 343% over the previous year, while in the Arab countries a million children still die annually before reaching one year of age, as a result of poverty, sickness and malnutrition. Their intake of essential food items such as proteins and vitamins is only one-tenth of that fed to dogs and cats in the United States of America.

With the ever growing chasm which separates a minority of rich who own the wealth and control the power of nations, and the vast majority worn out by exhaustion, toil, sickness and hunger, problems are daily growing more acute, conflicts becoming more sharp and bitter, popular explosions more frequent, and everywhere the struggle of developing peoples for freedom, independence and social equality a widespread phenomenon which is shaking the foundations of an imperialist system built on social, racial and sexual discrimination. In almost every country of the 'Third World' the conflict between classes in its open and clandestine, legal and illegal manifestations is growing with each passing day.

The Iranian Revolution of 1978-79, which swept before it the Pahlavi dynasty, is an indication that people in the underdeveloped countries are no longer able to stand the growing pressures of an economic crisis that is affecting wider and wider sections of the urban and rural workers, the middle classes, the intellectuals and the national bourgeoisie, and burdening the life of millions, both men and women, whose existence is already one long trail of suffering from birth to death. Yet in Iran the Shah was the self-proclaimed leader of a modernization process which, it was said, had brought increasing prosperity to the country, but which in fact had only engendered incalculable riches for a handful of corrupt, degenerate and sanguinary despots, and a train of misery and death for those who worked the fields, operated the machines, ran the schools and colleges, and turned the wheels of everyday administration and business in a country where oil revenues had attained $9 billion a year.

The Revolution in Iran, therefore, is in its essence political and economic. It is a popular explosion which seeks to emancipate the people of Iran, both men and women, and not to send women back to the prison of the veil, the kitchen and the bedroom. The Iranian Revolution has lifted the banners of Islam overhead, as banners of freedom from imperialist oppression in the economic, social and cultural life of more than thirty-seven million people. For Islam in its essence, in its fundamental teachings, in its birth and development under the leadership of Mahomet, was a call to liberate the slave, a call to social equality and public ownership of wealth in its earliest form, that of a 'House' or 'Bank' in which all surplus wealth was to be deposited and used for feeding and clothing and housing the poor. Early Islam laid the first foundations of what might be called a Primitive Socialism, for the money deposited in the 'House of Wealth' belonged to all Muslims equally, irrespective of their tribe or class. But Primitive Socialism in Islam did not last long. It was soon buried under the growing prosperity of the new classes that arose and thrived after Mahomet's death, and that increased their influence when the Muslim warriors burst beyond the narrow frontiers of the Arab desert and flowed out from the burning sands into the green valleys of Syria, Iraq and Egypt. Primitive Socialism received its first blows at the hands of Osman Ibn Affan, the Fourth Caliph of the Muslims and head of the Ommayad dynasty in Damascus.

Thus arose in Islam the struggle that began, and was never to end, between those who hoped or believed or fought for social justice, freedom and equality, and those who stood for class privilege, feudal oppression and whose descendants were later to side with the Turkish domination, with French, British, Italian and German colonialism and later with international imperialism headed by the United States of America.

Thus it came about that, from the time of Osman Ibn Affan in the Eighth Century A.D., history was to plunge the Arab Islamic peoples into a long night of feudal oppression and foreign domination reaching its darkest depths under the Turkish Empire which, ever since it conquered and ruled, has symbolized what is most corrupt, degenerate, obscurantist, inhuman and reactionary in the annals of the Arab peoples.

Thus it was also that women were condemned to toil, to hide behind the veil, to quiver in the prison of a Harem fenced in by high walls, iron bars, windowless rooms, and the ever present eunuchs on guard with their swords.

In their quest for liberation from the injustices and oppression exercised against them by foreign invaders and internal feudal rulers, the Arab peoples could see no hope except in the application of those principles of social equality, freedom and justice which constituted the essence of Islamic teachings. This explains why the great majority of revolutionary Arab leaders who fought against feudal despotism in its various forms, internal or external,

and later against colonialism, as well as the pioneers and thinkers who played
a role in the cultural and intellectual development of the Arab peoples particularly during the reawakening of the 19th and early 20th century were also
leaders and pioneers in Islam. We can cite as eminent examples Gamal El
Dine El Afghani, Abdel Rahman El Kawakbi, Abdallah Nadeem, and Sheikh
Mohammed Abdou. It is both interesting and significant to note that their
thought and action not only aimed at the liberation of Arab peoples from the
rapid expansion of colonialism in its economic, political and military forms,
and from the oppression of feudal regimes, but also dealt with problems
related to women's status and the need to draw them into the mainstream of
life and of the struggle for emancipation.

The Iranian Revolution of today, therefore, is a natural heritage of the
historical struggle for freedom and social equality among Arab peoples, who
have continued to fight under the banner of Islam and to draw their inspiration from the teachings of the Koran and the Prophet Mahomet. Thus it is that
Islam, a religion characterized not only by its philosophical and theological
content, but also by the fact that since the early days it penetrated into the
arena of politics and also embraced the economic and social aspects of everyday life, has been and still is the banner and inspiration for conflicting forces
— for feudalism, oppression and reaction on the one hand, and for the freedom fighters and martyrs in the cause of Arab liberation on the other.

The past years have witnessed a growing conflict which is being fought
out on the basis of Islam, between the forces of progress, and those of imperialism and reaction. As the contradictions in the world of today grow deeper
and more acute, the battle for people's minds and convictions is expanding
in scope and complexity. This battle is being fought in all areas. Islam is one
of the essential arenas because it spreads its influence over crucial regions of
the world, rich in resources and human potential. The conflicts within Islam
are directly related to the struggle for control of the oil fields.

Since Islam still exercises a profound influence over the eighty million
people who constitute the Arab world, both the forces of reaction and those
who stand for freedom and progress are waging a battle to win the support
of the vast majority who still base their attitudes and behaviour towards
many of the problems of society and of everyday life on the teachings of
Islam.

As a result, the last two decades have seen a vigorous revival in the political
and social movements of Islamic inspiration. These movements consider that
Islam can be an effective weapon in the hands of the Arab peoples against
oppression and exploitation. Parallel to this development, and related to it,
increasing efforts are being made to spread the effective utilization of Arabic
as the national language. The Algerian Revolution, which fought French
colonialism by mobilizing the Islamic potential, has also carried out a vigorous
Arabization campaign. This is characteristic also of other countries in North
Africa where French had replaced Arabic as the official language under the
colonial regime.

The movements aiming at cultural emancipation, independence and identity run parallel to and intertwine with the political and economic struggles waged by the peoples of underdeveloped countries. They are growing in depth and maturity both in North Africa and in Sub-Saharan Africa. Peoples everywhere are not only breaking the bonds of political and economic dependence, but also the cultural chains that imprison the mind. They are probing into their past, rediscovering their origins, their roots, their history; they are searching for a cultural identity, learning anew about their own civilization, moulding a personality genuine enough and strong enough and resolute enough to resist the onslaught of Western interests and to take back what was plundered over the centuries: natural resources, labour producing value, goods and profits, and the creations of intellect and culture . . . and to restore the roots that take their sustenance in the past and their nourishment in cultural heritage. For without these roots the life of a people dries up, becomes weak and futile like a tree cut off from the depths of the soil, and loses both its physical and moral force.

This vast, deep and sweeping movement for liberation is, nevertheless, exposed to serious reverses as a result of the blows directed against it from both external and internal enemies. Imperialism continues to fight back viciously and often effectively in defence of its interests in the Islamic and Arab world. In this conflict any and all weapons can be used to contain the rising movement of peoples fighting for their rights.

Among these weapons is the use of religion, the 'sword and the words of Islam'. Any ambiguity in Islamic teachings, any mistake by an Islamic leader, any misinterpretation of Islamic principles, any reactionary measure or policy by Islamic rulers can be grist to the mill of imperialist conspiracy, can be inspired by CIA provocations, can be blown up and emphasized by Western propaganda, and can be manipulated or born of intent in order to be used in fighting back against the forces of progress. Only a short while ago, the Western press orchestrated a campaign against the Iranian Revolution accusing it of being reactionary, of imposing on women the veil and the *chador,* of attempting to deprive them of the civil rights they had enjoyed under the rule of the Shah. It tried to depict what was happening in Iran as a social change geared towards the past, traditionalist, and fanatic, rather than as a political and economic movement advancing under the pressure of a militant popular uprising surprising in its depth and resoluteness. Such counter-revolutionary machinations are characterized by their variety, subtlety, and the thought given to understanding the complexity of each situation and to ways of playing skilfully on the various contradictions. Even revolutionary and leftist movements can be utilized in this 'game of nations' and become unwitting instruments in the hands of reactionary forces posing under the guises of democracy, liberalism, humanism, modernism, and human rights. The Western press suddenly discovered that 'human rights' had to be defended in Iran. Progressive feminist movements intervened on behalf of Iranian women, not realizing that sometimes the form and even the content of their intervention was being used to discredit the Iranian people's struggle against American intervention. At the same time

Western interests and agents are in fact encouraging the most conservative and orthodox forces of Islam so as to build up a rampart against the progressive wings of the Revolution by opposing Islam to the socialists and communists who are described as no more than atheistic tendencies in a society of believers.

Capitalist circles today are facing a dilemma. They are in need of Islam and utilize it as a buttress against progressive and socialist movements. But at the same time they realize that Islam has been an important force for people's liberation at various stages of its history, including contemporary Arab societies, and that once again it can play an important role in the struggle against exploitation and oppression. This explains why the United States of America has adopted such an ambiguous stance with regard to the Islamic movements in the Arab world and the Middle East, a two-faced stand characterized by an attempt to preserve and reinforce them at times, while criticizing, attacking, and weakening them at others. The essence of American policy in this regard is to strengthen the reactionary, obscurantist and fanatical wings of Islam, and to divide, weaken and distort those movements that mobilize the masses in the Arab world to take an anti-imperialist, anti-feudalist or a socialist position. Let us not forget that, at the very time of writing (mid 1979), Islamic movements in the Arab countries have opposed the Israeli/Egyptian 'Peace Treaty' which has been conceived, engineered and almost negotiated by the U.S. — a Treaty which, instead of bringing peace, has divided the Arabs, strengthened Zionism, turned the Middle East into a theatre for American military bases and intervention, and led Egypt further down the path to capitulation and a deepening political and economic crisis.

In this double dealing game with Islam, the Western powers are supported by those Islamic regimes and those political and religious leaders following in the path previously paved by their predecessors for Turkish domination, and later French and British colonialism, those who utilized Islam as an instrument of oppression against the people, and who maintained that religion believed in and defended class privileges and was opposed to disobedience against the ruler, the father, and the male, those who depicted revolt, revolution and the struggle fo freedom as the greatest of all crimes, and who considered dissatisfaction of the ordinary person with poverty, destitution and disease as heresy. For was it not God Almighty who bestowed the good things of life on people in the way which he saw fit, depriving some of the bare necessities and bestowing upon others riches and pleasure without end ? He who is a believer, therefore, must perforce accept the will of God with peace, calm and a deep satisfaction!

Religious teachings and campaigns have played, and continue to play, an important role in maintaining and reinforcing reactionary regimes. Religious obscurantism, superstition and fanaticism have been and still are dangerous instruments in the hands of those rulers or classes that wish to disarm and divide the Arab peoples, instilling in their minds and hearts the conviction that destiny is all powerful and that fatalism and resignation are the highest of virtues.

Yet all through the centuries that followed Mahomet's first establishment of Islamic rule in the Arab Peninsula, there have been religious thinkers and leaders who have insisted that Islam cannot be understood properly if it is taken simply as a conglomeration of unrelated precepts and statements. These brave people have opposed the isolation of sayings like 'And we have made you to be of different levels' or 'One above the other' or 'Men are responsible for women' from their general context and from the essential principles of Islam in order that they might be used to support backward interpretations of Islam.

The broad character of the Iranian Revolution today means that it has drawn into its ranks a wide spectrum of Islamic leaders and religious thinkers. Some of them are enlightened and progressive. Others are not and tend to cling to traditionalist Islamic beliefs. These latter are the source of the pressures being exerted on women, of interpretations that require the body and head to be covered by a *chador,* or the emancipated working woman to be isolated once more within the precincts of the house. These slogans are either upheld out of ignorance of the real principles of Islam or are part of a connected plan aimed at holding back change, dividing the ranks of the Iranian people, and facilitating the success of the numerous conspiracies that are being hatched against the Revolution behind the scenes.

There are rulers in certain Arab countries who continue to use religion against the interests of their peoples. The present Sadat regime in Egypt did everything in its power to help in the revival and strengthening of conservative Islamic movements since 1970, in order that they might be used against progressive and socialist tendencies within the country. The government not only abstained from interfering in any way with their activities, but also helped them by opening up channels for financial and political support. Women were encouraged to wear the veil, and female students wearing modernized forms of Islamic dress were a familiar sight in the streets of Egyptian cities and on the university campus. Long articles extolling the virtues of motherhood and the dangers of female participation in paid employment appeared in the newspapers, and special radio programmes talked incessantly about woman's role in the home.

The Egyptian ruling class, however, retreated rapidly from this position and envinced serious alarm bordering on panic when the same Islamic movements started to attack the Peace Treaty with Israel and to defend the rights of Palestininians. This alarm was magnified a hundred fold by the sweeping march of the Iranian people battling to destroy the heritage of a tyrannical dynasty that had ruled the country over 57 years. Since large sectors of the revolutionary forces were drawing their inspiration from Islam, it now became necessary to attack what had been defended with such remarkable ardour before.

At the same time, the Western press once again started to attack the 'fanaticism' of Islamic movements. An enthusiastic campaign was launched in defence of Iranian women condemned to the dark walls of the *chador.* Iran overnight became peopled by hundreds of thousands of women, impressive yet chilling as they stood clothed in their long black robes, while the incessant click of Western cameras carried this medieval sight to millions of readers all over the world. Yet this enthusiasm for women's rights, or even human rights, was sadly lacking when thousands of Iranian men and women were being shot to death by army guns, or assassinated or tortured in the underground cells of the Savak, or when a whole people – men, women and children – was forced to flee its land to settle in the tents of refugee camps, or when peaceful populations were being burnt to death with napalm or torn to pieces by cluster bombs.

No doubt, any attempt to force women back into the *chador* or the home is a reactionary policy, unworthy of any revolution that wishes to emancipate people and abolish exploitation and misery. It is necessary that women unite everywhere to strengthen and broaden their movement towards liberation. Solidarity between women can be a powerful force of change, and can influence future development in ways favourable not only to women but also to men. But such solidarity must be exercised on the basis of a clear understanding of what is going on in the underdeveloped countries, lest it be used to serve other purposes diametrically opposed to the cause of equality and freedom for all peoples. It is necessary at all times to see the close links between women's struggles for emancipation and the battles for national and social liberation waged by people in all parts of the 'Third World' against foreign domination and the exploitation exercised by international capitalism over human and natural resources. If this link is forgotten, feminist movements in the West may be used not to further the cause of women's liberation but instead to participate in holding back the forces of freedom and progress in the countries of Asia, Africa and Latin America.

Of course, I oppose the desire of certain religious leaders in Iran to see women covered in the *chador* or deprived of the civil rights they have gained over the years. Such religious leaders either do not understand Islam correctly or have accepted to serve a dubious cause. A religious leader is not a God, he is human and therefore liable to go wrong and to make mistakes. It is necessary that his words and actions be submitted to democratic control and critical appraisal by the people whose life he wishes to influence and even direct. He should be questioned and appraised by the women and men he is trying to lead. Iranian women have shown that they are capable of standing steadfastly against attempts to throw them back into the past. Supported by enlightened religious leaders and progressive men, they have succeeded in throwing back retrograde attempts against the status of women and their rights in society.

The religious movement of Iran is a concrete example on a higher and more advanced level of the age-long struggle that has continued in Islam between progressive political leaders and religious thinkers and those whose values and attitudes towards society are inspired by narrow class privileges and an orthodox traditionalist interpretation of Islam. An eminent leader may himself be the subject of inner contradictions so that his vision of certain aspects in the political and social struggle is enlightened, whereas his horizons in other areas remain limited and rigid. He may fight vigorously for the liberation of his country from foreign domination and yet look upon women as inferior creatures who should be subject to the will and fantasies of men. In this world of ours is it not true to say that very few are the men who not only intellectually believe in equality between men and women, but also are capable of practising it in everyday life? And is it not also correct to say that, even within the socialist movement itself, a backward position as far as women is concerned still remains characteristic and indicates that in many spheres socialist and Marxist thought and practice has still a long way to go?

Time and time again, life has proved that, whereas political and economic change can take place rapidly, social and cultural progress tends to lag behind because it is linked to the deep inner emotive and psychic processes of the human mind and heart. Men are very often the victims of such contradictions in their attitude towards women. The role of women's organizations, and of the political struggle of women, therefore continue to be crucial factors in any changes which will ultimately lead to the complete emancipation of women and to real equality between the sexes. Only through the influence exerted by political action and effective organization will this social and cultural change be possible. Such is the law of progress and the status of women is no exception. Men must come to realize, and even be compelled to make, the changes within themselves which are so necessary for human progress and which they seem so reluctant to make.

The feminist movements in the West which are devoting great efforts to the cause of women everywhere are beginning to understand the specific aspects of the situation in underdeveloped countries which have to be taken into account by women's liberation movements. For although there are certain characteristics common to these movements all over the world, fundamental differences are inevitable when we are dealing with different stages of economic, social and political development. In underdeveloped countries, liberation from foreign domination often still remains *the* crucial issue and influences the content and forms of struggle in other areas including that of women's status and role in society. Cultural differences between the Western capitalist societies and Arab Islamic countries are also of importance. If all this is not taken into account and studied with care, enthusiasm and the spirit of solidarity on its own may lead feminist movements to taking a stand that is against the interests of the liberation movements in the East, and therefore also harmful to the struggle for women's emancipation. This perhaps explains the fact that progressive circles among Iranian women adopted a somewhat neutral attitude to some American feminist figures who rushed to Iran in defence of their sisters against the reactionary male chauvinist regime 'that was threatening to imprison women behind the black folds of the *chador.*'

It is necessary to understand that the most important struggle that faces women in Arab Islamic countries is not that of 'free thought' versus 'belief in religion', nor 'feminist rights' (as understood sometimes in the West) in opposition to 'male chauvinism', nor does it aim at some of the superficial aspects of modernization characteristic of the developed world and the affluent society. In its essence, the struggle which is now being fought seeks to ensure that the Arab peoples take possession of their economic potential and resources, and of their scientific and cultural heritage so that they can develop whatever they have to the maximum and rid themselves once and for all of the control and domination exercised by foreign capitalist interests. They seek to build a free society with equal rights for all and to abolish the injustices and oppression of systems based on class and patriarchal privilege.

It is worth noting in this connection that it is precisely the current reactionary regime in Egypt, after having linked its fate to that of American and Zionist interests in the Middle East and abandoned the struggle of Arab peoples for a just and lasting peace, that started to attack the Iranian Revolution as opposed to the values of a modern civilization and the rights of women.

Our past experience has always shown that any strengthening of the links that bind the Arab peoples to Western interests inevitably leads to a retreat in all spheres of thought and action. Social progress is arrested and the most reactionary and traditionalist circles in society begin to clamour for a return to orthodoxy and dogma. The social and economic rights of the vast majority are subjected to attack, and women become the first victims of the general assault against freedom and progress. Radical social change is replaced by superficial modernization processes that affect the elitist and privileged groups in society, and the women belonging to these groups are transformed into a distorted version of the Western woman, while the vast majority of toiling women in industry, agriculture, government administration, commerce and trade, or in the teaching and liberal professions find themselves victims of increasing oppression and a sharp decline in their standards of living. Superficial processes of modernization, whether in the West or the East, will never lead to true equality between women and men in the economic, social, political and sexual aspects of life. Sexual rights as practised in many Western societies do not lead to the emancipation of women, but to an accentuated oppression where women are transformed into commercialized bodies and a source of increasing capitalist profits.

In addition, modernization processes in the West sometimes bestow 'equal rights' on that small minority of women belonging to the middle or upper classes. These find their way into business or the liberal professions and may even become Members of Parliament or Ministers. But usually such women are as conservative, if not more conservative, than the men to whose class they belong. The positions they enjoy do not serve to liberate women from the inferior position which is characteristic of such societies. On the contrary, they perpetuate inequality between men and women by masking the real situation and affording a pretence of change, whereas in fact no real change has taken place.

When Margaret Thatcher, leader of the Conservative Party, became the first woman Prime Minister of Britain during the month of May, 1979, the Western Press acclaimed this event as a significant development. And yet many people might feel that Margaret Thatcher's policies will probably lead to a deterioration in the situation of women, for it is not the mere fact of her being a woman which is important, but the class and policies she represents. A Conservative government will necessarily be antagonistic to the rights of working people, democratic liberties and socialism, and this inevitably leads to a similar position with regard to movements for women's emancipation. This will not only affect policies as regards women in England. Britain still exercises considerable influence in world affairs and particularly over a certain number of the countries in Africa and to a smaller extent in Asia.

The struggle of women in underdeveloped countries is not a narrow fanatical movement prejudiced in favour of the female sex and rising to its defence at any cost. We know that progress for women, and an improvement of their status, can never be attained unless the whole of society moves forward. We believe that fanaticism of any form should be opposed, whether religious, political or social. Victory in the long and difficult struggle for women's emancipation requires that women adopt a flexible attitude and be prepared to ally their efforts with all those who stand for progress. Women should be ready to co-operate with democratic and nationalist forces, progressive religious movements, as well as with socialist and Marxist oriented trends and organizations. It is the unified efforts of all these forces that permitted the Iranian people to carry through a successful revolution against the 57 year old rule of the Pahlavi dynasty, and it is this unified effort that remains the main guarantee for its future development. This explains why the enemies of the Iranian people are concentrating on attempts to divide these forces, to play one off against the other. In these divisive attempts, any slogan and any force can be utilized as long as it serves the main purpose — no matter whether that force be progressive or retrograde, capitalist or socialist, democratic or rigid and fanatical, chauvinistic and racialist or internationalist. The women's liberation movement is no exception.

Women have always been an integral part of the national liberation movement in the countries of Asia, Africa, the Middle East and Latin America. They fought side by side with the men in Algeria against French colonialism, and as part of the Palestine Liberation Organization's struggle against Zionist and imperialist aggressive policies aimed at depriving the Palestinian people of their national right to self-determination. And women fought too in Yemen against the British occupation and Arab reactionary intrigues, in Mozambique against Portuguese colonialism and Rhodesian punitive expeditions, in Vietnam against successive armed invasions of their country by the French, the Japanese, the Americans and now the Chinese.

Through their participation in the struggle for national liberation and for economic and social reconstruction they have gained many rights. Nevertheless, once the new systems of government are in place, whether national democratic or socialist, they very often cease to advance in a significant manner as far as women's status in society is concerned. This is noticeable in the socialist regimes of Eastern Europe, in Algeria after independence, and in other countries like North Korea, China and even Vietnam. This is due mainly to the fact that women have not succeeded in becoming a well organized political force capable of ensuring adequate representation for themselves at all levels of government and administration, as well as in the political institutions and structures built up after the national or social revolution in society. Despite the crucial role they play in all fields of economic and social endeavour in the factories, fields, social services, different professions and at home, and the fact that they represent half the population in each country, their representation within the political power structure is always limited to a minority, and sometimes even a very restricted minority.

The new ruling classes and governments are composed of men, and have a tendency quickly to forget the problems faced by women, or at least not to give them the attention and effort that are required. Instead of attempting to sweep away patriarchal class relations within the family, these are maintained in one form or another, and the values related to them continue to hold sway.

The changes that have taken place in the Arab countries are characterized by a shift from feudalistic structures to capitalism, and sometimes even to early stages of socialist orientation. These changes are usually accompanied by an accelerated industrialization which requires a rapid expansion of labour outside the home and which draws hundreds of thousands of both men and women into the production process and the numerous services and organizations that grow up. Families migrate in large numbers from the rural areas to the cities which tend to swell at a phenomenal rate (anything from a 4% to 13% annual increase in the population). Working women not only grow in numbers but they face a whole range of new problems resulting from the social changes to which they are exposed. They are deprived of the support, assistance and numerous functions that were previously afforded by the extended family system. Their children used to be cared for and looked after by members of the extended family whenever work called their mothers to the fields or elsewhere. Social, psychological and even financial support was forthcoming, and numerous tasks were undertaken in common so as to alleviate the burdens of every day life. The extended family carried out a wide variety of social functions. Migration to the city and social change in general are doing away with this unit, which is now being replaced by the nuclear family. But the nuclear family is incapable of performing the same role, and no other institution has grown up to substitute itself for the structures that once existed, and so be capable of undertaking what the extended family system once did for the family members and particularly the mother.

In this new situation, men have continued to wash their hands of any responsibility at home and to evade many of the responsibilities in society and public life, responsibilities related to the need for a new organization of social life capable of solving the problems faced by women both at work and in the home. Women continue to bear the double or even triple burden constituted by their new roles in society and at the work place, combined with their old roles at home, towards the husband, the children and sometimes relatives such as fathers, mothers, brothers, sisters and even cousins.

Whereas society has thrown overboard certain values that were an obstacle to the participation of women in the labour force, it has continued to uphold many old values with remarkable obstinacy, and in particular those values which ensure a continued exploitation of their efforts in caring for the home, husband and children, efforts which also continue to remain unpaid. It has extolled the work of women and their right to education, and torn down social walls and fences that prevented women from becoming a freely circulating part of the labour force. Nevertheless, it continues to reinforce those values that bind women to their children and husbands in servitude; it continues to sing the virtues of sweet motherhood, to maintain (as in some Islamic circles) that 'Paradise lies under the feet of mothers' and that obedience to the husband is the highest of qualities in a woman and a mark of obedience to Almighty Allah. To this very day, an Egyptian woman with work and a career, even if she be a Minister, is still governed by the law of obedience consecrated in the Egyptian Marriage Code. When a woman succumbs to the innumerable burdens in her job and in the home, or is unable to give her husband and children the care that is expected of her, she is not spared. Accusations are heaped on her head, not the least of which is that, by neglecting her children and not submitting herself to the husband's will and needs, she is contributing to the dissolution of 'sacred family bonds'.

Society pays great attention to preserving 'sacred family bonds' and yet cares little about what happens in matters without which the preservation of these 'sacred bonds' becomes no more than an illusion. The man's absolute right to divorce in Arab Islamic countries, to marriage with more than one wife and to a legalized sexual licentiousness all negate any real security and stability for children, and destroy the very essence of true family life. Society raises up 'motherhood' to the heavens and yet at the same time forgets to provide the facilities and means necessary for mothers to bring up their children appropriately. A woman is rarely given enough time to nurse her child, and the periods of leave afforded to her before and after giving birth to her baby are sadly inadequate.

The insistence that society has so far displayed in preserving the formal structure of the family, while depriving it of any genuine substantive content, is related to the desire of exploiting classes and the political powers that represent them to ensure that the economic functions of the family be maintained and that the family continues to bear the burden and costs of rearing children instead of these becoming the responsibility of the social system. The woman remains a source of free labour and of numerous services that would have to be compensated and paid for if other institutional arrangements were to take over her functions in the home. To prevent people from discovering the truths that lie at the basis of this touching attachment to the family system, society has all along reinforced the links between mother love or family love and the upkeep, nourishment and rearing of children. As though motherly or family affection must and can only express itself in assuming unaided responsibility for their economic needs. At the same time the inequality, injustice and poverty which characterize the lives of the vast majority of people in Arab countries deprive them of any real possibility of performing adequately the functions for which the family system was created and is still maintained. The vast majority of families cannot provide their children with the required economic means. Most mothers suffer hunger, deprivation and a state of exhaustion which renders them unfit to nourish their babies or even look after them. Without food their breasts dry up, without the basic needs of life their affection withers. Deprived of everything, they lose their capacity to give. Withered to the core by years of labour in the fields and in the home, their youth ebbs away in a matter of years, leaving a broken body and a drying soul — a useless forgotten human being whose lot it is to be cast aside for a younger and more attractive woman.

Women who are educated may find more rewarding occupations and a career. Nevertheless, in most cases, the husband will continue to dominate over her, to take possession of her earnings, and to threaten her with divorce whenever she tries to loosen his grip or refuses to respond to his fantasies. Patriarchal norms and values continue to reign in the home, the street, the school, the mosque and the place of work, and even in the concepts and attitudes propagated through radio programmes, T.V., films, the theatre, newspapers and magazines.

This is the situation of most women in the Arab countries. Yet I cannot agree with those women in America and Europe who draw sharp distinctions between their own situation and that of women in the region to which I belong, and who believe that there are fundamental differences. They tend to depict our life as a continual submission to medieval systems, and point vehemently to some of the rituals and traditional practices such as female circumcision. They raise a hue and cry in defence of the victims, write long articles and deliver speeches at congresses. Of course, it is good that female circumcision be denounced. But by concentrating on such manifestations there is a risk that the real issues of social and economic change be evaded or even forgotten, and that effective action be replaced by a feeling of superior humanity, a glow of satisfaction that may blind the mind and feelings to the concrete everyday struggle for women's emancipation.

I am against female circumcision and other similar retrograde and cruel practices. I was the first Arab woman to denounce it publicly and to write about it in my book, *Woman and Sex*. I linked it to the other aspects of female oppression. But I disagree with those women in America and Europe who concentrate on issues such as female circumcision and depict them as proof of the unusual and barbaric oppression to which women are exposed only in African or Arab countries. I oppose all attempts to deal with such problems in isolation, or to sever their links with the general economic and social pressures to which women everywhere are exposed, and with the oppression which is the daily bread fed to the female sex in developed and developing countries, in both of which a patriarchal class system still prevails.

Women in Europe and America may not be exposed to surgical removal of the clitoris. Nevertheless, they are victims of cultural and psychological clitoridectomy. 'Lift the chains off my body, put the chains on my mind.' Sigmund Freud was perhaps the most famous of all those men who taught psychological and physiological circumcision of women when he formulated his theory on the psychic nature of women, described the clitoris as a male organ, and sexual activity related to the clitoris as an infantile phase, and when he maintained that maturity and mental health in a woman required that sexual activity related to the clitoris cease and be transferred to the vagina.

No doubt, the physical ablation of the clitoris appears a much more savage and cruel procedure than its psychological removal. Nevertheless, the consequences can be exactly the same, since the end result is the abolition of its functions so that its presence or absence amount to the same thing. Psychological surgery might even be more malicious and harmful because it tends to produce the illusion of being complete, whereas in actual fact the body may have lost an essential organ, like a child born an idiot yet provided with brain substance. It can create the illusion of being free, whereas in actual fact freedom has been lost.

To live in an illusion, not to know the truth is the most dangerous of all things for a human being, woman or man, because it deprives people of their most important weapon in the struggle for freedom, emancipation and control of their lives and future. To be conscious that you are still a slave still living under oppression is the first step on the road to emancipation.

We the women in Arab countries realize that we are still slaves, still oppressed, not because we belong to the East, not because we are Arab, or members of Islamic societies, but as a result of the patriarchal class system that has dominated the world since thousands of years.

To rid ourselves of this system is the only way to become free. Freedom for women will never be achieved unless they unite into an organized political force powerful enough and conscious enough and dynamic enough to truly represent half of society. To my mind the real reason why women have been unable to complete their emancipation, even in the socialist countries, is that they have failed to constitute themselves into a political force powerful, conscious, and dynamic enough to impose their rights.

More and more women are being drawn into the struggle for social transformation in the Arab countries. Many of them, however, still believe that the cause of women's liberation is purely a woman's problem, or a particular social change related to the family, to the husband, or to children, a problem which is completely separate and distinct, unrelated to the major political issues in society, or to the struggle for socialism, freedom and democracy.

However, the experience and mistakes of the past have contributed towards a growing maturity among the women and men who are playing a leading role in progressive social movements and parties. Many of them are realizing more clearly the need to bridge the gap between political and civil life, between the general issues of society and the personal problems and needs related to each individual, between the broad functioning of government in society and the daily participation of people in the solution of their own problems and the running of their own affairs. They feel the need for a modern theory of social transformation that links thought to action, intellect to feeling and emotion, and that is able to build up a new and higher relationship between women and men in their struggle for a better world.

This new concept of society, and of the processes related to its transformation, must be able to concretize the relationships between the general oppression of both men and women, and the specific forms of oppression to which women alone are exposed for no other reason than that they are women. In other words, there is an urgent and vital need to visualize the links between the political, economic and social remoulding of society, and the cultural, moral, psychological, sexual and affective remoulding of the human being, and to blaze the trails along which this process must advance.

The creation of a woman's movement in each Arab country, capable of mobilizing the women in every home, village, town or city, of drawing into its ranks the illiterate peasant woman, the female factory worker, the educated professional woman, will mean that the Arab movement for democracy, progress and socialism is capable of reaching every woman, and is attaining the stage where it is a real mass movement and not just the instrument of a specific class.

It is Arab women alone who can formulate the theory, the ideas and the modes of struggle needed to liberate themselves from all oppression. It is their efforts alone that can create a new Arab woman, alive with her own originality, capable of choosing what is most genuine and valuable in her cultural tradition, as well as assimilating the progress of science and modern thought. Conscious Arab women who no longer live under the illusion that freedom will come as a gift from the Heavens, or be bestowed upon them by the chivalry of men, but understand that the road to freedom is long and arduous, and that the price to pay is heavy. Such women alone are those that will lead others to total emancipation. Such Arab women will not hesitate because they know that, if the price to pay for freedom is heavy, the price of slavery is even heavier.

Nawal El Saadawi
Cairo
1979

Introduction

Long years of medical practice in both urban and rural areas, and the men and women who day after day rang my door bell and stepped across the threshold of my home, carrying their load of psychological and sexual problems, have led me to write this book.

Many are those who might think that this study will deal only with women – their families, or children, or husbands – and the emotional and sexual stresses which face them in life. Traditionally studies dealing with women have occupied a place way down at the end of the list, because they were considered of a limited nature, dealing with a special group, and with problems that are inevitably narrow in scope. For is not the world of women limited to the family, to children and to the home? And how can this small world compete with the great political and human issues of our time: freedom, justice, or the future of socialism, which sway our passions and thoughts?

And yet any attempt to undertake an in-depth study of woman's status in society, if freed from the attitude which considers her only as a means of reproduction, will lead inevitably to an examination of a much broader range of issues related to all aspects of human life. It carries us into the realm of general concerns related to politics, or more precisely it becomes a political cause of the first order intertwined with the never ending struggle for freedom and truth.

For the 'higher' politics of any country are a construction built up of many small bricks, of details that weave themselves into the general pattern. These details are the personal needs, problems and desires of individuals. The personal lives of people and their requirements are the directing and motivating force which are translated in the final analysis into a political will, into policies, and into the politics of a country. This personal life obviously includes the intricacies of sex, the relations between man and woman, and the relations of production and division of labour. Those who see fit to underrate the problems of women, and of sex, ignore or do not understand the principles of politics. It is no longer possible to escape the fact that the underprivileged status of women, their relative backwardness, leads to an essential backwardness in society as a whole. For this very reason it is necessary to see the emancipation of women as an integral part of the struggle against all forms of oppression, and of the efforts made to emancipate all exploited

1

classes and groups in society, both politically and sexually.

Numerous are those who still deny that Arab women have lagged behind
in the social development of our region, and who refuse to see the problems
with which they are relentlessly assailed. Such an attitude, apart from its
fundamental dishonesty, is a serious disservice to the cause of progress in the
Arab countries. A sincere attachment to this cause requires that we expose
our weaknesses rather than attempting to cover them up. This is necessary
if we are to overcome them.

During the past years a number of serious studies have been published, and
have contributed to the unmasking of many social ills that require a radical
cure if Arab society is to attain real freedom in all fields of endeavour whether
economic, political, human, or moral. Among the studies carried out by Arab
scholars I would like to mention that of Halim Barakat published under the
title *The River With No Embankments*. He shows how Israel took advantage
of the 'sexual sensitivities' of traditionalist Palestinian Arabs to stir up the
waves of emigration during the successive wars that were fought between the
years 1948 and 1967. Apart from aerial bombardment, one of the factors that
forced the Arabs to leave the West Bank of Jordan during the 1967 war was
their desire to protect the 'honour' of their womenfolk. It is easy to understand therefore why some of the Arab militants insisted that the word *A'ard*
(honour) be replaced in the Arab dictionary by the word *Ard* (meaning land).*

It is thus that we come to realize the connection between a personal issue
such as female virginity and a critically salient political event such as the
migration of large groups of Arab refugees, which facilitated territorial
occupation of their lands by Israel. This is only one example among many
others which proves that importance should be given to the study of problems
related to girls and women, and to the different aspects of sexual and moral
relations in our society, by all those who have a genuine interest in the future
of our countries.

During the past years I have published a number of books in the Arab
countries dealing with these questions. But among all these books, it is
Woman and Sex which has aroused the widest interest among different
sections of public opinion. The first edition was rapidly exhausted and since
then several reprints have been necessary to meet a growing demand for the
book. Shortly after it appeared, I realized that I was now sitting on the edge
of a volcano, listening to its distant rumblings coming ever closer. And day by
day the avalanche of letters, telephone calls and visits from young and old,
men and women, grew steadily, most of them asking for a way out of problems, most of them friendly or desperate, and a few, very few, menacing.

I got used to the repeated rings of my door bell, to the dim form of letters
behind the glass of the small wooden box, to the subdued call of the
telephone, to the shy hesitant steps crossing the floor of my office or the hall

*See the preface written by Sabha el Khalili to the volume, *Woman and Sex*,
by Nawal el Saadawi published in Jerusalem by the Guy Printing Press
(May 1974).

in my small suburban apartment. Some started to come even from neighbouring Arab countries.

To those who came I opened my door, my thoughts and my heart. But as time went by I began to feel how heavy the burden had now become, how troubling the responsibility could be. For the problems of women and men in our society are without end, without solution unless a sustained and ever greater effort is made to lay bare our failings and to expose them right down to their root causes, their real causes in the political, social, economic, sexual and historical structures upon which our life has been built. Many letters demanded of me that I undertake these efforts and go further. For me this was a source of concern, but also a source of happiness and support. Now I had come to know more firmly than at any other time that the great majority of men and women in our society carry a thirst for greater knowledge and understanding, and a sharp hunger for further progress.

However it was also natural that a small minority express their fear, or even panic, at words written by a pen sharp as a scalpel that cuts through tissue to expose the throbbing nerves and arteries embedded deep in a body. It was the panic of those accustomed to darkness, faced suddenly by a searching light. Some of the letters I received called upon me to refrain from publishing the facts and knowledge which I had gathered with an impatient patience over many years. Their call was like a hand raised to shield the eyes from an unexpected light. And another minority from among 'those who wield power and authority' decided that I should be deprived of my job as Director of Health Education in the Egyptian Ministry of Public Health and of my right to publish the magazine, *Health*, whose Board had chosen me as Editor-in-Chief.

But such events, however painful they might be, have not and will not dampen my enthusiasm or slow down my efforts. My pen will continue to lay bare the facts, clarify the issues, and identify what I believe is the truth.

For I am firmly convinced that real harm only comes from an attempt to cover up the truth about 'Women and Sex', rather than searching for it and making it known. The truth sometimes shocks, or shakes the tranquillity of set ideas. But sometimes a good shake can awaken minds that rest in slumber, and open eyes to see what is really happening around them.

There is no doubt that to write about women in Arab society, especially if the author is herself a woman, is to tread on difficult and sensitive areas. It is like picking your way through territory heavy with visible and hidden mines. Almost every step might touch an electrified wire, a sanctified and sacred spot which is meant to be untouchable, a value that is not to be questioned because it is a part of the religious and moral structures that rear themselves up like heavy iron bars whenever questions related to women are raised and hands stretched out to set her free.

Religion, in particular, is a weapon often used in traditionalist societies to cut short, and even cut down, the efforts of researchers, and seekers after truth. I have come to see more and more clearly that religion is most often used in our day as an instrument in the hands of economic and political forces, as an institution utilized by those who rule to keep down those who

3

are ruled. In this it serves the same purpose as juridical, educational, police and even psychiatric systems used to perpetuate the patriarchal family, historically born, reinforced, and maintained by the oppression of women, children and slaves. Thus in any society it is not possible to separate religion from the political system, nor to keep sex separate from politics.

The trilogy composed of politics, religion and sex is the most sensitive of all issues in any society. This sensitivity is particularly acute in developing countries with a rural background and culture, and where feudal relations are predominant. The industrial, technological and scientific progress achieved in Europe played a vital role in ridding the culture of its peoples from the powerful influence of feudalism and outdated values in the realms of religion and sex. This process was only made possible through a bitter struggle against the church. The conflict was a reflection of the antagonism between the rising forces of capitalism and those vested interests which were linked to the Middle Ages and the institutions of feudalism. As in all social conflicts, victims were sacrificed on the way, men and women of culture and intellect some of whom were accused of defying the precepts of the church and burnt alive at the stake: men like Giordano Bruno, who proclaimed that the earth was sweeping the heavens in a continuous movement round the sun, or the ever famous Joan of Arc. But the day came when this conflict ended in the victory of the new capitalist forces over the church and its religious leaders. Such is the logic of human history, an inexorable logic where economic factors gain the upper hand even against religion.

For the life of people and their essential needs are dependent on economics and not on religion. Throughout human history the standards and values of religion have themselves been shaped by the economy. The oppression of women in any society is in its turn an expression of an economic structure built on land ownership, systems of inheritance and parenthood, and the patriarchal family as an inbuilt social unit. Yet although human history has proved time and again that the underprivileged position of women, and the oppression to which they have been exposed throughout most ages, are an offshoot of the socio-economic system, many writers and analysts maintain, even today, that religion is the root cause. This is particularly true when Western sources deal with the situation of Arab women, and try to explain the problems that beset them as arising from the attitudes and values and nature of Islam as compared with other religions. This belief is perhaps a result of an incomplete or biased understanding of Islam and of the role it has played in social change. It may even spring from a biased evaluation of Islamic precepts and systems, or constitute an attempt to conceal the real facts and to cover up the vested economic interests of certain ruling classes who are closely linked to the forces of neo-colonialism.

In some of the countries that constitute the Arab region, or come under the category of 'Third World', many local vested interests have co-operated with the forces of neo-colonialism in a continuous, carefully designed campaign that utilizes religion and its teachings to confuse, misguide and misinform the people. The banners of religion have been utilized in one way or another to pump more oil out of Saudi Arabia, to overthrow Mossadeq and restore the rule of the oil monopolies in Iran, to close down on Sukarno and perpetrate mass murder on an unprecedented scale in Indonesia, to crush Salvador Allende and establish a military dictatorship in Chile built on cannons, machine guns, prisons and the daily echo of heavy boots marching down the streets. Religion has played its role also in the assassination of Mujib Abdel Rahman in Bangladesh and in the fratricidal war being waged for long months in Lebanon, a war which is no more than a new conspiracy to stem the rising forces of nationalism, democracy and progress. In the name of religion thousands of people in the countries of the Arab region have faced, and are facing, a horrible death. And in Egypt, under the guise of religion, the forces of obscurantism, orthodoxy and exploitation are banding together in an attempt to deprive people of their daily bread, of their most vital necessities in order to serve the interest of the few. The very same forces simultaneously proclaim that the place of women is in the home, and seek to establish a more modern version of the harem. It is these forces which stand behind the barbaric circumcision to which girls are subjected in some Arab countries, even today. Amputation of the clitoris and sometimes even of the external genital organs goes hand in hand with brainwashing of girls, with a calculated merciless campaign to paralyze their capacity to think and to judge and to understand. For down the ages a system has been built up which aims at destroying the ability of women to see the exploitation to which they are subjected, and to understand its causes. A system which portrays the situation of women as a destiny prescribed by the Creator who made them as they are, females, and therefore a lesser species of the human race.

Any serious study of comparative religion will show clearly that in the very essence of Islam, as such, the status of women is no worse than it is in Judaism or in Christianity. In fact the oppression of women is much more glaring in the ideology of Christianity and Judaism. The veil was a product of Judaism long before Islam came into being. It was drawn from the Old Testament where women were abjured to cover their heads when praying to Jehovah, whereas men could remain bareheaded because they had been created in the image of God. Thus arose the belief that women are incomplete, a body without a head, a body completed only by the husband, who alone possesses a head.

From this followed the surgical and mental circumcision that was performed on girls and women in non-Islamic societies in the form of the chastity belt, a shield of steel locked around the lower belly, and in numerous forms of suppression and discrimination exercised over females ever since the patriarchal family came into being.

Before the patriarchal family, which was built on land ownership, inheritance, patrilineal relations, and the oppression of slaves and women, arose, man worshipped both male and female gods. In many of the more ancient civilizations, including that of Ancient Egypt, women occupied a special position in society and female gods ruled in many spheres. But as soon as the new economic systems and patriarchal family had become well entrenched, male gods enforced their monopoly in monotheistic religions. The ancient female gods disappeared, and the functions of priesthood and prophecy became the exclusive domain of men.

The emancipation of Arab women cannot be achieved unless the root causes of, and conditions leading to, oppression are swept away. Real emancipation can only mean freedom from all forms of exploitation whether economic, political, sexual or cultural. Economic emancipation alone is not sufficient. A socialist system where women work and receive equal pay to that of men does not necessarily lead to their complete emancipation, as long as the patriarchal family remains dominant and carries with it a whole train of consequences in the relationships between women and men. There is no doubt that freedom from economic exploitation is an important contribution to the total cause of women's emancipation, but it must be linked to freedom from all other forms of oppression, whether social, moral or cultural, so that women, and men also, may really become free.

Nawal El Saadawi
Cairo
1977

PART 1
The Mutilated Half

1. The Question That No One Would Answer

I was six years old that night when I lay in my bed, warm and peaceful in that pleasurable state which lies half way between wakefulness and sleep, with the rosy dreams of childhood flitting by, like gentle fairies in quick succession. I felt something move under the blankets, something like a huge hand, cold and rough, fumbling over my body, as though looking for something. Almost simultaneously another hand, as cold and as rough and as big as the first one, was clapped over my mouth, to prevent me from screaming.

They carried me to the bathroom. I do not know how many of them there were, nor do I remember their faces, or whether they were men or women. The world to me seemed enveloped in a dark fog which prevented me from seeing. Or perhaps they put some kind of a cover over my eyes. All I remember is that I was frightened and that there were many of them, and that something like an iron grasp caught hold of my hand and my arms and my thighs, so that I became unable to resist or even to move. I also remember the icy touch of the bathroom tiles under my naked body, and unknown voices and humming sounds interrupted now and again by a rasping metallic sound which reminded me of the butcher when he used to sharpen his knife before slaughtering a sheep for the *Eid*[1] .

My blood was frozen in my veins. It looked to me as though some thieves had broken into my room and kidnapped me from my bed. They were getting ready to cut my throat which was always what happened with disobedient girls like myself in the stories that my old rural grandmother was so fond of telling me.

I strained my ears trying to catch the rasp of the metallic sound. The moment it ceased, it was as though my heart stopped beating with it. I was unable to see, and somehow my breathing seemed also to have stopped. Yet I imagined the thing that was making the rasping sound coming closer and closer to me. Somehow it was not approaching my neck as I had expected but another part of my body. Somewhere below my belly, as though seeking something buried between my thighs. At that very moment I realized that my thighs had been pulled wide apart, and that each of my lower limbs was being held as far away from the other as possible, gripped by steel fingers that never relinquished their pressure. I felt that the rasping knife or blade was heading straight down towards my throat. Then suddenly the sharp metallic edge

7

seemed to drop between my thighs and there cut off a piece of flesh from my body.

I screamed with pain despite the tight hand held over my mouth, for the pain was not just a pain, it was like a searing flame that went through my whole body. After a few moments, I saw a red pool of blood around my hips.

I did not know what they had cut off from my body, and I did not try to find out. I just wept, and called out to my mother for help. But the worst shock of all was when I looked around and found her standing by my side. Yes, it was her, I could not be mistaken, in flesh and blood, right in the midst of these strangers, talking to them and smiling at them, as though they had not participated in slaughtering her daughter just a few moments ago.

They carried me to my bed. I saw them catch hold of my sister, who was two years younger, in exactly the same way they had caught hold of me a few minutes earlier. I cried out with all my might. No! No! I could see my sister's face held between the big rough hands. It had a deathly pallor and her wide black eyes met mine for a split second, a glance of dark terror which I can never forget. A moment later and she was gone, behind the door of the bathroom where I had just been. The look we exchanged seemed to say: 'Now we know what it is. Now we know where lies our tragedy. We were born of a special sex, the female sex. We are destined in advance to taste of misery, and to have a part of our body torn away by cold, unfeeling cruel hands.'

My family was not an uneducated Egyptian family. On the contrary, both my parents had been fortunate enough to have a very good education, by the standards of those days. My father was a university graduate and that year (1937) had been appointed General Controller of Education for the Province of Menoufia in the Delta region to the North of Cairo. My mother had been taught in French schools by her father who was Director-General of Army Recruitment. Nevertheless, the custom of circumcising girls was very prevalent at the time, and no girl could escape having her clitoris amputated, irrespective of whether her family lived in a rural or an urban area. When I returned to school after having recovered from the operation, I asked my classmates and friends about what had happened to me, only to discover that all of them without exception, had been through the same experience, no matter what social class they came from (upper class, middle or lower-middle class).

In rural areas, among the poor peasant families, all the girls are circumcised as I later on found out from my relatives in Kafr Tahla. This custom is still very common in the villages, and even in the cities a large proportion of families believe it is necessary. However, the spread of education and a greater understanding among parents is making increasing numbers of fathers and mothers abstain from circumcising their daughters.

The memory of circumcision continued to track me down like a nightmare. I had a feeling of insecurity, of the unknown waiting for me at every step I took into the future. I did not even know if there were new surprises being stored up for me by my mother and father, or my grandmother, or the people around me. Society had made me feel, since the day that I opened my eyes on life, that I was a girl, and that the word *Bint* (girl) when pronounced by anyone is almost always accompanied by a frown.

Even when I had grown up and graduated as a doctor in 1955, I could not forget the painful incident that had made me lose my childhood once and for all, and that deprived me during my youth and for many years of married life from enjoying the fullness of my sexuality and the completeness of life that can only come from all round psychological equilibrium. Nightmares of a similar nature followed me throughout the years, especially during the period when I was working as a medical doctor in the rural areas. There I very often had to treat young girls who had come to the out-patients clinic bleeding profusely after a circumcision. Many of them used to lose their lives as a result of the inhuman and primitive way in which the operation, savage enough in itself, was performed. Others were afflicted with acute or chronic infections from which they sometimes suffered for the rest of their days. And most of them, if not all, became the victims later on of sexual or mental distortions as a result of this experience.

My profession led me, at one stage, to examine patients coming from various Arab countries. Among them were Sudanese women. I was horrified to observe that the Sudanese girl undergoes an operation for circumcision which is ten times more cruel than that to which Egyptian girls are subjected. In Egypt it is only the clitoris which is amputated, and usually not completely. But in the Sudan, the operation consists in the complete removal of all the external genital organs. They cut off the clitoris, the two major outer lips (*labia majora*) and the two minor inner lips (*labia minora*). Then the wound is repaired. The outer opening of the vagina is the only portion left intact, not however without having ensured that, during the process of repairing, some narrowing of the opening is carried out with a few extra stitches. The result is that on the marriage night it is necessary to widen the external opening by slitting one or both ends with a sharp scalpel or razor so that the male organ can be introduced. When a Sudanese woman is divorced, the external opening is narrowed once more to ensure that she cannot have sexual relations. If she remarries, widening is done again.

My feeling of anger and rebellion used to mount up as I listened to these women explaining to me what happens during the circumcision of a Sudanese girl. My anger grew tenfold when in 1969 I paid a visit to the Sudan only to discover that the practice of circumcision was unabated, whether in rural areas, or even in the cities and towns.

Despite my medical upbringing and my education, in those days I was not able to understand why girls were made to undergo this barbaric procedure. Time and again I asked myself the question: 'Why? Why?' But I could never get an answer to this question which was becoming more and more insistent, just as I was never able to get an answer to the questions that raced around in my mind the day that both my sister and I were circumcised.

This question somehow seemed to be linked to other things that puzzled me. Why did they favour my brother as regards food, and the freedom to go out of the house? Why was he treated better than I was in all these matters? Why could my brother laugh at the top of his voice, move his legs

freely, run and play as much as he wished, whereas I was not supposed to
look into people's eyes directly, but was meant to drop my glance whenever
I was confronted with someone? If I laughed, I was expected to keep my
voice so low that people could hardly hear me, or better, confine myself to
smiling timidly. When I played, my legs were not supposed to move freely,
but had to be kept politely together. My duties were primarily to help in
cleaning the house and cooking, in addition to studying since I was at school.
The brothers however, the boys, were not expected to do anything but study,

My family was educated and therefore differentiation between the boys
and girls, especially as my father was himself a teacher, never reached the
extent which is so common in other families. I used to feel very sorry for my
young girl relatives when they were forced out of school in order to get
married to an old man just because he happened to own some land, or when
their younger brothers would humiliate and beat them for no reason at all,
except that as boys they could afford to act superior to their sisters.

My brother tried to dominate me, in turn, but my father was a broadminded man and tried as best he could to treat his children without discrim-
inating between the boys and the girls. My mother, also, used to say that a
girl is equal to a boy, but I used to feel that in practice this was often not the
case.

Whenever this differentiation occurred I used to rebel, sometimes violently,
and would ask my mother and father why it was that my brother was accorded
privileges that were not given to me, despite the fact that I was doing better
than him at school. My father and mother, however, never had any answer to
give me except: 'It is so . . .' I would retort: 'Why should it be so?' And back
would come the answer again, unchanged: 'Because it is so . . .' If I was in an
obstinate mood, I would repeat the question again. Then, at the end of their
patience, they would say almost in the same voice: 'He is a boy, and you are
a girl.'

Perhaps they thought that this answer would be enough to convince me, or
at least to keep me quiet. But on the contrary it always made me persist more
than ever. I would ask: 'What is the difference between a boy and a girl?'

At this point my old grandmother, who very often paid us a visit, would
intervene in the discussion, which she always described as being an 'infringe-
ment of good manners', and scold me sharply: 'I have never in all my life seen
a girl with such a long tongue as you. Of course you are not like your brother.
Your brother is a boy, a boy, do you hear? I wish you had been born a boy
like him!'

No one in the family was ever able to give me a convincing answer to my
question. So the question continued to turn around restlessly in my mind, and
would jump to the forefront every time something happened that would
emphasize the fact that the male is treated everywhere and at all times as
though he belongs to a species which is superior to that of the female.

When I started to go to school, I noticed that the teachers would write my
father's name on my notebooks, but never that of my mother. So I asked
my mother why, and again she answered, 'It is so.' My father, however,

explained that children are named after their father, and when I sought to find out the reason he repeated the phrase that I knew well by now: 'It is so.' I summoned up all my courage and said: 'Why is it so?' But this time I could see from my father's face that he really did not know the answer. I never asked him the question again, except later on when my search for the truth led me to ask him many other questions, and to talk to him about many other things that I was discovering on the way.

However from that day onwards I realized that I had to find my own answer to the question that no one would answer. From that day also extends the long path that has led to this book.

References

1. *Eid* is a four day festival which follows the month of fasting (Ramadan) among Muslims. It is an occasion of great festivities. Another *Eid* is that celebrated about one and a half months later, *Eid El Adha,* the Festival of Sacrifice, in which a sheep or lamb is sacrificed. This is a repetition of Abraham's sacrifice of a lamb in place of his son.

2. Sexual Aggression Against the Female Child

All children who are born healthy and normal feel that they are complete human beings. This, however, is not so for the female child.

From the moment she is born and even before she learns to pronounce words, the way people look at her, the expression in their eyes, and their glances somehow indicate that she was born 'incomplete' or 'with something missing'. From the day of her birth to the moment of death, a question will continue to haunt her: 'Why?' Why is it that preference is given to her brother, despite the fact that they are the same, or that she may even be superior to him in many ways, or at least in some aspects?

The first aggression experienced by the female child in society is the feeling that people do not welcome her coming into the world. In some families, and especially in rural areas, this 'coldness' may go even further, and become an atmosphere of depression and sadness, or even lead to the punishment of the mother with insults or blows or even divorce. As a child, I saw one of my paternal aunts being submitted to resounding slaps on her face because she had given birth to a third daughter rather than a male child, and I overheard her husband threatening her with divorce if she ever gave birth to a female child again instead of giving him a son.[1] The father so hated this child that he used to insult his wife if she used to care for her, or even just feed her sufficiently. The baby died before she had completed forty days of her life, and I do not know whether she died of neglect, or whether the mother smothered her to death in order to 'have peace and give peace', as we say in our country.

The rate of infantile mortality remains very high in rural areas, and overall in most Arab countries, as a result of the low standards of living and education. But the proportion is much higher in female children than it is in males, and this is often due to neglect. However the situation is improving as a result of better economic and educational standards,[2] and the disparity in infantile mortality rates between female and males is rapidly disappearing.

A female child may be met with much less gloom and more human feelings if born into an educated Arab family living in a city. Nevertheless, from the moment she starts to crawl or stand on her two feet, she is taught that her sexual organs are something to fear and should be treated with caution, especially the part that much later in life she begins to know as the hymen.

12

Female children are therefore brought up in an atmosphere that is full of warning and fear when it comes to exposing or touching their sexual parts. No sooner does the hand of a female child fumble over her sexual organs in those exploratory movements that are normal and healthy in all children, since it is their way to knowledge, than it will be exposed immediately to a short, sharp tap or blow from the watchful fingers or hand of the mother, and sometimes the father. The child might even be taken unawares by a slap on the face, but the more reasonable of parents may limit themselves to a quick warning or a stern word.

The education that a female child receives in Arab society is a series of continuous warnings about things that are supposed to be harmful, forbidden, shameful or outlawed by religion. The child therefore is trained to suppress her own desires, to empty herself of authentic, original wants and wishes linked to her own self, and to fill the vacuum that results with the desires of others. Education of female children is therefore transformed into a slow process of annihilation, a gradual throttling of her personality and mind, leaving intact only the outside shell, the body, a lifeless mould of muscle and bone and blood that moves like a wound up rubber doll.

A girl who has lost her personality, her capacity to think independently and to use her own mind, will do what others have told her and will become a toy in their hands and a victim of their decisions.

Now who are these others we are talking about? They are the males in her family, and sometimes males outside the family who happen to come in contact with her at one or other stage of life. These males who are of different ages, extending from childhood to old age, and who may be of different backgrounds, have one thing in common. They are also victims of a society that segregates the sexes, and that considers sex a sin and a shame which can only be practised within the framework of an official marriage contract. Apart from this permitted avenue for sexual relations, society forbids adolescents and young men to practise sex in any form, other than that of nocturnal emissions. This is almost word for word what is taught to adolescents in Egyptian secondary schools, under a chapter entitled 'Customs and Traditions'.[3] It is also mentioned that masturbation is forbidden because it is harmful and, more precisely, as harmful as practising sex with prostitutes.[4] Young men therefore have no alternative but to wait until they have accumulated sufficient money in their pockets to permit them to marry according to Allah's directives and those of the Prophet.

Since, however, the accumulation of some money in the pockets of a young man, whether the sum be relatively big or small, takes a certain number of years spent in education and work, especially in cities, the age of marriage there has gone up considerably as compared to rural areas. The sons or daughters of the more affluent sections can of course get married earlier, but this rarely happens. For other people, the inhibiting factors — apart from education and employment — are the steep rise in the cost of living, an extreme scarcity of housing, and exorbitant rents. The result is an increasing number of young men who are unable to get married for economic reasons, and a growing gap therefore between their biological maturity and sexual needs on the one hand, and their economic maturity and chances of marriage on the other. This gap, on average, is not less than a span of ten years. A question therefore arises. How are young men supposed to satisfy their natural sexual needs during this period in a society which warns against masturbation and forbids its practice as being harmful to them physically and mentally, and which also does not allow sexual relations with prostitutes because of the dangers to health, especially with the rapid spread in venereal diseases since prostitution has been made illegal in many Arab countries. In addition the price of a session with a prostitute has now become prohibitive for the vast majority of young men. Sexual relations outside marriage and homosexuality both being severely condemned by society, young people are left with absolutely no solution.

The only female whom a young boy or man can probably find within easy reach is therefore his young sister. In most homes she will be sleeping in the adjoining bed, or even by his side in the same bed. His hand will start touching her while she is asleep, or even awake. In any case it does not make much difference since, even when awake, she cannot stand up to her elder brother because of fear of his authority which is consecrated by custom and law, or fear of the family, or as a result of a deep-seated feeling of guilt arising from the fact that she may be experiencing some pleasure under the touches of his hand, or because she is only a child, not able to understand exactly what is happening to her.

Most female children are exposed to incidents of this type. They may be exactly similar, or very different, according to circumstances. The male in question may be the brother, the cousin, the paternal uncle, the maternal uncle, the grandfather or even the father. If not a family member, he may be the guardian or porter of the house, the teacher, the neighbour's son, or any other man.

These incidents of sexual assault may take place without any force being used. If the girl however is grown up she may resist, in which case the aggressor has recourse either to a mixture of tenderness and deceit, or to his physical strength. In most cases the girl surrenders and is afraid to complain to anyone, since, if there is any punishment to be meted out, it will always end up by being inflicted on her. It is she alone who loses her honour and virginity. The man never loses anything, and the severest punishment he can expect (if he is not a member of the family) is to be obliged to marry the girl.

Most people think that such incidents are rare or unusual. The truth of the matter is that they are frequent, but remain hidden, stored up in the secret recesses of the female child's self, since she dare not tell anyone of what has happened to her; neither will the man ever think of admitting what he has done.

Since these sexual aggressions usually happen to children or young girls, they are forgotten through the process known as 'infantile amnesia'. The human memory has a natural capacity to forget what it wishes to forget, especially if related to painful incidents or accompanied by a feeling of guilt or regret. This is particularly true of certain happenings that have occurred in childhood, and which have not been discovered by anyone. But this amnesia is never complete in most cases since something of it remains buried in the subconscious, and may come to the surface for one reason or another, or during a mental or moral crisis.

References

1. This was around the year 1942, in my village Kafr Tahla, province of Kalioubia.
2. *Report of the Ministry of Health in Egypt, 1971.* Infantile mortality was 127 per 1,000 live births in 1952 and dropped to 115 in 1977.
3. Ministry of Education, *Textbook of Psychology for Students in the Third Year* (Secondary level, Arts and Literature). Written by Dr. Abdel Aziz El Kousy and Dr. Sayed Ghoneim, (Cairo, 1976).
4. *Ibid.,* Chapter 11, pp.123-74.

3. The Grandfather With Bad Manners

The numerous cases which I saw in my clinic made me decide to devote a good part of my life to the task of unmasking the double face of the society in which we live, a society which preaches virtue and morality in the open, and practises something very different in secret.

Since I am a medical doctor my work has taught me to undress the patient before examining him or her if the malady is physical, or to remove all the masks with which people cover their real selves if the illness or disturbance is mental.

In both situations, when the body becomes naked or when the self is unveiled and exposed, the person concerned is seized with panic. That is why most people refuse to be undressed, either physically or mentally, and quickly pull up the bedclothes over their bodies or rearrange their public mask, hoping thereby to stop people from seeing who they really are, and to keep their real being hidden in the deep and labyrinthine recesses of the self. However this hope, this attempt to hide the real self, is often impossible. For truth, though it may be buried in distant depths, remains living. Its breathing is perceptible as long as the human being remains alive and drawing breath. The truth may suddenly stick out its head like a worm buried in the earth, at a moment when the person is off guard. Human beings are very often off their guard, no matter how careful they are, as happens in moments of anger, passion or fear. In these moments they forget to don their mask quickly enough, and discerning eyes can get a clear vision of what is underneath.

This is particularly the case when a person is ill, for he or she then becomes incapable of maintaining the mask in place. It has to come down, and the body and soul laid bare. The loss of clothing, of the mask, of the veil, of the fig leaf, the nakedness of the body and the self, now becomes much less threatening than the dangers of disease. Now health and life must be preserved at any cost.

One of the cases that I remember is that of a tall girl with wandering thoughtful eyes. She was complaining of various physical and mental pains. I do not propose to go into the details of her malady, but her story has remained vivid in my memory. She told it to me, one cold winter night, as we sat with shutters drawn and the heater on in my sitting room.

'I remember that I was five years old when my mother used to take me to

16

visit her family. They lived in a big rambling house in the district of Zeitoun near Heliolopolis [in Cairo].

'My mother used to spend the time talking and laughing with her mother and sisters while I played with the children of the family. The house was full with the merry clamour of voices until the moment when the door bell rang, announcing the arrival of my grandfather. Immediately voices became hushed, my mother would speak in low tones, and the children would disappear. My grandmother then tiptoed to my grandfather's room where she would help him to remove his clothes and shoes, standing in front of him silently with lowered head.

'Like the rest of the family, whether elders or children, I feared my grand-father and never played or laughed in his presence. But after lunch, while the older people were having their siesta, he would call me in a voice that was a little less harsh than usual: 'Come, let us pick some flowers from the garden.'

'When we reached the far corner of the garden, his voice would become as gentle as that of my grandmother, and he would ask me to sit by his side on the wooden bench, facing the bed of roses. He would hand me a few red and yellow flowers and when I became engrossed in their petals and colours, seat me on his lap, and start caressing me or singing to me until I closed my eyes like one going to sleep. But I never fell asleep, because each time I could feel his hand creeping tenderly and stealthily under my clothes, and his finger disappearing to a hidden spot under my knickers.

'I was only five years old, but somehow I realized that what my grand-father was doing was wrong and immoral, and that if my mother found out, she would be angry with me and would scold me. I understood vaguely that I probably should have jumped off my grandfather's knees and refused to go with him into the garden when he called me.

'Other ideas occurred to me. Even though only five years old, the feeling that I was not a well-mannered child grew on me, for I used to remain seated on his knees instead of jumping off. Furthermore I derived some pleasure from the movements of his hand beneath my underclothes. When he heard my mother's voice calling me, he would hastily draw away his hand, shake me as though he was waking me up from my sleep, and say: "Your mother is calling you." I used to open my eyes as though waking from sleep and run to my mother with the open face that a small child of five is wont to have. She would ask me: "Where were you?" And I would answer with the innocent tones of a child: "With grandfather in the garden."

'She would feel relaxed and secure the moment she learnt that I had been with my grandfather in the garden. She used to caution me against going down into the garden alone, and never tired of repeating her warnings about "that man", the gardener, who wore a flowing robe and used to spray water over the flowers, which led me to fear not only the gardener but even the water drops that used to fill the air from his can.

'Once my grandfather had climbed the stairs back into the house, he would put on his usual personality once more, the personality that all feared including myself. The yellow prayer beads would start slipping through his fingers. In my imagination I almost came to believe that the grandfather that used to caress me in the garden was not the grandfather who sat at the table, and whom I feared. Sometimes I even used to think I had two grandfathers.

'When I was ten years old, my grandfather died. I was not sad at his death, and on the contrary felt a strange obscure happiness and ran around skipping and playing and laughing with the children. But my mother scolded me and locked me up in the house with the words: "Do you not know that your grandfather died? Have you got no manners?"

'I was on the point of asking her: "Did my grandfather know what it meant to have good manners?", but I did not have the courage to do it, so I kept quiet and the secret remained locked in my heart. This is the first time, Doctor, that I am telling the story to anyone.'

I have not given a complete account of what the woman told me on that night many years ago. She only opened her heart to me when she felt sure that I would not think of passing a moral judgement on her. Many of the girls and women who came to my clinic were hesitant at the beginning, to unveil the secrets they kept hidden within themselves. But once confidence and trust were established, they would gradually start to lighten themselves of many of the painful things they had carried with them for years.

4. The Injustice of Justice

The number of incidents of this kind that come to light is only a very small proportion as compared with the number that actually occur. The child or young girl locks her secret up within herself out of fear or shame. Even if she says something, or if the man is caught at the actual moment of sexual aggression, the family will hush up what has happened and refuse to go to a court of law, in order to preserve the honour of the family and its reputation intact.

The reputation and standing of a family may be irrevocably lost if one of the daughters loses her hymen prematurely, even though a victim of rape. This is why an incident of rape is kept a close secret and rarely divulged, thus enabling the aggressor to escape scot free. The real criminal remains safe, out of reach, protected from the hands of the law, whereas the victim who loses her virginity, the girl who loses her hymen — for whatever reason, even as a result of rape, or at any age, even that of early childhood — is doomed to lose her honour for life. Her hymen is her honour and, once lost, it can never be replaced.

It is a well known fact that in our society young girls are often exposed to various degrees of rape. Even female children below the age of seven years are frequently the victims of an unexpected or unrecognized aggression from grown-up men and youths, who are often members of the family, such as the brother, the uncle or even the father, or from a servant or porter in the building.

The tragedy inherent in such incidents is intensified by the fact that the male aggressor not only refrains from protecting his young victim, but is sometimes actually a party to whatever punishment is meted out to her, or even the hand that is raised against her in execution. It is thus that he tries to evade the eyes of suspicion and appear as the protector of the family honour. Such sad incidents are quite common and are brought to the attention of researchers and writers despite attempts to hush them up.

I personally have come across a number of heart-rending stories. One of the most gruesome is that of the uncle who was strongly attracted to his brother's daughter and had sexual relations with her. When the fact became known, the two brothers conspired together and poisoned the young girl to forestall the shame that threatened the family honour, were it to become known that she

19

had lost her virginity.

Most of the crimes related to such matters remain a closely guarded secret and rarely come to the notice of the police or the courts of justice. Even when brought before a tribunal, the judges often decide to close the case in an attempt to protect the reputation of the victim and her family. As a result the aggressor is safe. In some cases he is prevailed upon to marry the girl as the 'best way out of a delicate situation'. It is not uncommon to meet with similar cases in schools frequented exclusively by girls. The culprit is then one of the male teachers, and the solution arrived at is usually restricted to his being transferred to another school or a distant area.

I remember an incident involving a teacher who sexually assaulted nine female school children whose ages ranged from seven to twelve years. The case appeared before the courts but the judges decided to suspend the proceedings in order to avoid the scandal that would inevitably have involved a number of families. The accused was merely transferred from his profession to a job of a different nature.[2]

The decision to close the case ran as follows:

> Despite the fact that all the evidence goes to show that the accused was guilty, which would normally necessitate that he be indicted and sentenced for having committed rape on a number of young female children, the court has decided to close the case. A number of the victims are very young in age, and should not be brought before a criminal court to bear witness. The counsel for the prosecution is indeed sorry that he is obliged to request the closure of the case against the accused, and to limit his demands to transferring him from his job of teaching in a girls' school to another job.

In the question of rape Tunisia has moved ahead with its legislation much more rapidly than other Arab countries. The legislation related to rape has been considerably modified. Proceedings against the accused, however, are still dropped if he agrees to marry the victim.[3]

In 1973 I began a research study in the College of Medicine, Ein Shams University, Cairo.[4] The study covered 160 Egyptian girls and women, drawn from different social categories including educated and uneducated families. One of the findings of the research showed that sexual aggression by grown-up men on female children or young girls is a common occurrence. The percentage in uneducated families is as high as 45% and drops in educated families to 33.7%, which is not a low figure since it means that one-third even of these children were exposed to such aggression. This proportion is higher than that elicited by a similar study carried out by Kinsey in the United States in 1953 where the figure was 24%.

It is very difficult to compare these two studies for several reasons, including the time gap of some twenty-five years, the wide differences between the two societies and the circumstances of the groups that were studied in Egypt and the USA, the variations in approach and methodology etc.

But what can be said without hesitation, on the basis of the figures obtained in both research studies, is that incidents of this nature are very widespread. This completely contradicts the common view upheld by those who prefer to bury their heads in the sand and say that no such thing occurs and that, even if it does, it is extremely rare. I differ very strongly with such ideas and maintain on the contrary that such incidents are a feature of all societies, including Arab societies. They are not as infrequent as many people insist, especially if we keep in mind that in most cases whatever occurs is kept a close secret by all concerned.

On the basis of my experience as a woman who has tried to open her mind and heart to people's problems, I can say without risk of exaggeration that many girls in our society are exposed during their childhood to different kinds of sexual aggression, extending from caresses and love play with the hands, to complete sexual intercourse. A female child may lose her virginity without realizing it. She ends up by forgetting what has happened, or remembering it only as a frightful dream or nightmare that torments her and erodes her mental health throughout her life. This is the case if she escapes the punishment that waits, ready to pounce on her when she grows up, and the husband or parents discover that she is not virgin on the marriage night.

During my research I spent some time in the Department of Forensic Medicine at the Ministry of Justice. One of the researchers read to me excerpts from a register dealing with various forms of sexual aggression committed against female children and girls. For example, a teacher in a girls' school had one degree or another of sexual relations with all the girls in his class. With some of them he had limited himself to caresses, but with others he had had complete sexual relations. She also drew my attention to the story of a mother who one day came to her in a state of panic, saying that her daughter, who was three years of age, had been sexually assaulted by the porter of the apartment building in which they were living. He was carrying the child and fondling her, and had used his finger to touch her private parts.

During my visits to the asylums in Cairo, I asked to see the records of some of the cases of rape where the patient was diagnosed as suffering from a mental disease. The records revealed a strange aspect of the situation. Most of the patients were either students in religious institutes or people who were teaching religion in schools. One of them who was in tears throughout the interview said to me:

> I am deeply religious and I am an honourable man. I never practised masturbation in my life, and I hide my face when confronted by a girl, so that my ablutions remain pure. This was the first mistake in my life, and it was bad luck that brought it to light. All human beings make mistakes. No one is perfect except Allah, whose name be praised and raised to the heavens.

A young man among the patients of the ward who had collected around me, whispered in my ear:

Allah is merciful and compassionate. But people have no pity. Take my case as an example. I was sitting under a tree in the field, and a small girl came up to me and started playing with me. I put my finger there without meaning any harm. She did not scream; on the contrary she seemed to be happy at what I was doing. But they saw me. People collected around and beat me up. Then they accused me of rape, and brought me to this place.

Among the cases that I examined during my research study on women and neurosis was that of a young female doctor who had just graduated. She had been engaged and then married to one of her colleagues. On the marriage night her husband discovered that she was not a virgin. She explained to him that she had lost her virginity while still a child and that her father was the culprit. But her husband was unable to take the shock in his stride and divorced her. The young woman returned to her parents' home. She was unable to tell her mother the truth out of fear for the father. The good woman accused her of being perverted and the father zealously joined in, heaping blame upon his daughter. The girl, at her wits' end, wept and finally confessed to her mother all that had happened. In turn the poor woman, exposed to the terrible shock of finding out what her husband had done, almost collapsed. The father, however, accused his daughter of lying and beat her savagely. She was seized with a nervous breakdown which the father used to his advantage. He accused the girl of being insane and sent her off to a hospital for mental disease. The psychiatrist in charge of the case put his trust in the father's story and refused to believe the girl. The result was that she ended up by losing not only her integrity and honour, the man who was her husband, and her whole future, but also her reason, since for some people at least she was now considered mentally unbalanced.

An almost unending stream of incidents, stories and cases have been brought to my notice over the years. Some of them have faded in my memory with time, but others remain vivid. And still others I have kept in records and files, like the woman who was sexually assaulted by her uncle when she was still a child. He pounced upon her near the chicken coop the family had built on the roof top, and trembling with fear she submitted to his caresses. But the incident remained a secret for life. When the man died, she had grown up. No visible signs of sorrow could be seen on her face and she refused to go into mourning or wear black despite her mother's injunctions and admonitions. Her mother beat her and insisted that she was abnormal, and the father added his blows to those of the mother and accused her of being mad. However, she was more fortunate than other women in her situation might have been. She was not packed off to an asylum, nor did her husband discover that she was not a virgin when the day for her to get married came along. She was wise enough at least to have repaired the damage that had been done to her physically.

If sexual assaults on young girls and female children are frequent, it is natural that the stratagems necessary to conceal the loss of virginity should also be practised quite often. The methods used may be either a surgical repair of the hymen, or a simulation of the blood that spurts out during defloration. The most unfortunate of women are of course those girls who lack the material means to undergo an operation, or are not experienced enough to put on some comedy on the marriage night. One of the most numerous categories of poor girls are the domestic servants who are usually of rural origin.[5] They leave their native villages for the towns and cities in search of a job, usually as servants in the houses of middle and upper class families. These girls become the only sexual object available to the young males, and sometimes even the elder males, in the family. The adolescent boys find them much more suitable to their needs than a sister, cousin or female student at school or in college. The boys are less liable to feel guilty if sex is practised with a servant girl, and in addition they are not doing wrong to somebody of their own class, but to a creature who is socially very much their inferior. In addition, she is preferable to a prostitute since sex with her is free of charge and does not threaten them with the chances of venereal disease.

The head of the family — the respected husband and father — may in his turn creep to the bed of the maidservant during his wife's illness or when she is away from the house, or during the periods of her menstrual cycle and pregnancy. Or his wife may be neither absent, nor pregnant, nor menstruating but only sexually frigid. In fact most wives are frigid because of their upbringing and the sexual and physical suppression to which they are exposed since childhood, or because of the lack of real love and affection or at least of understanding and refined treatment between husband and wife. Most marriages are contracted for economic reasons, which in itself is sufficient to explain why there is rarely any genuine feeling between the couple. If we add to this the patriarchal nature of the family, with the man acting as the supreme authority, and enforcing his dominion, there is little chance for a warm emotional and physical relationship to develop.

The small maidservant, therefore, is the only remaining 'sex avenue' for the hungry males that are panting with the thirst of sexual frustration, and lying in wait for any chance or hope of satisfying it.

When I was working in my clinic as a physician, first in Benha and later in Giza,[6] or in the different general hospitals where I spent years practising my profession, I very often came across the small maidservant whose age usually did not exceed fifteen or sixteen years, and yet whose belly was already swollen with an illegitimate pregnancy.

This child becomes in the eyes of society an unmarried woman, pregnant with child, or in other words a fallen depraved girl, devoid of virtue or honour. She faces the world alone and her life may terminate in suicide, or in a murder committed by her father or another male member of the family. Alternatively she may die during an abortion carried out by one of the primitive rural methods so often resorted to despite all its dangers. If she survives the abortion, she is liable to be prosecuted legally since abortion is not permitted by the law, and if she has to bring up her child, life becomes an interminable, long drawn out source of humiliation and misery.

On the other hand the master of the house, the dignified son of the family

23

the respected husband highly admired by those who know him, the pillar of society, who in the dark of night swooped over the defenceless body and lay with it, in other words the man, remains safe, unsullied, and continues to emjoy his life in dignity and honour, well out of the reaches of a law which is in reality unlawful and a justice which is unjust. It is sometimes thought that incidents of this nature are rare. But researchers and specialists who are interested in the life of women and young girls know that this is very far from the truth. For a segregated society with strict separation between the sexes creates widespread sexual frustration and suppression. One of the few ways in which desire can find its expression, especially in the absence of natural relations between boys and girls, and between men and women, is by seeking channels within the family to which such opportunities are restricted. The most vulnerable family members are young female children and girls who, through ignorance, fear and submission to authority, do not dare to protest, no matter what may befall them. This is particularly true of the poorer social classes where promiscuity is a common phenomenon due to severe over-crowding. A family of eight to ten members often lives in a single room; the mother, the father, the brothers and sisters and often other members of the family live almost 'body to body' and this situation leads to numerous problems of a sexual nature.

References

1.   *El Akhbar,* daily newspaper, 10 May 1972.
2.   *Akhbar El Yom,* daily newspaper, 23 February 1974.
3.   Tunisian law No. 21, promulgated on 27 March 1969, amending Article 227 of the Criminal Code, No. 12, 25-28 March 1969, p.369: 'A man who has sexual intercourse with a girl whose age is less than 15 years, even if violence is not used on his part, will be sentenced to 15 years' penal servitude. The sentence will be reduced to five years' penal servitude if his age is between 15 and 20 years. However if he accepts to marry the girl, legal proceedings against him will be dropped, and any sentence that has been passed will be rendered null and void.'
4.   The Research Study extended over the two years 1973-74.
5.   These constitute the majority of women members of the active labour force employed in the 'services' sector. Their percentage in this sector is 89.3%. See *Al Mara'a Al Misria fi Eishreen Aaman 1952-1972,* Markaz El Abhath wal Dirasat Al Soukaneya — Al Gihaz El Markazi Lilta'abia wal Ihsa'a.
6.   Benha is a small city 30 miles north of Cairo and, Giza is a province adjoining Cairo on its southern side.

5. The Very Fine Membrane Called 'Honour'

Every female Arab child, even today, must possess that very fine membrane called a hymen, which is considered one of the most essential, if not *the* most essential, part of her body. However, the mere existence of the hymen is not in itself sufficient. This fine membrane must be capable of bleeding profusely, of letting out red blood that can be seen as a visible stain on a white bed sheet the night a young girl is married.

No girl can be more unfortunate than she whom nature has endowed with an elastic hymen, capable of widening and stretching at the moment when the man's finger or his sexual organ penetrates upwards in the vagina, for such a hymen will not bleed. No girl can suffer a worse fate than she whom nature has forgotten to provide with a hymen, or whose hymen is so delicate that it is torn away and lost by repeated riding on a bicycle or a horse, or by masturbation, or by one of those minor accidents that happen so often in childhood. No human being can know greater misery and humiliation than a girl whose hymen is thick, deprived of an orifice, and elastic. For then neither the male finger nor the man's penis can draw blood as it pushes the hymen before it like a rubber membrane.

One day, when I still had my clinic in Benha, I was confronted with a case of the latter type. My 'patient' was a young girl, about sixteen years old, pale and so thin that she looked as though she had barely passed the age of twelve. It appeared to me as though undernourishment had prevented her body from filling out normally. The husband who had accompanied her during the visit explained to me that they had married about a year before, and that she was complaining of a fullness in the belly, which led him to think that she was probably pregnant.

However, when I examined the girl, I could not find any signs of pregnancy. On the other hand, I noticed that she had been born with a thick, elastic and and non-perforated hymen. The swelling of her belly was therefore due to the menstrual flow that had accumulated in her vagina, month after month, since the age of puberty, which she had apparently reached some time after marriage. The absence of an orifice in the hymen had prevented this flow from being discharged out of her body. With a jab of my sharp lancet I made an opening in the hymen, and let the old accumulated dark blood rush out through it.

It transpired, in the discussion that followed after the girl had got off the operating table, that the husband had accused her of not being a virgin, since she had not bled from the external genital organs on the night of marriage. If unmarried she might have found herself in an even worse position where others might have jumped to the conclusion that she was pregnant with an illegitimate child, since her parents would most probably have noticed the unusual swelling of her belly.

This reminds me of a story I read many years later in the newspapers. The police had discovered the dead body of a young pregnant girl. It was thought that she had been murdered to defend the 'honour' of her family as very often happens in such cases. However, when the body was dissected by a medico-legal expert in the mortuary, his report showed that the girl had not been pregnant. The swelling detected in her belly was, as in the case I treated, due to the accumulated menstrual flow held back by a thick unperforated hymen.

If we keep in mind the high percentage of anomalies that affect the hymen at the time when the embryo is still developing, and which are therefore born with female children, it is easy to imagine what sufferings a girl may undergo without even knowing what has gone wrong. For it is known that 11.2% of girls are born with an elastic hymen, 16.16% with so fine a membrane that it is easily torn, 31.32% with a thick elastic hymen, and only 41.32% with what may be considered a normal hymen.[1]

A mother once awakened me at dead of night in a panic. She wanted to know whether boiling water had any effect on the 'membrane of virginity', as it is called in Arabic, since her child had fallen into a deep tub of boiling water and the whole of her lower half had been immersed. The mother was more concerned with the poor child's hymen than she was with her life.

The number of husbands, fathers and mothers who at one time or another turned up in my clinic to ask me about the hymen of a young bride or daughter cannot be counted. Very often the father or the mother would ask me for a medical certificate indicating that the daughter was a virgin, or that her hymen had been torn while she was playing some sport, or as a result of an accident (not related to sex, of course).

Arab society still considers that the fine membrane which covers the aperture of the external gential organs is the most cherished and most important part of a girl's body, and is much more valuable than one of her eyes, or an arm, or a lower limb. An Arab family does not grieve as much at the loss of a girl's eye as it does if she happens to lose her virginity. In fact if the girl lost her life, it would be considered less of a catastrophe than if she lost her hymen.

A girl who does not preserve her virginity is liable to be punished with physical death, or moral death, or at least with being divorced if she is found out at the time of marriage. Such divorce is of course accompanied by a scandal, usually restricted to family circles, but which very often inevitably spreads far and wide. Yet such a girl may be completely innocent of any sexual relation, but incapable of proving her innocence. This is due to the fact that patriarchal class society has imposed premarital virginity on girls and ensured that the very honour of a girl, and her family, is closely linked to the preservation of this virginity. If virginity is lost, this brings almost everlasting shame which can only be 'wiped out in blood', as the common Arab saying goes.

Virginity is a strict moral rule which applies to girls alone. Yet one would think that the first criterion of a moral rule, if it is indeed to be moral, should be that it applies to all without exception, and does not yield to any form of discrimination whether on the basis of sex, colour or class.

However, moral codes and standards in our societies very rarely apply to all people equally. This is the most damning proof of how immoral such codes and standards really are.

In history the ruling classes of by-gone days imposed the moral values of abstinence, stoicism and a renunciation of worldly pleasures on wage-earners to ensure that they were satisfied with their meagre pay, and would willingly join up to fight in armies for the defence of privileges which belonged to others. In the upper classes, however, all was permitted and the values of greed, lust, extravagance and pleasure were allowed to flourish on the misery of the toiling masses.

Since it is men who rule over women, they in turn permitted themselves what they forbade to women. Thus it was that chastity and virginity were considered essential for women, whereas freedom and even licentiousness were looked upon as natural where men were concerned.

There are many people in Arab society who, to this very day, firmly believe that virginity can only be destined for girls and not for boys. God has provided them with a hymen as a means to proving virginity. Such reasoning is only a reflection of the backwardness that prevails in many aspects of our life. The anatomical and biological constitution of human beings, whether men or women, can have no relation to moral values. Moral values are in fact the product of social systems or, more precisely, of the social system imposed by the ruling class with the aim of serving certain economic and political interests, and ensuring that the situation from which that class draws benefit and power is maintained. The anatomical and biological characteristics of the body are aimed at something else, namely at fulfilling certain vital physiological functions related to the protection and maintenance of life.

By what figment of imagination can we profess that the hymen was created in order to block the passage of the male sexual organ when it seeks to penetrate through the external genital organs of the female into the vagina, during the period prior to marriage? Such a function can only be considered a social and moral one, in no way related to the vital biological and physiological functions exercised in this part of the body.

As a matter of fact, the hymen can be compared to the appendix since it has no real bodily functions to fulfil. If it had an important function we would not have found so many girls born without any hymen at all, or others with just a remnant. Indeed, if the hymen were so important an organ for the preservation of virginity, God or nature would surely have ensured that all hymens bleed at the first copulation, whereas in fact a very high proportion

27

seem to suffer from an innate anaemia. More than 30% of girls have no bleeding at all during their first sexual act. What can this mean? Surely God has not sought to punish these girls by not providing them with the right kind of hymen, with a hymen capable of bleeding, and therefore of indicating virginity! What justice is it that punishes a girl because she had a different anatomical constitution from others, or a wider hymenal aperture than is usually the case?

It is well known that the organs of the human body, whether related to the reproductive system or to any other system, vary widely as regards size and even shape. No body completely resembles another. No body is an identical mould or finger-print of another. Each one of us has his or her own unique physical constitution, and leaves our own characteristic finger-prints on anything we may touch. Thus it is that the penis of one man differs from that of another. Similarly, the aperture of the hymen differs from female to female and so from virgin to virgin. What irony of fate, therefore, if a girl with a wide hymenal orifice marries a man with a diminutive penis!! Can this possibly be a sufficient reason for divorce or disgrace or even death, as it commonly is in societies where virginity is still considered a supreme value?

Fortunately education, and in particular the education of an increasing number of girls, as well as the fact that more and more females are seeking paid work outside the home, are both contributing to relatively rapid changes in the personality of Arab women. These changes are making them more independent, more respectful of their own minds and bodies, less prone to submit their lives to unjust moral values imposed by a male dominated society. Such developments are leading to changes in the attitudes of society towards women, and are bringing to life new generations of Arab youth where the males no longer judge a girl by her hymen, or the flow of blood on the night of marriage.

Change is taking place. But the vast majority of Arab men still insist on virginity in their partner at marriage. A girl who has lost her virginity runs a great danger if it is discovered at the time of marriage, especially in Upper Egypt, where her fate is often death at the hands of her own family. If a girl happens to have been provided by nature with an elastic hymen which does not bleed on the first night of marriage, ignorance will be her executioner. For the rituals of marriage require that defloration be performed by the husband with his finger and that 'red blood be shed on the white sheet'.

Very few people understand that the hymen varies in texture, size and consistency from one girl to another, just as the male sexual organ differs from man to man. Luck may have it that a girl with an elastic hymen marries a man with a diminutive sexual organ and, if finger defloration is not done, the inference will be that she is not a virgin, since no bleeding will occur. An educated husband will sometimes take his young wife to be examined by a doctor if he wishes to reassure himself of her virginity. Since gynaecological examination of virgins is rare, doctors do not often get a chance to see different types of hymens and are therefore liable to make mistakes. I remember the case of a medical doctor who was asked by a newly married husband to examine his bride. The family of the bride were waiting outside the examination room, and when the doctor came out and informed them that the girl was not a virgin the news to them was like a stroke of lightning. One day later she was murdered by her cousin despite her protestations of innocence. Her body was examined by the coroner and it transpired too late that the doctor's diagnosis had been incorrect.[2] Another victim had been sacrificed in the name of 'virginity'.

Many a husband rang the bell of my clinic in Giza and walked into my consultation room accompanied by a weeping young girl. In angry nervous tones he would explain to me that on the first night of marriage no 'red blood' could be discerned after sexual intercourse. Numerous were the nights which I spent by the side of a young girl in a small country house or mud hut during my years in rural Egypt, treating a haemorrhage that had resulted from the long dirty finger nail of a *daya* cutting through the soft tissues during the process of defloration. For in many villages this ritual ceremony in honour of virginity is performed by an ugly old crone, the *daya* who earns her living by amputating the clitoris of children, and tearing open the vagina of young brides. The father of the bride then holds up a white towel stained with blood, and waves it proudly above his head for the relatives assembled at the door to bear witness to the fact that the honour of his daughter and of the family is intact.

I used to attend some of these marriage ceremonies in order to follow at close quarters what was taking place. On one occasion the *daya* embedded her long nail in the hymen, but only a few drops of scanty blood were forthcoming. To my horror, she pushed her finger up the vagina and the blood welled out in a steady stream. The white towel bathed in crimson flapped out over the father's head, the drums beat, and female voices emitted the long drawn out shrieks of joy. I realized that she had cut through the wall of the vagina. At the end of the night, in answer to my questions, she explained to me that on marriage nights she was very much in demand. Her fame, built up on her capacity for bringing forth a vigorous flow of blood in the process of defloration, had earned her an unusual popularity and a steady income from such auspicious occasions.

When the finger of a rural husband replaces that of the *daya,* then defloration becomes even more brutal. His only experience in the use of his hands is related to gripping the thick handle of the plough or the harrow. The *daya* at least has some notion of the female body. And nothing can be more brutal than a thick coarse finger plunging mercilessly into the external opening of the vagina, and boring up in an unknown direction. Thus it was that, on a cold winter's night, a young girl was carried into my clinic bleeding profusely between her thighs, only for me to discover that the husband's finger had perforated the interior vaginal wall into the urinary bladder.

Yet this brutal orthodoxy in relation to women is accompanied, on the other hand, with almost unlimited licence for men. The Arab proverb goes: 'Only the pocket of a man can bring him shame.' For our society, therefore, shame is only the result of poverty, where men are concerned. Male ego grows in proportion to the number of his female conquests, and his sexual relations are a source of pride and occasions for boasting.

Education has contributed to greater enlightenment in matters relating to sex and the situation of women in Arab society, and yet many educated men still maintain their traditionalist attitudes and values in this sphere. I personally have met many men who have higher degrees or have pursued their studies abroad and travelled widely, yet their emotional and mental constitution remains rigid and backward in so far as women are concerned. An engineer who had spent five years in West Germany, on his return to Egypt noticed what he thought were signs of pregnancy in his seventeen year old sister. He searched her room and found a bottle of medicine in the wardrobe which he carried to the nearby drugstore. The chemist informed him that the medicine he had brought for examination is used in attempts to induce abortion. The engineer rushed back to his house in a state of uncontrollable agitation, seized hold of a knife from the kitchen and stabbed his sister to death. In the post mortem examination it transpired that she was still a virgin and no evidence of pregnancy was detectable. Counsel for the defence, in his submission to the court, pleaded for the engineer's release on the grounds that his motive in committing the crime had been the defence of his family's honour. He had been assailed by doubts about his sister's conduct and this had led him to commit the crime. His doubts had been misplaced, but his intentions were good. The court set him free without bail.[3]

So once again we see a situation where, even in case of a murder, a man escapes retribution because he is covered by traditionalist conceptions of honour, whereas these very conceptions lead to punishment where girls and women are concerned. The law is almost always on the side of men, and courts of justice very often dissolve marriages because the bride was found to have lost her virginity before marriage.[4]

Where women are concerned, harshness and even cruelty are the rule whenever the law is applied. I have known a court of law pass sentence on a teacher because she entered a bathroom in which her female colleague was lying naked in the tub without knocking on the door. Another notable case was that in which severe legal punishment was meted out to a school teacher because she took her class and spent some time with them in a waterside cafe.[5]

The murky fate which awaits a girl who loses her virginity often forces her to find some way out of the dilemma. The daughter of a rich family can go to a gynaecologist and pay a large sum of money to undergo a plastic repairal of the hymen. Whereas a poor village girl will depend on the subterfuges of the *daya,* which include fixing the date of marriage at the time of menstruation or placing a small bag full of chicken's blood at the opening of the vagina to ensure a red flow at the time of defloration.

One day a young girl came to my clinic for a consultation. She was carrying a five months pregnancy, but when I examined her the hymen was still intact. She explained to me that the pregnancy had occurred after repeated superficial sexual intercourse and asked me to remove the child through an abdominal operation (a *Caeserean section*). I refused to comply with her request, so she left. Many years later I met her accidentally, and she explained

to me that after my refusal she had been to another doctor who performed
the operation for her. Now she was married to a successful engineer and had
two children by him. In my imagination I often evoke the picture of this
engineer, whom I never met, carrying out the ritual defloration on the first
night of marriage with care, to make sure that his bride was a virgin, and
happy to discover that her hymen was intact. For him, the incision extending
perpendicularly along the abdomen mattered little, just as an incision in her
heart or liver or even brain would have been of little significance, whereas a
small tear in the hymen, a millimetre long, would have been sufficient to
upset his whole world.

There is a distorted concept of honour in our Arab society. A man's
honour is safe as long as the female members of his family keep their hymens
intact. It is more closely related to the behaviour of the women in the family,
than to his own behaviour. He can be a womanizer of the worst calibre and
yet be considered an honourable man as long as his womenfolk are able to
protect their genital organs. There are certain moral standards for females
and others for males, and the whole of society is permeated by such double
moral standards. At the root of this anomalous situation lies the fact that
sexual experience in the life of a man is a source of pride and a symbol of
virility; whereas sexual experience in the life of women is a source of shame
and a symbol of degradation.

It is not difficult to realize the consequences of this double standard of
morality. The males are let loose in search of sexual experience, in any form
and no matter at what price, in an attempt to prove their virility and bolster
their masculine pride, which are motives as strong as the satisfaction of
sexual desire *per se*. Men are engaged in a perpetual chase after women and
have recourse to declarations of passionate love, or showering them with
gifts. In this continuous urge to possess a woman, the male will tempt a poor
servant, or land himself with a syphilitic prostitute, or victimize a young
child, or entice a girl with promises of marriage. If the latter believes in his
promises and surrenders herself to him, she is trapped. For then he will
usually refuse to marry her because she has lost her virginity and society now
considers her a fallen woman. She is abandoned to the sad fate of a dishonoured female carrying an illegitimate child, whereas the male moves on to
new conquests.

This picture is typical of a large sector of urban society, and of the upper
classes in rural areas. However when we consider the working class in the
cities and towns, and the peasants and agricultural labourers in the villages,
many of the phenomena mentioned previously are rarely discernible. Early
marriage, continuous hard work and the difficulties of life leave little room
for sexual licence, although other manifestations of discrimination against
women and sexual oppression remain an integral part of social behaviour.

It is not difficult to understand why, under such circumstances, girls live
in continuous anxiety and fear of losing their virginity. The upbringing of
girls in Arab families is calculated to keep them away from men, and to warn
them of the dangers and subterfuges to which they are liable to fall victims

31

at any moment. Physical circumcision, therefore, has as its corollary another form of circumcision that we may call 'educational circumcision' to which we must now turn.

References

1. Statistics of the Institute of Forensic Medicine, Baghdad, Iraq, 1940-1970, published in *The Iraqi Medical Journal* dated 21 February 1972.
2. *The Iraqi Medical Journal,* article by the medico-legal specialist, Dr. Wasfy Mohammed Ali, 21 February 1972.
3. *Akhbar El Yom,* weekly edition, 18 May 1974, p.10, under the title: 'He killed his sister and then discovered she was a virgin'.
4. *Akhbar El Yom,* weekly edition, 6 March 1976, p.10, under the title: 'The court of Appeal abolishes the contract because the wife was not a virgin.'
5. *Akhbar El Yom,* weekly edition, 9 August 1975, p.10.

6. Circumcision of Girls

The practice of circumcising girls is still a common procedure in a number of Arab countries such as Egypt, the Sudan, Yeman and some of the Gulf states.

The importance given to virginity and an intact hymen in these societies is the reason why female circumcision still remains a very widespread practice despite a growing tendency, especially in urban Egypt, to do away with it as something outdated and harmful. Behind circumcision lies the belief that, by removing parts of girls' external genital organs, sexual desire is minimized. This permits a female who has reached the 'dangerous age' of puberty and adolescence to protect her virginity, and therefore her honour, with greater ease. Chastity was imposed on male attendants in the female harem by castration which turned them into inoffensive eunuchs. Similarly female circumcision is meant to preserve the chastity of young girls by reducing their desire for sexual intercourse.

Circumcision is most often performed on female children at the age of seven or eight (before the girl begins to get menstrual periods). On the scene appears the *daya* or local midwife. Two women members of the family grasp the child's thighs on either side and pull them apart to expose the external genital organs and to prevent her from struggling — like trussing a chicken before it is slain. A sharp razor in the hand of the *daya* cuts off the clitoris.

During my period of service as a rural physician, I was called upon many times to treat complications arising from this primitive operation, which very often jeopardized the life of young girls. The ignorant *daya* believed that effective circumcision necessitated a deep cut with the razor to ensure radical amputation of the clitoris, so that no part of the sexually sensitive organ would remain. Severe haemorrhage was therefore a common occurrence and sometimes led to loss of life. The *dayas* had not the slightest notion of asepsis, and inflammatory conditions as a result of the operation were common. Above all, the lifelong psychological shock of this cruel procedure left its imprint on the personality of the child and accompanied her into adolescence, youth and maturity. Sexual frigidity is one of the after-effects which is accentuated by other social and psychological factors that influence the personality and mental make-up of females in Arab societies. Girls are therefore exposed to a whole series of misfortunes as a result of outdated notions and values related to virginity, which still remains the fundamental criterion of a girl's honour. In recent years, however, educated families have begun to realize the harm that is done by the practice of female circumcision.

Nevertheless a majority of families still impose on young female children the barbaric and cruel operation of circumcision. The research that I carried out on a sample of 160 Egyptian girls and women showed that 97.5% of uneducated families still insisted on maintaining the custom, but this percentage dropped to 66.2% among educated families.[1]

When I discussed the matter with these girls and women it transpired that most of them had no idea of the harm done by circumcision, and some of them even thought that it was good for one's health and conducive to cleanliness and 'purity'. (The operation in the common language of the people is in fact called the cleansing or purifying operation.) Despite the fact that the percentage of educated women who have undergone circumcision is only 66.2%, as compared with 97.5% among uneducated women, even the former did not realize the effect that this amputation of the clitoris could have on their psychological and sexual health. The dialogue that occurred between these women and myself would run more or less as follows:
'Have you undergone circumcision?'
'Yes.'
'How old were you at the time?'
'I was a child, about seven or eight years old.'
'Do you remember the details of the operation?'
'Of course. How could I possibly forget?'
'Were you afraid?'
'Very afraid. I hid on top of the cupboard [in other cases she would say under the bed, or in the neighbour's house], but they caught hold of me, and I felt my body tremble in their hands.'
'Did you feel any pain?'
'Very much so. It was like a burning flame and I screamed. My mother held my head so that I could not move it, my aunt caught hold of my right arm and my grandmother took charge of my left. Two strange women whom I had not seen before tried to keep me from moving my thighs by pushing them as far apart as possible. The *daya* sat between these two women, holding a sharp razor in her hand which she used to cut off the clitoris. I was scared and suffered such great pain that I lost consciousness at the flame that seemed to sear me through and through.'
'What happened after the operation?'
'I had severe bodily pains, and remained in bed for several days, unable to move. The pain in my external genital organs led to retention of urine. Every time I wanted to urinate the burning sensation was so unbearable that I could not bring myself to pass water. The wound continued to bleed for some time, and my mother used to change the dressing for me twice a day.'
'What did you feel on discovering that a small organ in your body had been removed?'
'I did not know anything about the operation at the time, except that it was very simple, and that it was done to all girls for purposes of cleanliness, purity

and the preservation of a good reputation. It was said that a girl who did not undergo this operation was liable to be talked about by people, her behaviour would become bad, and she would start running after men, with the result that no one would agree to marry her when the time for marriage came. My grandmother told me that the operation had only consisted in the removal of a very small piece of flesh from between my thighs, and that the continued existence of this small piece of flesh in its place would have made me unclean and impure, and would have caused the man whom I would marry to be repelled by me.'

'Did you believe what was said to you?'

'Of course I did. I was happy the day I recovered from the effects of the operation, and felt as though I was rid of something which had to be removed, and so had become clean and pure.'

Those were more or less the answers that I obtained from all those interviewed, whether educated or uneducated. One of them was a medical student from Ein Shams School of Medicine. She was preparing for her final examinations and I expected her answers to be different, but in fact they were almost identical to the others. We had quite a long discussion which I reproduce here as I remember it.

'You are going to be a medical doctor after a few weeks, so how can you believe that cutting off the clitoris from the body of a girl is a healthy procedure, or at least not harmful?'

'This is what I was told by everybody. All the girls in my family have been circumcised. I have studied anatomy and medicine, yet I have never heard any of the professors who taught us explain that the clitoris had any function to fulfil in the body of a woman, neither have I read anything of the kind in the books which deal with the medical subjects I am studying.'

'That is true. To this day medical books do not consider the science of sex as a subject which they should deal with. The organs of a woman worthy of attention are considered to be only those directly related to reproduction, namely the vagina, the uterus and the ovaries. The clitoris, however, is an organ neglected by medicine, just as it is ignored and disdained by society.'

'I remember a student asking the professor one day about the clitoris. The professor went red in the face and answered him curtly, saying that no one was going to ask him about this part of the female body during examinations, since it was of no importance.'

My studies led me to try and find out the effect of circumcision on the girls and women who had been made to undergo it, and to understand what results it had on their psychological and sexual life. The majority of the normal cases I interviewed answered that the operation had no effect on them. To me it was clear that in the face of such questions they were much more ashamed and intimidated than the neurotic cases were. But I did not allow myself to be satisfied with these answers, and would go on to question them closely about their sexual life both before and after the circumcision was done. Once again I will try to reproduce the dialogue that usually occurred as faithfully as possible.

'Did you experience any change of feeling or of sexual desire after the operation?'

'I was a child and therefore did not feel anything.'

'Did you not experience any sexual desire when you were a child?'

'No, never. Do children experience sexual desire?'

'Children feel pleasure when they touch their sexual organs, and some form of sexual play occurs between them, for example, during the game of bride and bridegroom usually practised under the bed. Have you never played this game with your friends when still a child?'

At these words the young girl or woman would blush, and her eyes would probably refuse to meet mine, in an attempt to hide her confusion. But after the conversation had gone on for some time, and an atmosphere of mutual confidence and understanding had been established, she would begin to recount her childhood memories. She would often refer to the pleasure she had felt when a man of the family permitted himself certain sexual caresses. Sometimes these caresses would be proffered by the domestic servant, the house porter, the private teacher or the neighbour's son. A college student told me that her brother had been wont to caress her sexual organs and that she used to experience acute enjoyment. However after undergoing circumcision she no longer had the same sensation of pleasure. A married woman admitted that during intercourse with her husband she had never experienced the slightest sexual enjoyment, and that her last memories of any form of pleasurable sensation went back twenty years, to the age of six, before she had undergone circumcision. A young girl told me that she had been accustomed to practise masturbation, but had given it up completely after removal of the clitoris at the age of ten.

The further our conversations went, and the more I delved into their lives, the more readily they opened themselves up to me and uncovered the secrets of childhood and adolescence, perhaps almost forgotten by them or only vaguely realized.

Being both a woman and a medical doctor I was able to obtain confessions from these women and girls which it would be almost impossible, except in very rare cases, for a man to obtain. For the Egyptian woman, accustomed as she is to a very rigid and severe upbringing built on a complete denial of any sexual life before marriage, adamantly refuses to admit that she has ever known, or experienced, anything related to sex before the first touches of her husband. She is therefore ashamed to speak about such things with any man, even the doctor who is treating her.

My discussions with some of the psychiatrists who had treated a number of the young girls and women in my sample, led me to conclude that there were many aspects of the life of these neurotic patients that remained unknown to them. This was due either to the fact that the psychiatrist himself had not made the necessary effort to penetrate deeply into the life of the woman he was treating, or to the tendency of the patient herself not to divulge those things which her upbringing made her consider matters not to be discussed freely, especially with a man.

In fact the long and varied interchanges I had over the years with the majority of practising psychiatrists in Egypt, my close association with a large number of my medical colleagues during the long periods I spent working in health centres and general or specialized hospitals and, finally, the four years I spent as a member of the National Board of the Syndicate of Medical Professions, have all led me to the firm conclusion that the medical profession in our society is still incapable of understanding the fundamental problems with which sick people are burdened, whether they be men or women, but especially if they are women. For the medical profession, like any other profession in society, is governed by the political, social and moral values which predominate, and like other professions is one of the institutions which is utilized more often than not to protect these values and perpetuate them.

Men represent the vast majority in the medical profession, as in most professions. But apart from this, the mentality of women doctors differs little, if at all, from that of the men, and I have known quite a number of them who were even more rigid and backward in outlook than their male colleagues.

A rigid and backward attitude towards most problems, and in particular towards women and sex, predominates in the medical profession, and particularly within the precincts of the medical colleges in the Universities.

Before undertaking my research study on 'Women and Neurosis' at Ein Shams University, I had made a previous attempt to start it at the Kasr El Eini Medical College in the University of Cairo, but had been obliged to give up as a result of the numerous problems I was made to confront. The most important obstacle of all was the overpowering traditionalist mentality that characterized the professors responsible for my research work, and to whom the word 'sex' could only be equated to the word 'shame'. 'Respectable research' therefore could not possibly have sex as its subject, and should under no circumstances think of penetrating into areas even remotely related to it. One of my medical colleagues in the Research Committee advised me not to refer at all to the question of sex in the title of my research paper, when I found myself obliged to shift to Ein Shams University. He warned me that any such reference would most probably lead to fundamental objections which would jeopardize my chances of going ahead with it. I had initially chosen to define my subject as 'Problems that confront the sexual life of modern Egyptian women', but after prolonged negotiations I was prevailed to delete the word 'sexual' and replace it by 'psychological'. Only thus was it possible to circumvent the sensitivities of the professors at the Ein Shams Medical School and obtain their consent to go ahead with the research.

After I observed the very high percentages of women and girls who had been obliged to undergo circumcision, or who had been exposed to different forms of sexual violation or assault in their childhood, I started to look for research undertaken in these two areas, either in the medical colleges or in research institutes, but in vain. Hardly a single medical doctor or researcher had ventured to do any work on these subjects, in view of the sensitive nature of the issues involved. This can also be explained by the fact that most of the research carried out in such institutions is of a formal and superficial nature, since its sole aim is to obtain a degree or promotion. The path of safety is therefore the one to choose, and safety means to avoid carefully all subjects of controversy. No one is therefore prepared to face difficulties with the responsible academic and scientific authorities, or to engage in any form of struggle against them, or their ideas. Nor is anyone prepared to face up to those who lay down the norms of virtue, morals and religious behaviour in society. All the established leaderships in the area related to such matters suffer from a pronounced allergy to the word 'sex', and any of its implications, especially if it happens to be linked to the word 'woman'.

Nevertheless I was fortunate enough to discover a small number of medical doctors who had the courage to be different, and therefore to examine some of the problems related to the sexual life of women. I would like to cite, as one of the rare examples, the only research study carried out on the question of female circumcision in Egypt and its harmful effects. This was the joint effort of Dr. Mahmoud Koraim and Dr. Rushdi Ammar, both from Ein Shams Medical College, and which was published in 1965. It is composed of two parts, the first of which was printed under the title *Female Circumcision and Sexual Desire*,[2] and the second, under the title *Complications of Female Circumcision*.[3] The conclusions arrived at as a result of this research study, which covered 651 women circumcised during childhood, may be summarized as follows:

(1) Circumcision is an operation with harmful effects on the health of women, and is the cause of sexual shock to young girls. It reduces the capacity of a woman to reach the peak of her sexual pleasure (i.e. orgasm) and has a definite though lesser effect in reducing sexual desire.

(2) Education helps to limit the extent to which female circumcision is practised, since educated parents have an increasing tendency to refuse the operation for their daughters. On the other hand, uneducated families still go in for female circumcision in submission to prevailing traditions, or in the belief that removal of the clitoris reduces the sexual desire of the girl, and therefore helps to preserve her virginity and chastity after marriage.

(3) There is no truth whatsoever in the idea that female circumcision helps in reducing the incidence of cancerous disease of the external genital organs.

(4) Female circumcision in all its forms and degrees, and in particular the fourth degree known as Pharaonic or Sudanese excision, is accompanied by immediate or delayed complications such as inflammations, haemorrhage, disturbances in the urinary passages, cysts or swellings that can obstruct the urinary flow or the vaginal opening.

(5) Masturbation in circumcised girls is less frequent than was observed by Kinsey in girls who have not undergone this operation.

I was able to exchange views with Dr. Mahmoud Koraim during several meetings in Cairo. I learnt from him that he had faced numerous difficulties while undertaking his research, and was the target of bitter criticism from some of his colleagues and from religious leaders who considered themselves the divinely appointed protectors of morality, and therefore required to shield society from such impious undertakings, which constituted a threat to established values and moral codes.

The findings of my research study coincided with some of the conclusions arrived at by my two colleagues on a number of points. There is no longer any doubt that circumcision is the source of sexual and psychological shock in the life of the girl, and leads to a varying degree of sexual frigidity according to the woman and her circumstances. Education helps parents realize that this operation is not beneficial, and should be avoided, but I have found that the traditional education given in our schools and universities, whose aim is simply some certificate, or degree, rather than instilling useful knowledge and culture, is not very effective in combating the long-standing, and established traditions that govern Egyptian society, and in particular those related to sex, virginity in girls, and chastity in women. These areas are strongly linked to moral and religious values that have dominated and operated in our society for hundreds of years.

Since circumcision of females aims primarily at ensuring virginity before marriage, and chastity throughout, it is not to be expected that its practice will disappear easily from Egyptian society or within a short period of time. A growing number of educated families are, however, beginning to realize the harm that is done to females by this custom, and are therefore seeking to protect their daughters from being among its victims. Parallel to these changes, the operation itself is no longer performed in the old primitive way, and the more radical degrees approaching, or involving, excision are dying out more rapidly. Nowadays, even in Upper Egypt and the Sudan, the operation is limited to the total, or more commonly the partial, amputation of the clitoris. Nevertheless, while undertaking my research, I was surprised to discover, contrary to what I had previously thought, that even in educated urban families over 50% still consider circumcision as essential to ensure female virginity and chastity.

Many people think that female circumcision only started with the advent of Islam. But as a matter of fact it was well known and widespread in some areas of the world before the Islamic era, including in the Arab peninsula. Mahomet the Prophet tried to oppose this custom since he considered it harmful to the sexual health of the woman. In one of his sayings the advice reported as having been given by him to Om Attiah, a woman who did tattooings and circumcision, runs as follows: 'If you circumcise, take only a small part and refrain from cutting most of the clitoris off . . . The woman will have a bright and happy face, and is more welcome to her husband, if her pleasure is complete.'[4]

This means that the circumcision of girls was not originally an Islamic custom, and was not related to monotheistic religions, but was practised in societies with widely varying religious backgrounds, in countries of the East and the West, and among peoples who believed in Christianity, or in Islam, or were atheistic . . . Circumcision was known in Europe as late as the 19th century, as well as in countries like Egypt, the Sudan, Somaliland,

Ethiopia, Kenya, Tanzania, Ghana, Guinea and Nigeria. It was also practised in many Asian countries such as Sri Lanka and Indonesia, and in parts of Latin America. It is recorded as going back far into the past under the Pharaonic Kingdoms of Ancient Egypt, and Herodotus mentioned the existence of female circumcision seven hundred years before Christ was born. This is why the operation as practised in the Sudan is called 'Pharaonic excision'.

For many years I tried in vain to find relevant sociological or anthropological studies that would throw some light on the reasons why such a brutal operation is practised on females. However I did discover other practices related to girls and female children which were even more savage. One of them was burying female children alive almost immediately after they were born, or even at a later stage. Other examples are the chastity belt, or closing the aperture of the external genital organs with steel pins and a special iron lock.[5] This last procedure is extremely primitive and very much akin to Sudanese circumcision where the clitoris, external lips and internal lips are completely excised, and the orifice of the genital organs closed with a flap of sheep's intestines leaving only a very small opening barely sufficient to let the tip of the finger in, so that the menstrual and urinary flows are not held back. This opening is slit at the time of marriage and widened to allow penetration of the male sexual organ. It is widened again when a child is born and then narrowed down once more. Complete closure of the aperture is also done on a woman who is divorced, so that she literally becomes a virgin once more and can have no sexual intercourse except in the eventuality of marriage, in which case the opening is restored.

In the face of all these strange and complicated procedures aimed at preventing sexual intercourse in women except if controlled by the husband, it is natural that we should ask ourselves why women, in particular, were subjected to such torture and cruel suppression. There seems to be no doubt that society, as represented by its dominant classes and male structure, realized at a very early stage that sexual desire in the female is very powerful, and that women, unless controlled and subjugated by all sorts of measures, will not submit themselves to the moral, social, legal and religious constraints with which they have been surrounded, and in particular the constraints related to monogamy. The patriarchal system, which came into being when society had reached a certain stage of development and which necessitated the imposition of one husband on the woman whereas a man was left free to have several wives, would never have been possible, or have been maintained to this day, without the whole range of cruel and ingenious devices that were used to keep her sexuality in check and limit her sexual relations to only one man, who had to be her husband. This is the reason for the implacable enmity shown by society towards female sexuality, and the weapons used to resist and subjugate the turbulent force inherent in it. The slightest leniency manifested in facing this 'potential danger' meant that woman would break out of the prison bars to which marriage had confined her, and step over the steely limits of a monogamous relationship to a forbidden intimacy with another man, which would inevitably lead to confusion in succession and inheritance, since there was no guarantee that a strange man's child would not step into the waiting line of descendants. Confusion between the children of the legitimate husband and the outsider lover would mean the unavoidable collapse of the patriarchal family built around the name of the father alone.

History shows us clearly that the father was keen on knowing who his real children were, solely for the purpose of handing down his landed property to them. The patriarchal family, therefore, came into existence mainly for economic reasons. It was necessary for society simultaneously to build up a system of moral and religious values, as well as a legal system capable of protecting and maintaining these economic interests. In the final analysis we can safely say that female circumcision, the chastity belt and other savage practices applied to women are basically the result of the economic interests that govern society. The continued existence of such practices in our society today signifies that these economic interests are still operative. The thousands of *dayas,* nurses, para-medical staff and doctors, who make money out of female circumcision, naturally resist any change in these values and practices which are a source of gain to them. In the Sudan there is a veritable army of *dayas* who earn a livelihood out of the series of operations performed on women, either to excise their external genital organs, or to alternately narrow and widen the outer aperture according to whether the woman is marrying, divorcing, remarrying, having a child or recovering from labour.[6]

Economic factors and, concomitantly, political factors are the basis upon which such customs as female circumcision have grown up. It is important to understand the facts as they really are, and the reasons that lie behind them. Many are the people who are not able to distinguish between political and religious factors, or who conceal economic and political motives behind religious arguments in an attempt to hide the real forces that lie at the basis of what happens in society and in history. It has very often been proclaimed that Islam is at the root of female circumcision, and is also responsible for the under-privileged and backward situation of women in Egypt and the Arab countries. Such a contention is not true. If we study Christianity it is easy to see that this religion is much more rigid and orthodox where women are concerned than Islam. Nevertheless, many countries were able to progress rapidly despite the preponderance of Christianity as a religion. This progress was social, economic, scientific and also affected the life and position of women in society.

That is why I firmly believe that the reasons for the lower status of women in our societies, and the lack of opportunities for progress afforded to them, are not due to Islam, but rather to certain economic and political forces, namely those of foreign imperialism operating mainly from the outside, and of the reactionary classes operating from the inside. These two forces cooperate closely and are making a concerted attempt to misinterpret religion and to utilize it as an instrument of fear, oppression and exploitation.

Religion, if authentic in the principles it stands for, aims at truth, equality, justice, love and a healthy wholesome life for all people, whether men or women. There can be no true religion that aims at disease, mutilation of the bodies of female children, and amputation of an essential part of their reproductive organs.

If religion comes from God, how can it order man to cut off an organ created by Him as long as that organ is not diseased or deformed? God does not create the organs of the body haphazardly without a plan. It is not possible that He should have created the clitoris in woman's body only in order that it be cut off at an early stage in life. This is a contradiction into which neither true religion nor the Creator could possibly fall. If God has created the clitoris as a sexually sensitive organ, whose sole function seems to be the procurement of sexual pleasure for women, it follows that He also considers such pleasure for women as normal and legitimate, and therefore as an integral part of mental health. The psychic and mental health of women cannot be complete if they do not experience sexual pleasure.

There are still a large number of fathers and mothers who are afraid of leaving the clitoris intact in the bodies of their daughters. Many a time they have said to me that circumcision is a safeguard against the mistakes and deviations into which a girl may be led. This way of thinking is wrong and even dangerous because what protects a boy or a girl from making mistakes is not the removal of a small piece of flesh from the body, but consciousness and understanding of the problems we face, and a worthwhile aim in life, an aim which gives it meaning and for whose attainment we exert our mind and energies. The higher the level of consciousness to which we attain, the closer our aims draw to human motives and values, and the greater our desire to improve life and its quality, rather than to indulge ourselves in the mere satisfaction of our senses and the experience of pleasure, even though these are an essential part of existence. The most liberated and free of girls, in the true sense of liberation, are the least preoccupied with sexual questions, since these no longer represent a problem. On the contrary, a free mind finds room for numerous interests and the many rich experiences of a cultured life. Girls that suffer sexual suppression, however, are greatly preoccupied with men and sex. And it is a common observation that an intelligent and cultured woman is much less engrossed in matters related to sex and to men than is the case with ordinary women, who have not got much with which to fill their lives. Yet at the same time such a woman takes much more initiative to ensure that she will enjoy sex and experience pleasure, and acts with a greater degree of boldness than others. Once sexual satisfaction is attained, she is able to turn herself fully to other important aspects of life.

In the life of liberated and intelligent women, sex does not occupy a disproportionate position, but rather tends to maintain itself within normal limits. In contrast, ignorance, suppression, fear and all sorts of limitations exaggerate the role of sex in the life of girls and women, and cause it to swell out of all proportion and to end up by occupying the whole, or almost the whole, of their lives.

References

1. This research study was carried out in the years 1973 and 1974 in the School of Medicine, Ein Shams University, under the title: *Women and Neurosis.*
2. *Female Circumcision and Sexual Desire,* Mahmoud Koraim and Rushdi Ammar, (Ein Shams University Press, Cairo, 1965).
3. *Complications of Female Circumcision,* the same authors, (Cairo, 1965).
4. See *Dawlat El Nissa'a,* Abdel Rahman El Barkouky, first edition, (Renaissance Bookshop, Cairo, 1945).
5. Desmond Morris, *The Naked Ape,* (Corgi, 1967). p.76.
6. Rose Oldfield, 'Female genital mutilation, fertility control, women's roles, and patrilineage in modern Sudan', *American Ethnologist,* Vol. II, No. 4, November 1975.

7. Obscurantism and Contradiction

In the first stages of its life a child cannot depend on itself, but later on it gradually learns how to do without others, when seeking to satisfy some of its needs. In this process of becoming independent, it therefore loses its passivity and becomes more and more self-reliant. This inevitably leads to the development of positive reactions, the ability to choose, to decide and to act with freedom. All these changes together constitute growth or development, both physical and mental. Mental and psychological development is in its essence a movement towards greater independence of the personality, the ability to make choices, personal freedom and a sense of responsibility.

But the strongly patriarchal relations in Arab society, coupled with its hierarchical class nature, have subjected women to a great deal of discrimination and caused them to be victims of a very marked degree of suppression, both physical and mental. Arab society also suppresses children, and even men, but the load carried by women is multiplied by the severe physical and psychological constraints which surround their lives. As a result, the mental and psychological development of a woman is greatly retarded, and she is unable to free herself from passive attitudes and the habit of depending on others. She remains like a child in the early stages of its life, but differs in the fact that her body has grown, and that she may have reached the age of thirty, forty or even fifty years.

The forms of suppression exercised against women are manifold. Most of them rely on fear and intimidation, on subtle or direct forms of obscurantism, on keeping her in the dark, ignorant, deprived of true knowledge. For a woman, right from the early stages of childhood and during the years of growth, adolescence and youth, is deprived of any real knowledge about her body and herself.

Ignorance about the body and its functions in girls and women is considered a sign of honour, purity and good morals and if, in contrast, a girl does know anything about sex and about her body, it is considered something undesirable and even shameful. A mature woman with experience and knowledge of life is looked upon as being less worthy than a simple, naive and ignorant woman. Experience is looked upon almost as a deformity to be hidden, and not as a mark of intrinsic human value.

Women, therefore, tend to nurture their ignorance and simplemindedness so that society continues to look upon them as being virtuous and of good reputation. Parents also encourage ignorance in their daughters, and want them to be simple and naive, to remain 'blind pussy cats' as the Egyptians would say. For a 'blind pussy cat' is what an average Egyptian man would consider the kind of girl best suited to be a wife.

This cult of ignorance does not apply to matters related to sex and men alone, but is advocated in so far as all matters related to the female body are concerned. Arab girls are therefore brought up in an environment of darkness and silence concerning everything related to the body and its functions. They are often seized with nervous shock, therefore, on the day when, opening their eyes in the morning, they perceive a trickle of red blood between their thighs and a scarlet stain on the white sheet beneath their buttocks.

It would be difficult for anyone to imagine the panic that seized hold of me one morning when I woke to find blood trickling down between my thighs. I can still remember the deathly pallor of my face in the mirror. My arms and legs were trembling violently and it appeared to me as though the disaster which had frightened me for so long was now a fact. That somehow, in the dark of night, a man had crept into my room while I was sleeping and succeeded in causing me harm. This eventuality had never left my thoughts and each night, before going to bed, I used to close the window overlooking the street as tightly as possible.

An amusing aspect of this situation is that on the previous day at school we had been given a lesson on the subject of bilharzia. This is a parasitic disease that infects the urinary tracts of rural folk in Egypt. At one of its stages in the life cycle, the parasite lodges in the soft tissues of a water snail, and is released into the water of streams and canals where it penetrates the body by piercing the skin of the legs. One of the symptoms of this disease is blood in the urine and it occurred to me that I might have become infected with it, which would explain the red trickle emanating from the opening between my thighs.

I was then ten years old and thought that, if this was so, all I had to do was to wait until the disease cured itself. But the flow of blood did not stop. On the contrary, it increased from hour to hour and on the following day I was obliged to overcome the fear and shame that possessed me and speak to my mother. I asked her to take me to a doctor for treatment. To my utter surprise she was calm and cool and did not seem to be affected by her daughter's serious condition. She explained this was something that happened to all girls and that it recurs every month for a few days. On the last day when the flow ceased, I was to cleanse myself of this 'impure blood' by having a hot bath. Her words echoed in my ears: 'monthly condition', 'a hot bath' to rid me of the 'impure blood'. I was therefore to understand that in me there was something degrading which appeared regularly in the form of this impure blood, and that it was something to be ashamed of, to hide from others. So I stayed in my room for four consecutive days, unable to face anybody. When I opened the door on my way to the bathroom, I would look around to make sure that nobody was in sight, and before returning I would wash the floor carefully as though removing the marks of a recent crime, and under my arms and between my legs, several times, to make sure that no smell of this impure blood remained.

These incidents are typical of the life of Arab girls who are brought up in an atmosphere of sexual fear and kept in ignorance of their reproductive organs and of the natural physiological functions carried out by different parts of the body. Girls are made to feel the difference between themselves and boys from early childhood. A brother can go out and play and jump around. But a girl must remain indoors, and, if her skirt rises just one centimetre above the prescribed level, her mother will throw threatening glances at her and put her to shame.

Her thigh is a source of evil, a taboo that must be hidden from sight. From a young age a girl is made to feel that her body is something impure, obscene and must remain invisible, unseen. Newspapers, magazines and the mass media instil religious conceptions that portray the female body as an obscenity that should be hidden carefully. Only the face and palms of the hand should appear and, for this reason, many girls take to the wearing of veils.

Yet despite these rigid and orthodox teachings which deny sex in the life of a girl and aim at moulding her into an asexual being, a parallel and contradictory educational process is going on all the time which seeks to make her an instrument of sex and a mere body which should be adorned and made beautiful so as to attract men and arouse their desire. A girl is trained, again from early childhood, to be almost wholly preoccupied with her body, her hair, her eyelashes, and clothes, at the expense of her mind and thoughts and her future as a human being. Arab girls are reared for the role of marriage which is the supreme function of women in society, whereas education, work and a career are considered secondary matters which should in no way divert her from her primary functions as a wife whose job is to cook, serve her husband and look after her children.

As a child I had to struggle against the whole family so that I could be permitted to read and develop my mind. I used to refuse cooking and cleaning in the house and insist on going to school. I would rebel against long hair, coloured ribbons and plaits, and wonder why my mother paid so much attention to my clothes and dresses. I used to surpass my brothers at school and gain high marks, yet nobody seemed to be happy or think of congratulating me. Yet if I once cooked a bad meal, everyone would criticize me.

The moment I took refuge in my own small world of illustrated books and coloured pencils, my mother would drag me to the kitchen and mumble: 'Your future lies in marriage and you must learn to cook.' Your future is in marriage, marriage! That ugly word that my mother would never tire of repeating until I hated it with all my being. No sooner pronounced, I would imagine before my eyes a man with a swollen belly full of food. The smell of the kitchen for me was the smell of men. So I learnt to hate the smell of men, and the smell of food.

For me, everything my mother said seemed to be contradictory. How come that she should always be warning me about sex and men, and yet always be so careful about my appearance and clothes, with the sole aim of making me more desirable to them? I was mortally afraid of men, and used to avoid them like the plague. I believed that proximity to a man could only bring shame and be a danger to my reputation as a good respectable girl. Yet, at the same time, I felt deep inside me a tremendous force that attracted me to the opposite sex. The passionate songs full of yearning and love, or the films which we saw now and again, only served to increase my obscure desires. Many a time I would conjure up a scene in my mind in which an unknown man would hold me in his arms, and at the very next moment I would be overpowered by a feeling of guilt and shame, a feeling that was magnified by the pleasure I derived from these daydreams. I could not understand myself or assimilate the inherent contradictions in my thoughts and actions. Inside me there would be a burning flame and, on the outside, a picture of cool indifference.

Yet this calm indifference was not a pose. I hated men, yet somehow the man of my dreams was different. I could not define in what way he differed from other men for, in appearance, he resembled them completely.

What I experienced as a girl, though different in some ways, is a replica of the trials that affect all girls in our society. Love and yearning are a constant theme in Arab songs and films and leave a deep impression on the mental and emotional make-up of a girl. At the same time she is exposed to a whole system of traditional and religious values. But the moment she falls in love with a young man, her reputation is at stake, her name is bandied around in a scandalous way, and she falls victim to the values of a puritanical and corrupt society.

Her fate is a hundred times worse if she happens to fall in love with a *poor* man. On the other hand if he is rich, the family may encourage the love affair and help her to attract the man into marriage. For decision-making in marriage is still largely a family matter and most fathers are still prepared to sell their daughters into wedlock for a good price. Parental authority is shamefully misused when the matter concerns daughters. The Arab family being highly patriarchal, both socially and legally, the authority of the father over his daughters is absolute. In the name of a good marriage young girls are given to old decrepit husbands just because they can pay a big dowry.

In recent years, with the spread of consumer values, and with money flowing through the hands of speculators, black marketeers, oil barons etc., many poor girls have been sold into prostitution under the legal cover of arranged marriages. The case of the young girl whose father forged a birth certificate to show that her age was eighteen and not twelve, in order to marry her to an old man in exchange for a large sum of money, is no longer an isolated case.[1]

This absolute authority enjoyed by the father permits him to act with impunity and to ensure that the law is on his side, even if right is on the side of the daughter.

As an example I would like to cite a story published in one of our morning newspapers under the title 'The Court decides on divorce because the wife married without her father's consent.' The bride was over twenty-one years old and had decided to marry the man she loved, without the prior consent of her father. The marriage contract and ceremony were presided over by a *maazoun* (religious dignitary), according to Islamic law, in the presence of two witnesses. The marriage was therefore regular in both its legal and religious aspects. Subsequently the father initiated juridical proceedings in which he requested that the marriage contract be considered null and void because the daughter had not sought his consent. Despite the fact that the girl had come of age, and was therefore perfectly free to choose her own partner, the court nevertheless accepted the father's plea, basing its decision on the fact that, according to tradition and custom in the country, the consent of the father is essential, and that this consideration should be sufficient to overrule the fact that the marriage was fully in accordance with the civil and religious legal provisions. (In addition, it was also current practice for the father, or another male member of the family like the uncle or brother, to represent the daughter at the wedding ceremony.)[2]

In fact the only reason why the father had opposed this marriage was the fact that the bridegroom belonged to a poor family and the marriage ran counter to the original plan of finding a rich husband for the daughter. A genuine attachment to human values would have required the father to be rebuked for his mercenary attitude which meant that, for him, the daughter was no more than a commodity for sale. Thus a marriage built on mutual love and understanding, and on a contract in complete compliance with the law, was flouted and arbitrarily overruled by the court, in order to uphold the authority of a father and a social system based on class, sex and mercenary discrimination.

Parents and educational systems pay lip-service to human values, to equality, freedom and work. But the vast majority of families, in practice, pay little attention to these values when a decision has to be taken on the marriage of a daughter. Here tradition, custom, class and money remain the overriding considerations.

Since the fifties, there have been enlightened Arab men and women who have expended great efforts to change the backward traditions and unjust laws that govern the life and destiny of women. Their contribution to progress has brought with it whatever rights women now enjoy. Nevertheless a long road lies ahead, for women are still deprived of many essential human rights. The social forces that oppose true equality for women still have recourse to moral and religious values. And yet everyday these very values are violated on the screens of cinemas and television sets, and on the posters of commercial advertisements, the pages of political and social studies and through floods of pornographic literature and a never ending stream of songs and radio broadcasts. And yet here again the men who represent these social forces remain silent, and sometimes even participate openly or indirectly in propagating ideas which are the negation of the principles they profess.

These double standards in the moral attitudes and values of Arab society are characteristic of the present situation. The life of individuals and of society as a whole is shot through with deep contradictions:—

1. A rush of films that depend for their attraction on sexual stimulation, vulgar dances, nakedness and disguised pornography. The same tendency is reflected in T.V. programmes, magazines, advertisements etc.

2. An orchestrated religious campaign spreading rapidly to all means of communication and which permeates every aspect of educational, cultural and informational activity. As part of this campaign, young girls in Egypt are reverting to the veil, there is a growing crescendo voicing demands for 'a return to Islamic law', 'prohibition', 'the woman's place is at home', 'punish immoral women'.

3. Parallel with this religious campaign, moral looseness in all spheres of life is also a noticeable phenomenon: disguised forms of prostitution that involve girls in schools and universities and a noticeable increase in the white slave trade, sometimes covered up by false marriage certificates, etc.

For with the rapid infiltration of commercial values the barriers constructed by religious and moral standards are easily swept away, and in the commercial race women's bodies are an important commodity and a source of 'super profits'.

This fundamental hypocrisy in contemporary Arab society inevitably has its victims, and women above all are made to suffer, perhaps more than ever before. They are crushed in the mill of contradiction between lip service to traditional religious and moral precepts, and the invasion of their lives by vested political and economic interests whose first and foremost aim is profit at any cost, and in the shortest possible time.

Arab women are sacrificed on the altars of God and Money from the moment of birth to the hour of death. Children are made to suffer more than their elders, poor people more than the rich, women more than men and those that are ruled more than those who wield the reins of power. For, in order to fight back in a society torn by such contradictions, a person must be armed either with money, or authority, or masculinity, or legal backing, or age. If deprived of all such weapons, they will be helpless in the face of powerful and furious forces, rushing on blindly to crush those who are defenceless.

It is not difficult to imagine what can be the fate of a female illegitimate child born in poverty when faced with a society where such blind forces are being let loose. Death is perhaps a merciful end when compared with the life that faces such a child, born by a will over which she has no control.

A female child, even if legitimate, will remain underprivileged as compared with her brother. To this day most families, whether urban or rural, are happy at the birth of a male child and disappointed when the child is a girl.

A daughter does not bring with her the advantages of a son. The son carries the name of his family and provides it with continuity, whereas a girl ends up as a member of her husband's family. A daughter may become a source of dishonour, for honour is still closely linked with premarital virginity and fidelity to the husband after marriage.

References

1. *Akhbar El Yom*, weekly edition, August 1975, p.10.
2. *Akhbar El Yom*, weekly edition, 5 January 1974, p.10.

8. The Illegitimate Child and the Prostitute

In its essence real honour is in contradiction with all forms of slavery, subjugation and imposition, and with all forms of trade and commercialization of human beings, whether they be slaves, women, or children. True honour is fundamentally against transforming a human being into an instrument, or an object, or a commodity for sale. The marriage customs and laws followed in our patriarchal and class society are the negation of true honour, for they have transformed woman into merchandise, which can be bought in exchange for a dowry and sold at the price of an alimony. Sometimes she can even be sold for nothing, and we only have to read the text of Article 67 of the *Common Law on Marriage* to realize that this last statement is no exaggeration. This article says:

> No alimony is liable to a wife if she refuses to yield herself to her husband and is not within her rights when so doing, or is obliged to refuse herself to him for a reason which is not inherent in the husband himself. She is also not entitled to an alimony if put in jail, even though unjustly, or in a concentration camp, or if she is the victim of a rape, or if she changes her religion, or if prevented from living with her husband by her parents, or if she is suffering from any condition which might prevent the husband from utilizing her as a wife. [*sic*].

The term 'not utilizable as a wife' lays bare the true nature of the relationship which exists between a man and a woman after marriage. It is a relationship built on the utilization of the woman by the man, on her exploitation by him, in a manner which is more inhuman than the exploitation by a landowner of his labourers or a master of his slave. The master was expected to treat his slave if the latter fell sick, but a wife has no rights and can be treated, or is very often treated, much worse than a slave or a labourer, since she works in her husband's house and serves his children without being given any pay. If she should happen to fall seriously ill the husband can, according to the marriage law, send her back to her parents, since he is not legally responsible for ensuring that she receives the necessary care.

The phenomenon of 'illegitimate' children stands out in history as one of the crimes committed by the patriarchal class system. Some of the more advanced capitalist countries have been obliged to face this problem by instituting the system of adoption which has now become quite common in some Western countries. This change runs parallel to, or follows, the increased participation of women in the active labour force and their tendency to move more and more out of the home and take up paid work. The law in some of these countries, therefore, accords them the right to give their names to their children and thus spare them the misery from which illegitimate children used to suffer before. Economic rights help to change the status of women and to make them equal to men so that even their name receives an equal standing and is sufficient to carry with it 'honourability', social approval and legal rights to the children.

Islamic societies do not permit adoption, and a child cannot ever give proof of its parentage by referring to adoption. Islam insists that every child must be attributed to its father and states that those whom you only declare to be your children cannot be considered so, for that is only word of mouth. 'Allah speaks the truth and shows you the right path . . . Relate them to their fathers for that is more acceptable to Allah. If you do not know their fathers, however, relate them to your brothers in religion.'[1]

Tunisia, however, has forged ahead in this area by establishing a system of adoption, whereas the law in other Islamic Arab countries still forbids it. In Morocco, for example, the Family Law peremptorily declares that 'Adoption has no juridical value, and does not lead to any of the effects of affiliation [son and daughter]'.[2]

Many illegitimate children were born as a result of the sexual freedom enjoyed in Islamic societies. The laws of affiliation by which descent from parents is regulated were therefore obliged to encompass and draw into the fold of legitimacy a large number of these victims. The substance and the letter of the marriage laws and their logical and juridical basis have thus to be openly flouted. The affiliation of a child to its father, according to Islamic legislation, can therefore be decided in one of the following ways:—

1. Sexual intercourse with a woman who is legally the man's wife.
2. Inferred or suspected sexual intercourse with a woman.
3. The confession or acknowledgement of the man.
4. If trustworthy people bear witness that the child is that of a particular man.

A Legally Sound Marriage Contract

If a man has had sexual intercourse with his wife and ejaculated in such a way that part of the semen could have reached the uterus (or if he spent some time alone with her in a situation which fulfils the conditions of the Sunnite rites), and if a minimum pregnancy time of six months has elapsed from the date of intercourse, and if the woman has not surpassed the maximum period of pregnancy, which is one year from that date (two years in the Hanafi theological school and four years for the Shafei's and the Maliki's), then the child is that of the man.[3]

By laying down this ruling, Islamic society tried to reduce the number of illegitimate children as much as possible. Another idea that reinforced this tendency was the concept of what was known as the 'sleeping child', built on the Islamic saying, 'a child is the son of the bedding', and which also conformed with the Prophet's dictum: 'the child is of the bedding'. Two explanations were put forward for this saying. The first maintained that it indicated a new need to affiliate the child to the father whereas the custom previously had been to seek the line of descent from the mother. The second was built on the assumption that any child born of a married woman had to be automatically considered the child of her husband. The Imam Abou Hanifa maintained that a marriage contract alone, irrespective of its period of duration, was sufficient to indicate that any child born of the woman was from the husband. Even if a married woman had a child in the absence of the husband, an absence which could last as much as four years, he was still considered legally the father. In the same way, if a woman gave birth to a child only three or four months after marriage, the husband was again named as the father. Such a child received the appellation 'sleeping child'.

However, modern scientific knowledge about the normal length of pregnancy and the number of months during which an embryo can remain alive in the womb of its mother, as well as the large number of both legitimate and illegitimate children who were being born, led Islamic Arab society to discard the concept of 'the sleeping child'.

Until 1929, Egyptian society followed the teachings of Abou Hanifa who considered that any child born of a married woman should be attributed to her husband, and that the marriage contract was alone sufficient to prove the fatherhood and parentage of the child. This later changed and the condition laid down by the three Imams, Ahmed Ibn Hanbal, El Shafei and Malik, namely proof that intercourse had taken place between husband and wife or that it had possibly taken place, was added in determining the parentage of a child.

Tunisia and Morocco have also rejected the idea of 'the sleeping child' in their modern legislation. One of the articles in the Moroccan Family Law stipulates that:

The maximum duration of pregnancy is one year calculated from the date of repudiation (divorce) or death [of the husband]. If at the end of the period of one year, there is still some doubt as to the pregnancy, the case will be submitted to a judge by the interested party. The judge will then consult experts from the medical profession.[4]

Affiliation through Legalized Adultery
If a man has sexual intercourse with a woman to whom he is married without knowing that she is not really his wife, or with a woman forbidden to him although he thought she was his wife, or with a woman whom he has married by contract without realizing that legally she cannot become his wife, and if, as a result of one of these sexual relations, the woman becomes pregnant, no adultery is considered to have been committed by the couple, since at the

time of their relationship they were ignorant of the fact that they were not really married. The child then is legally attributed to the man and he is considered the legal father.[5] [It is implied, of course, that the father recognises his marriage with the woman, and the child born of this marriage.]

The above stipulations demonstrate how lenient towards the sexual freedom of men most Islamic laws are. A man can have relations with any woman who is not his wife, without being considered to have committed adultery, and be the legal father of the child that ensues from this relation, on condition that at the time he believed that the woman was really his wife! Is such a situation possible? It is true that all sorts of things can happen, but the least we can say is that a case like this must be very difficult to come across. It is possible for a man to have sex with a woman and not know whether she is his wife or not? Perhaps, under the influence of drink, but no provision for alcohol is made in Islam since in any case it is *haram* (forbidden).

If a man can be in such a state that he cannot differentiate between his wife and another woman, is it not possible to conceive of a woman, in her turn, being unable to tell her husband from another man? Is it not possible to allow for such a situation with women especially, since according to religious teaching they are inferior in mind and religious conviction, whereas men are provided with a greater degree of reason and wisdom, and therefore less liable to lose track of what they are doing?

If we follow this reasoning to its logical conclusion, it means that any man who practises sexual relations with a woman other than his wife can escape the accusation of adultery merely on the grounds that he did not realize who the woman really was at the time. If this is so, to whom then will the law on adultery be applicable?

Confession or Acknowledgement of the Man

Affiliation of children to their parents may be determined by acknowledgement, that is if the man declares that he is the father of the child and if there is no other man to dispute his claim. The child need not acquiesce to this fatherhood if he or she is still small, but once grown up, such acquiescence is essential.

Thus it is that an unmarried man without a wife can still have legitimate children. A woman in the same situation, however, does not have the same privileges. The children born of her relationship with a man who is not her husband will be considered illegitimate unless he confesses to being the father, and on condition that no other man competes with him for the child or children.

Trustworthy Witnesses

Lines of descent in general, and the parentage of children in particular, can be determined if trustworthy witnesses agree to give testimony. These witnesses are usually two in number. So if two brothers testify that a child is the son of their dead brother, that is sufficient evidence. The two trustworthy witnesses in this case are male members of the family. On the other hand, testimony of the woman who gave birth to the child is not considered valid.

If the man is accorded the right to testify to his fatherhood, he is also given exactly the same prerogative in denying his parentage of a child, even if it is only a question of doubt as far as he is concerned. A man who is sure that he is not the father of a particular child is compelled, according to religious law, to deny his parentage. It is strictly forbidden for him to claim to be father of a child whom he knows has definitely been born of another father.

A husband may deny his fatherhood if a child is born earlier than six months after sexual intercourse with the woman or later than the maximum time limit for a full term pregnancy (usually considered as one year). If, however, the child has not been born earlier than the minimum or later than the maximum of these periods, and if the marriage contract with the woman is a permanent one, then the way of denying his parenthood of the child is by a procedure of repudiation called *La'an* (derived from *Lan* which means 'curse').[6] This procedure consists in the father sending a complaint to the legal ruler (the religious-political leader) in his region or area, denying his fatherhood of the child, upon which the ruler will ask him to stand before him and testify to the fact. He must repeat four times: 'I testify before Allah, that I am telling the truth when I maintain that this child is not of me [of my issue].' After having repeated these words the requisite number of times, he is supposed to add: 'May I be accursed by Allah if I lied when I accused my wife, and said that the child was not mine.' After the husband has born witness, it is the turn of the wife. In conformity with the instructions of the ruler, she is supposed to say four times: 'I swear to Allah that my husband is lying when he accuses me of adultery.' Then, after having completed her testimony, she is supposed to say: 'May Allah's wrath smite me if my husband is telling the truth.'

Judgement is then passed as a result of the *La'an*. Such a judgement may include denial of the man as parent of the child and perpetual separation between the man and the woman concerned.[7]

According to these Islamic legal provisions it is clear that not only an unmarried man, but even a husband, can repudiate his own son, born of his wife, if he merely repeats the words of the *La'an* four times in succession. This can happen even if the marriage contract is perfectly in order, the minimum and maximum periods of pregnancy are in consonance with what is required by the law, and even if the wife swears to the fact that the child is his and no one else's. The ruler who passes judgement on both of them is a man, and not a woman, and the society within which he operates is male dominated and strongly patriarchal. Who therefore would believe a woman and place the lie with the man? A man, in the eyes of the law and religious custom, is much closer to the truth and reason and what is right, and a woman much more prone to lies and deceit and to a lack of understanding and awareness. And yet, as we saw earlier, it was the man who showed a strange lack of awareness when the point in question was his right to have sexual relations with a woman other than his wife, and his right to accept or repudiate the parentage of a child born as a result of sexual relations within or outside the framework of marriage.

The procedure of *La'an* permits a man to deny his fatherhood of a child simply because he is assailed by doubts about the loyalty of his wife, and the laws of parentage give the man an absolute right to refuse to give his name to a child just because he had not signed a marriage contract with the mother.

The law punishes a woman for committing adultery much more heavily than it does a man. In Egypt her punishment could be a maximum prison sentence of two years. A man, however, is not punished for adultery as long as it is committed outside the home in which his wife is living with him. Even if he is caught having sexual relations with another woman in the very same house, his sentence cannot exceed six months' imprisonment.[8] Usually the woman alone is punished, since infidelity in a woman towards her husband is branded by the law, by custom and by religious precepts as an inexcusable crime. The disloyalty of a husband towards his wife, however, is looked upon much more lightly, and can even be tacitly permitted by law, custom and religous precepts. Adultery in a woman has dangerous consequences for the established system; it may lead to confusion between the descendants and in inheritance, both of which together constitute the cornerstone of the patriarchal system.

According to Egyptian law, if a man is caught in sexual intercourse with a prostitute he is not put in jail, but is used as a witness against her, whereas she is sentenced to a term of imprisonment. When such kinds of inequality exist no law can be just. Therefore all the laws that are promulgated within the framework of the patriarchal system with the aim of regulating the relationsnip between man and woman are forcibly unjust.

Prostitution means sexual intercourse between a man and a woman aimed at satisfying the man's sexual and the woman's economic needs. It is obvious that sexual needs, even in a male dominated system, are not as urgent and important as economic needs which, if not satisfied, lead to disease and death. Yet society considers the woman's economic need as less vital than the man's sexual one. This situation can only arise where inequality exists. The needs of the rulers or owners of property will always be more important than the needs of those who are ruled over by others, or of people who are mere wage-earners. The need of the master for recreation or pleasure is more vital than the need of the servant or slave for food or sleep. The need of the ruling classes for colour television is much greater than the need of the rural masses for pure water. The need of a man for sexual pleasure is more important than the need of his wife for food or medical care, and more vital than the need of a prostitute for a loaf of bread or for clothing with which to cover her body. She can therefore be put in jail, while he must go free and be enabled to continue his quest for other women.

Historically, prostitution started with the patriarchal system, with the division of society into landowners and slaves. At the same time there arose the earliest regulation of sexual relations through primitive forms of marriage. Prostitution in fact is the opposite face of the coin to marriage. Men needed marriage to identify their children, but they also wanted to give free rein to their sexual desires. The chastity belt and marital fidelity were therefore imposed on women alone. It is indeed fascinating to follow how man was able to condone his going to a woman other than his wife. In order to do this he cloaked his desire behind the mask of religion and made out of sex with the prostitute a religious rite and an act of sanctity.

Later on, the ruler or the King was the representative of God on earth and in some countries it was his right to have the first night with every virgin who was getting married.[9] To this very day the Sheikh ruling one of the Arab countries is provided with a virgin for one night every month, after which he never sees her again. Subsequently the male members of the upper-class families compete for the hand of this young woman because she has had the signal honour of having slept with the Sheikh and because she is, as a result of this event, the recipient of a very substantial allowance.

In Europe, during the Middle Ages, it became the right of the feudal lord to spend the first night with any young girl who was getting married if her family were living on his property or if the man she was marrying happened to be one of his serfs. The feudal lord was accorded this right by the King, Ruler or Prince. This system of the first night was known in Latin as *Jus Prunae Noctus.*[10]

Among certain tribes it was the function of the father to deflorate the young girl on her wedding night. He was thus able to satisfy his sexual passion for a young girl under the guise of a religious ceremony or ritual. The Babylonians believed that the gods were in the habit of paying a nightly visit to devout women in order to ensure that they gave birth to sons.[11] Sacred or religious prostitution continued to be practised until the 4th Century A.D., but in the year 325 A.D. the Emperor Constantine abolished it by decree.

In Ancient Egypt the noble families used to choose the most beautiful of their daughters and bestow them as a gift on the God Amoun whose temple was in Thebes. As the years passed and the young girl grew into an older woman, incapable of giving satisfaction to the priests, she was relieved of her duties amidst great marks of respect and ceremonial rites, was married to a man in the community and was welcomed in the most elevated of homes and families. These sacred prostitutes constituted a class of high priestesses and were known as the Harem (or Women) of the God Amoun.[12]

Sacred or temple prostitution has continued to exist during our present era in certain countries such as India and Japan. The temples in certain parts of India still accept girls who have agreed to devote their lives to the service of the gods, and allow them to live in the precincts of the temple where they carry out various functions. Some of these young women are chosen for the purpose of secretly satisfying the sexual needs of the priests and others even undertake to cater for a certain number of influential visitors or pilgrims. Fathers in ancient Phoenecia used to offer their daughters to visitors as a token of welcome. This form of prostitution was known and spread to Europe, continuing until the Middle Ages. Governments had a special category of prostitutes to look after important visitors for which purpose certain Municipal or Town Councils in the 14th Century used to run special houses.

Even today, in most countries of the East and West, as well as in Arab countries, there are various agencies operated by the state, such as intelligence agencies, special police forces (secret police, political police etc.) and embassies, which continue to use prostitution for obtaining information, influencing people and winning them over to certain points of view, blackmailing them etc.[13] Women are offered to special guests, political personalities and others and sometimes this is almost a routine procedure as, for example, in some of the Asian countries.

Houses of prostitution have continued throughout the ages to fulfil functions which appear vital to patriarchal society for at no time in history have they disappeared. In the early part of the period when Christianity spread over the whole of Europe, vestiges of a religious relationship between prostitution and the church still survived.[14]

A study of the history of prostitution, and of the changes that have affected moral and religious values in relation to the social and economic system, greatly enhances our understanding of the factors which have led to the subjection of women and the social and economic oppression to which certain classes in society are exposed and the motivating forces which have contributed so much towards shaping relations between the sexes.

For example, the oppression of women in India was so severe and cruel that until very recently it was customary to burn the widow alive after her husband's death. Even today, isolated cases occur where a widow is prevailed upon by social pressures to burn herself after the loss of her husband. The priests used to insist that this was the right thing to do, especially when the widow was rich, since her money according to law would pass to the temple!

In all ages it has been possible for people to change the system of marriage and the relationships between the sexes according to economic necessities without having any qualms about the question of moral standards or values. During periods of widespread poverty and stringency, parents are allowed to rid themselves of children by killing them, abortion becomes rife, sexual relations outside marriage strictly prohibited, while people are encouraged not to marry, or to marry and practise birth control. Society is, and always has been, capable of choosing from religion those values that are consonant with and serve to fulfil its economic interests. When there is a period of relative prosperity and labour is scarce, things change again and people are encouraged to have lots of offspring, whether inside or outside the marriage relationship.

In certain areas of Southern India, I visited poor tribal communities who forbade polygamy and allowed polyandry so that a woman would have more than one man, but each man had to be satisfied with only one woman. Thus a number of men, often brothers, became the husbands of one woman. This served a double purpose: it reduced expenditure and limited the number of children. Polyandry, was widespread for relatively long periods in history, but the economic reasons for its prevalence used to vary according to circumstances. In the Arab region before Islam and in the Spartan Republic of Ancient Greece, the law allowed a woman to have several husbands, on condition that she only had one child. The excess children in Sparta were killed off by the state, buried alive in the cemetery called Taigitos.

The inhabitants of Ancient Greece were allowed to practise all conceivable types of extra-marital sexual relations on condition that they had no deleterious effect on the wealth of the husband and did not lead to his inheritance falling into the hands of people from a lower social class or going to the children of another man.

In Roman society it was the man's right to adopt a son whose mother was unknown, the boy then becoming his legal son. The woman, however, could not adopt a boy whose fatherhood was not known. The reasons for this differentiation were purely economic and were related to questions of property and inheritance.

When the prolonged war between Athens and Sparta broke out at the end of the 5th Century B.C., it devoured a large number of men who had been absent from their homes for a long time, and who had left behind women living on their own. Thereupon the men who had not gone to war, but remained behind, started to think of some way that would allow them to have sexual relations with these women. Within a relatively short space of time ideas that called for, and defended, sexual freedom for women were being widely proclaimed and the best brains actively sought for plausible arguments in support of this new cause. Among them was the famous physician of Ancient Greece, Hippocrates, the father of medicine, who conveniently discovered that the womb needed continuous nourishment from the man (till then no man had evinced any particular interest in the fate of the uterus) and that if it were deprived of this necessary nourishment, the woman was liable to be seized with a nervous condition which he called 'hysteria' (derived from the Greek word for womb). Women before that time had lived in a condition of almost continuous sexual deprivation, but nobody had thought of the need to keep them satisfied. However now, as a result of this new terrible disease called hysteria, the non-combatants who were left behind, or who had chosen to stay in order to pay attention to the more important affairs of state, once more decided to sacrifice themselves for a noble cause, and enter into sexual relations with the unfortunate women who had been left on their own, and whose health would be in dire danger if no way were found of satisfying their sexual needs in time. The sexual needs of the men, of course, were not a matter taken into account!

At the time when the chastity belt was in vogue for women, especially during the Middle Ages, simultaneously sexual licence and prostitution spread like a prairie fire. Most husbands travelled widely, and often, in those days, for commerce had become a lucrative occupation and more and more families were turning to trade. Commercial travellers and merchants perforce had to leave their wives on their own and so man's ingenuity invented the chastity belt, made of iron. It was worn over the external genital organs of the woman and locked by the loving hands of the husband with a key which he carried away with him in his pocket. No doubt the feel of the key between his fingers helped to set his mind at rest, and allowed him to concentrate on the difficult job of making money, now that the property left behind was safely guarded.

However, a close analysis of merchant travels will show that very often the time and energy devoted by the husband during his travels to sexual enter- tainment with mistresses and prostitutes was more than that which he expended on his commercial activities. But this did not have to worry him unduly, since the children who might be born of such relations could not ever claim a share in his inheritance.

Men of religion, and priests, in their turn, were no less active in so far as sexual preoccupations were concerned. Immorality became widespread, the number of prostitutes multiplied at a vertiginous rate and hordes of illegitimate children were born. Those wearing the frock of the monk and the friar, or the flowing robes of the priest, despite the fact that they had taken an oath of lifetime chastity and renunciation of worldly pleasures, contributed with distinction to the sexual orgies that characterized these Middle or Dark Ages. The time came when the prostitute became an inseparable part of life and society, a necessity that could not be foregone, either in peace or war.

Politicians and rulers realized very early that it was not possible to muster an army, to ensure that it confronted the enemy with fortitude, and to conserve the health of its soldiers, if their sexual needs were not adequately taken care of. It therefore became the duty of those who raised and comman- ded these armies, not only to ensure that they were provided with arms, ammunition, food and clothing, but also to supply them with hundreds and even thousands of prostitutes, upon whom they could throw themselves with frenzy before the battle or after it was over. Therefore it is said that prosti- tution as a profession prospered and flourished extensively during the period of the successive Crusades. It was indeed gratifying to think that women were able to contribute so effectively to these wars, fought so ardently for a Holy Cause, namely that of opening the routes captured by the Arabs to the traders of Europe. In one year alone, the Crusades had to pay the expenses of food and shelter for over 13,000 prostitutes. When the war was over European society was faced with a new problem, namely that of again providing food and shelter to a veritable army of these women.

Many priests were engaged in running houses of prostitution during this period in Europe's history. Among them was a man called Menez of whom it was said that 'the number of prostitutes in the houses owned by him was equal to the number of books he had in his library'.[15]

It was natural that with these developments venereal disease should spread very widely and take on the form of an epidemic which constituted a mortal danger to the health of almost all communities. One of the European Emperors of the time made a solemn declaration in which he proclaimed that these diseases were a manifestation of God's wrath against the people who had flouted religion and surrendered to the devil of sex.

The real causes of this disease were as yet unknown and therefore it was attributed to the women and appropriately named the 'disease of Venus' (after Venus the Greek Goddess of Love). Later on, the same nomenclature was used for all venereal diseases, including gonorrhoea and syphilis which are known in Europe today as venereal diseases (Venere-Venus).

Thus, once more, just as sex and sin were attributed to Eve, diseases that spread as a result of sexual relations were attributed to Venus. Man remained pure and innocent, whereas women continued to be the source of evil, sin and disease.

Throughout the Middle Ages prostitution continued to be an integral part of social life. In the year 1414 when the Emperor Sigismund, at the head of his army, paid a visit to Berne, in Switzerland, the doors of the houses of prostitution were thrown wide open to receive him and his troops, as a resounding indication of the welcome which was considered his due, upon which the Emperor stood up amidst the general festivities and thanked the respectable higher authorities for their warm hospitality.[16]

In the 18th Century, when there began to develop the system which is known today as the police, houses of prostitution were placed under the supervision of this new state apparatus. This was more than a natural development, since the ruling class wished to exercise effective supervision over the institution it had created for its own purposes to ensure, since this was a particularly sensitive area, that it did not get out of control. The next step was to pass a series of laws regulating the practice of prostitution and ensuring the necessary medical supervision so that venereal disease did not infect the men who spent their nights with the prostitutes. In addition, there was no reason why the prostitutes should not pay towards the upkeep of the state that was looking after their interests, and so, with time, this profession was in its turn made to pay taxes. Government was convinced that prostitution was a profitable occupation and that, as the supreme authority exercising its power and dominion in the name of the ruling class, there was no reason why it should not get its share of these super profits, even if they were the fruit of sin and debasement. The state felt no shame in plunging its fingers into the handbags of the prostitutes, just as the pimps do today. Any who attempted to escape from paying her dues soon landed in jail convicted of the crime of practising prostitution!

The number of prostitutes multiplied rapidly as a result of the almost limitless need of husbands for sexual relations outside marriage, the growing realization among women that their value was greater, and their price higher, on the prostitution market than on the marriage market, and the increasing degree of poverty which accompanied more extensive and more organized class exploitation. This widespread prostitution, coupled with its 'venereal consequences' which had begun to take on alarming proportions, itself became a danger to the economy of society, and to the health of its members. As a result, governments began to promulgate legislation which made prostitution illegal.

In Egypt prostitution was legal and supervised by the state until the year 1951, when the government decided to prohibit it. Today prostitution in most Arab countries is illegal, although it is carried on clandestinely, or sometimes even openly. A prostitute is safe if she is under the protection of the police or of somebody with influence. Prison is her fate only if she is poor

61

or if she refuses to comply with the wishes of the police or someone else in power.

All these victims, whether prostitutes, abandoned women or illegitimate children, are sacrificed at the altar of a male dominated patriarchal civilization, be it in the West or the East, a civilization where man is God and decides how best to satisfy his interests, his desires and his whims. What can be more disconcerting than the fact that a man who towered high above the heads of others in modern society, a genius like Picasso, should have left a fortune calculated at around £140,000,000, and yet have decided in his will to deprive two of his illegitimate children, the girl Paloma and the boy Claude whose mother Francoise Gilot — was his mistress, of their right to a share in the inheritance?[17]

References

1. *The Koran, Sourat Al Ahzab . . .*,Verse 4-5.
2. *Morocco's Family Code*, 1957, Article 83, para. 3. Translated from the French.
3. El Sheikh Mohammed Mahdi Shams El Dine, *Al Islam wa Tanzeem El Osra*, Al Ittihad El Aalami Li Tanzeem El Walideya, I.P.P.F. Regional Office for the M.E. and North Africa, 1974, Vol. 2, p.77.
4. *Morocco's Family Law*, Article 76. Also the *Family Law of Tunisia*, Article 35 of Book III, 'Statut Personnel', August 1950. Translated from the French.
5. El Sheikh Mohammed Mahdi Shams El Dine, *Al Islam Wa Tanzeem El Osra*, I.P.P.F. Regional Office for the M.E. and North Africa, 1974, Vol. 2, p.77.
6. *Ibid.*, p.79.
7. *The Egyptian Criminological Magazine*, March 1965. See the article by Samir El Ganzouri on crimes committed against the family and sexual morals.
8. Mohamed Niazi Hetata, *Garaim El Bagha'a*, (Dar El Shaab Printers, Cairo, 1961), p.9.
9. *Ibid.*, p.10.
10. *Ibid.*, p.13.
11. *Ibid.*, p.17.
12. *Ibid.*, p.19
13. See the story published by Ihsan Abdel Kouddous in the issue of *El Ahram*, dated 9 December 1976, p.3, under the title 'Al Seid fi Bahr El Asrar.'
14. T.E. James, 1951, p.21.
15. Salah Hafez, *Al Tarikh Al Ginsi Lil Insan*, Al Kitab Al Dahaby, (Roz El Youssef, Cairo, 1973), p.82.
16. *Encyclopaedia Britannica, op. cit.*, Vol. 22, 'Prostitution. . .'
17. *Al Ahram*, Cairo, 27 March 1974, the first page under the title 'Akhbar El Sabah' (Morning News).

9. Abortion and Fertility

Reproduction of children, like any other form of production in society, is influenced by the economic system as well as by nutritional and material resources. If such resources become scarce in comparison with the number of inhabitants, society impelled by its fear of hunger or death will allow what was strictly forbidden, and even considered unholy before, in order to restore the balance between material production and human reproduction. This it does in one of two ways: either by increasing the level of production of material and nutritional resources, or by reducing the number of births and so of children.

In ancient times, science and technology had not advanced far enough to be able to increase nutritional resources substantially when required, nor did people know much about birth control and abortion. The only solution therefore was to kill children after they were born. This procedure was not considered in those days criminal or even immoral, but on the contrary was looked upon as a highly desirable and laudable act. Maternal or paternal feelings did not appear to stand in the way of what seems to us a very cruel and gruesome practice, for necessity is the midwife of behaviour. Feelings and emotions, like moral values, change and adapt themselves according to economic and social necessities. People cannot develop a real awareness of issues related to morals and religion until they have eaten, satisfied their vital needs and are more or less physically and mentally relaxed. A hungry man will not envisage buying a veil to cover his wife's face until he has had his loaf of bread to eat.

The woman's problem lies in the fact that her body, or more precisely her womb, is the only receptacle within which human life can be reproduced. The state, in order to be in control of the means of reproducing human beings, and in order to submit these means to the interests of the economic system which happens to be in force at the time, has been obliged to extend its control and subjugation to that of women's bodies. She has therefore lost the real ownership of her own body, it having been taken over by the state which, in modern society, has inherited much of the authority and functions which at one time were those of the father in the primitive patriarchal system.

Since most of the world's states in more recent history have been capitalist or feudalist, the body of woman has become, through the enforcement of a very strict legislation, the property of the capitalist and feudal classes which reign over society. These laws, however, are very often changed according to the state's requirements for more labour, or the opposite, to enforce policies that counter the growing fear resulting from a rapid increase in population.

Sexual freedom which allows for the birth of children, whether within wedlock or outside of it, is considered equally virtuous and desirable in a married or unmarried mother living in the Swedish society of today, for Sweden is now facing an acute shortage of people, and therefore of labour.

However, in countries which are faced with the problem of over-population, such as India and Egypt, the married mother (the unmarried mother here is, of course, completely out of bounds) is very likely to be punished if she gives birth to more than two or three children. In Egypt today the working woman is deprived by law of her maternity benefits after the third child, and more and more voices have been raised recently wanting also to deprive her of other rights, such as promotion, periodic salary increase etc. if she gives birth to more than two children.

In Tunisia and Somalia, despite the fact that they are both Islamic countries, abortion has been legalized as one of the means for combating high population growth. Yet in most Islamic countries abortion is still illegal, on the assumption that the Moslem religion considers it contrary to its principles.

If we study the relationship between religion and the state at different stages of human history, and in different types of society, we will discover that it is perfectly possible for a single religion to uphold diametrically opposing principles and positions, even on crucial issues. Principles and positions seem to vary much more with the socio-economic structures of states than they do with the religion in force. This is evident from the way in which the Christian church changed its position continuously and radically on many questions, to suit the transition from feudalism to capitalism. It is also powerfully illustrated by the extreme versatility of Moslem religious authorities in adapting their ideas and positions to the requirements of the various Arab governments at different periods, when the system shifted from slavery to feudalism, from feudalism to capitalism and then, finally, from capitalism to socialism.

The Islamic religious authorities have added one more contradictory position to a never ending series in their attitude towards birth control and family planning. Some of them actually maintain that Islam approves of family planning and even abortion; yet others hold firmly to the position that Islam not only opposes abortion, but even the utilization of contraception.

Gamal Abdel Nasser, in the National Charter of 1962, included a passage expressing the need for family planning (*Tanzeem El Osra*) 'because one of the most important obstacles facing the Egyptian people in raising the level of production and therefore the standard of living is rapid population increase'. In 1965, the Supreme Council for Family Planning was established in full sight and hearing of the religious authorities, and not one of them raised a voice to oppose this Presidential Decree. On the contrary, some of them entered into a zealous competition and came forward with proof of the fact that there were many arguments in Islam to support the practice of family planning. The newspapers, radio broadcasts and television, through speeches and Koranic verses, echoed these arguments assiduously and the governmental structure for family planning functioned regularly over a period of ten years. Gamal Abdel Nasser died in September 1970, that is only five years later, and suddenly without warning the Constituent Assembly of the World Islamic Association promulgated a resolution which stigmatized family planning as *Haram.* This resolution[1] was couched in the following terms:

> It has been proved medically that taking the drugs that are used to prevent pregnancy causes great harm to the mother, and to her children if they are born despite the use of these drugs. Various superficial arguments have been put forward to support birth control, such as overpopulation, the difficulty of providing adequate nutrition, and the low standards of education. All these should be ignored for the verse of the Holy Koran has the answer 'Do not kill your children for fear of heresy. He will provide for both you and them. Your needs depend on Allah and he will provide them. He who avoids Allah's wrath, Allah will find a way out for him, and will provide for him in a way he had not expected.'[2]

Nevertheless the Family Planning Council in Egypt has continued to function. Certain religious authorities even oppose the above statement. And other Islamic countries have permitted birth control, such as Morocco, Tunisia, Iran, Turkey, and some of them have even gone as far as permitting abortion.

As far as the essence of Islam is concerned, there is nothing in the Koran that supports or opposes birth control or contraception. The Koran is considered the primary source of Islamic jurisprudence and theological orientation. Next in order come the sayings and teachings of the Prophet, followed by the consensus of religious thinkers and leaders, and last of all the methods of inference and analogy. These are the three valid sources utilized as complementary to the Koran when it is desired to take a position on any problem. Some of the sayings of Mahomet (*Ahadith*) call upon people to multiply and reproduce, whereas on other occasions he advises a reduction or limitation in the number of children. The same applies to the thinkers and legislators of Islam. The contradictions or differing opinions which are discernible in Mahomet's teachings indicate that they were calculated to deal with different situations, and were expressed at different times and in varying contexts. The verses of the Koran also very often express varying, or even irreconcilable opinions, since here again there were differences, both as to time and place, when they descended on Mahomet as an inspiration from Heaven. Religion cannot be understood properly if it is looked upon as a series of isolated principles, teachings and directives sent by God, without attempting to see them in their interconnections with specific situations, each of which is characterized by its own social, economic and cultural setting. It is always necessary to study carefully the context in which God has spoken to people and explained to them what they should do.

At the beginning of Islam, one of Mahomet's foremost tasks was to establish the Moslem state and strengthen the Moslem nation. He therefore called upon the people to multiply and reproduce, since at that time a superiority in numbers was a source of strength and helped to build up powerful armies. Mahomet in his teachings during this period enjoined people to 'marry and multiply. For I will be proud of you among the nations on the day of Judgement.'[3] He also said to the men: 'Marry she who is affectionate and fertile.'

Some of the Moslem theologians and legislators draw support from verses of the Koran in order to oppose birth control and contraception, verses like 'Just as a camel does not carry in itself the wherewithal to live, Allah provides for you and it.'[4] Or 'Allah provides generously for those among His worshippers whom he sees fit to pick out.'[5] Also, 'Your God provides generously for whom He desires, for He is all powerful.'[6]

In support of such ideas it is often mentioned that the Prophet declared as a certainty that on the fourth month of the development of the embryo in the womb of the mother, that is after one hundred and twenty days, 'Allah sends an Angel who takes a decision for the child's future life in four crucial matters: its means of livelihood, its lifespan and a happy or unhappy life.'[7]

However Mahomet was very conscious of the fact that numbers had to be accompanied by good health and strength, and should not result in weakness, internal struggles and divisions, or merely be a quantitative and therefore useless addition. This is natural thinking for the leader of a nation who wishes to help the people and make them stronger so that they can overcome obstacles and enemies.

In one of his very famous sayings Mahomet is often quoted as having made clear that 'the greatest of catastrophies is many children and meagre sustenance'. This phrase was picked up by the Family Planning Council in Egypt as one of its slogans. The Prophet on another occasion left another famous saying: 'The nations are falling upon you just as the eaters fall upon the pot.' So one of those present asked him, 'But are we so few on such a day?' And the Prophet replied, 'No, you are many, but in shreds, like the froth of a stream.'[8] By this he meant that a great number of people by itself was like froth, thrown up by a stream of water, useless and without strength,

At the time of Mahomet, the Moslems used to practise contraception by the method known as pre-ejaculatory withdrawal or external ejaculation. In the book, *Al Sahihain,* Gaber is quoted as having said: 'At the time of Allah's Prophet when the Koran was descending upon him from Heaven, we used withdrawal.'[9] In *Sahih Mossalam* he said: 'We were wont to practise withdrawal during the time of the Prophet. When he heard of this he did not order us to abstain from so doing.'[10] The religious Imam El Ghazali, is quoted as saying: 'For us it is correct to say that withdrawal is allowed.'[11]

The theologians and legislators of the Maliki school of Islam agree that withdrawal is permissible to prevent pregnancy, but insist on the acquiescence of the wife to this procedure, whatever her age.[12]

The school which is predominant in Yemen, as mentioned by the Imam Zeid Ibn Ali Zein El Abedeen, allows withdrawal if the wife has no objection. In addition, the Imam Yehia Ibn Zeid supported withdrawal without reservation, if the aim was to prevent pregnancy.[13]

In Iraq, Pakistan, Afghanistan and Syria the most popular school of Islamic theology is that of *Al Shia El Ga'afareya*. In their writings, withdrawal aimed at avoiding pregnancy is condoned if agreement has been reached with the wife at the time of marriage.[14]

According to Mahomet, withdrawal should not be practised with a 'free woman' unless she agrees.[15] The disciples of Abdallah Ibn El Temimy (known as the *Abadeya*) who inhabit the region of Oman in the eastern part of the Arabian Peninsula, and some areas of North Africa, permit withdrawal on condition that the wife does not object. They maintain 'that withdrawal is permissible in order to escape the birth of a child, for fear of having too many children and causing harm to the infant . . .'

Some of the legislators and thinkers of Islam have permitted birth control by means other than that of withdrawal. One of them is for the woman to close the opening of the uterus to prevent 'water' (semen) from reaching it, so that pregnancy is avoided. This is said to have been expounded by Ibn Abdine as the opinion of Saheb El Bahr, one of the legislators of the Al Hanafi school of Islamic doctrine. Here again the prior agreement of the wife had to be sought.[16]

El Zarkashi is quoted as having spoken of causing the embryo to drop as a result of the use of a special medicament. On the use of medicaments after ejaculation he says: 'As regards the use of methods that prevent pregnancy by acting for example before ejaculation during sexual intercourse, there is no objection to this.'[17]

The Committee on *Fatwa's* (religious doctrinal directives or explanations) at the University of El Azhar declared:

> The use of medicaments to prevent pregnancy for a temporary period of time is not forbidden, according to the views expressed by the El Shafei School of Islamic doctrine. For this reason the committee supports this view, since it will make things easier for people, and prevent any feeling of shame, especially if there is fear of excessive pregnancies in the woman, or weakness as a result of repeated pregnancies. Allah the Almighty has said: 'Allah wishes to ease your burdens not to make things more difficult.'[18]

Throughout the Middle Ages Moslem physicians were in the habit of advising people about methods of contraception. One of the famous physicians was Abou Bakr Al Razi, a Persian Moslem who was born near Tehran in the middle of the 9th Century. He is considered the greatest medical physician in Islam, and the foremost practitioner of the Middle Ages. In his book called *Al Hawi* ('that which encompasses or is comprehensive') he has described different methods of birth control:

Sometimes it is important to prevent the semen from penetrating the uterus when, for example, pregnancy is dangerous to the woman. There are several ways to prevent the semen from reaching the uterus. The first method is coitus interruptus. The second method is to prevent ejaculation completely, and this is practised by some people. The third procedure is to place some medicaments at the opening of the uterus before penetration of the woman. These medicaments either close up the opening, or expel the semen and therefore prevent pregnancy. Examples of this are tablets or suppositories of cabbage, hanzal, kar, bull's gall, the wax secreted by animal's ears, the droppings of elephants, and calcium water. In addition, these medicaments may be used separately, or in various combinations.[19]

Another of the greatest medical practitioners of the Abbaside Caliphate in Baghdad was Ali Ibn El Abbas El Megousi who wrote, sometime in the middle of the 10th Century, supporting birth control:

Medicaments that prevent pregnancy, although they should really not be mentioned in order to prevent women of bad reputation from making use of them, yet there is no escape from utilizing them for women with a small womb, or who suffer from an illness that would make pregnancy risky for them to the extent of endangering their lives during labour.[20]

Despite Ali Ibn El Abbasi's outstanding knowledge of medicine, his understanding of society, the patriarchal family and the tragedy of illegitimate children was superficial. Otherwise he might have realized that the women he called 'those of bad reputation' (meaning prostitutes) needed more than anyone else to use birth control methods. Thus they could save their children from vagrancy, shame, and even death, and protect their own health and morale from the burdens of an illegitimate child, born of intercourse with men, an intercourse they were forced to accept as a result of the situation into which they had been cornered by the inhuman structure of class society built on the patriarchal family unit.

Another very well known thinker and man of science in Islam was Avicenna (Ibn Seena) who died in the year 1037 A.D. Ibn Seena, in his book *El Kanoun fil Tib* (the Laws of Medicine), described twenty different methods of contraception in a remarkably accurate and detailed manner considering the relatively early stage of scientific development at which he was writing.[21] These methods had been used for hundreds of years, and very often surpassed other methods prescribed by those who came after him. However, as in the case of most, if not all, medical scientists and practitioners, he prescribed these methods of contraception for medical reasons only. He was in no way concerned with the social and economic reasons for the practice of birth control, even at the individual or family level.

European medicine inherited much of the knowledge and techniques discovered or followed by the Arab physicians in Islam. It also delved into such sources as *Al Irshad* by Ibn Gami'i, *Tazkarat Daoud Al Antaki*(the prescriptions of David of Antioch), Ismail El Girgani and *Kitab El Malki*.

Many people are misinformed and think that methods of contraception and ideas of birth control were once again inventions of Western thought and science. Others are convinced that the rubber condom worn by men during intercourse was invented in the West, whereas the Imam El Ghazali mentioned in his writings long ago, the 'skin sack of the male' or the 'preventive retainer' which was made out of gut.

The position taken by Arab countries on the question of birth control varies according to population size and growth rates and their relationship to production and to the economic and material resources of the country. In Kuwait and Saudi Arabia contraception is only advised for medical reasons. However in other countries, like Egypt and Tunisia, the government is carrying out a family planning programme. This is also the case in Moslem countries like Pakistan, Iran and Turkey. The crux of the question, and the reasons for which one or other position is taken, do not therefore relate to religion but rather to economic factors.

The issues of family planning and birth control were first raised in the Egyptian press over forty years ago, on the 29th January 1937, when Mufti El Diyar El Masria (Egypt's religious head who explains doctrine) was asked for a clarification of the position of Islam in relation to birth control and abortion from both the medical and social aspects.[22] The answer of the Mufti was as follows:—
1. It is the right of the married couple to take individual measures of birth control for medical or social reasons. The acquiescence of both partners is not essential.
2. Before a period of sixteen weeks has elapsed since the beginning of pregnancy, it is permissible to take measures or medicines conducive to abortion without the mother being exposed to any danger if she is provided with adequate guidance.
3. All religious Imams have agreed that under no circumstances should abortion be carried out after this period has elapsed.

Thus it is clear that contraception, and abortion during the first sixteen weeks of pregnancy, were permitted by the religious authorities of Egypt in 1937, at a time when in most European countries they were prohibited by law. During the same year the Egyptian Medical Association organized a seminar, the aim of which was to study these questions in all their aspects, whether medical, social, legal, religious or statistical.

While Egyptian legislation permits the practice of contraception by established methods, to this day abortion remains illegal. Some Arab countries, such as Tunisia and Somalia, have legalized abortion, but the majority of them still prohibit legal abortion although clear-cut views supporting it before the end of the sixteenth week as a religiously acceptable measure have been voiced by various Islamic authorities in a number of countries including as we have seen, Egypt.

The Imam El Ghazali (of the El Shafei School of Doctrine) and Ibn Gazey (from the Maliki School of Doctrine) represent the two tendencies that vigorously oppose abortion at any period of pregnancy.

Some religious authorities in Islam consider that abortion is not prohibited by religion within the first 120 days of pregnancy as mentioned in the writings of the Hanafi school quoted by El Kamal Ibn El Hamam.[23]

The religious authorities who consider that abortion can be performed before the end of the fourth month base their reasoning on the contention that the embryo up to that time does not enfold a human life. The Prophet is said to have made it clear that *El Rouh* (life) does not awaken within the embryo before the 120th day.[24] Ibn Wahban El Hanafi in his teachings mentioned the following directive: 'It is indeed a grievous difficulty if her breast milk dries up after pregnancy, whereas the father of the boy has no money to hire a goat or a camel, and so fears that his child may die.' Then he goes on to say: 'In such a case permitting abortion can be considered no more than a fault, which means that it is not condemned as the crimes of killing would be.'[25]

If the first four months of pregnancy have passed, however, the religious authorities are unanimous in condemning abortion, and insist that a fine be paid if an abortion is done — unless it is proven that the abortion was essential to save the mother, 'who cannot be sacrificed to save the child since she is at the origin of its life.' Such cases are placed under a category known as committing the lesser of two ills, which is one of the general principles of religious jurisprudence and legislation. Moroccan criminal law bases itself on this Islamic legal principle. Article 453 states: 'Abortion is not a punishable offence if it is necessary in order to save the life of the mother when in danger, as long as it is performed openly by a medical practitioner or a surgeon after officially informing the administrative authorities.'[26]

One of the most important problems to which an Arab woman is exposed, whether within her married life or outside it, is pregnancy and child birth. If a poor girl becomes pregnant without having been married, then she is indeed to be pitied. She may pay the price of her mistake with her life, even though the fault is not really hers, even though she is simply a poor helpless child, violated or deceived by a man coming from the rich upper class. A girl from a rich family will usually not be exposed to such a fate since her parents will very quickly find a solution if such a problem arises. She will probably be married off to a man of lower social position who will come forward wearing the mask of chivalry since he is 'saving' the poor girl, whereas in fact he is quite happy to marry a wife with money. Alternatively, if the man who was responsible for what happened refuses to marry her, and if no one suitable volunteers, they can always take her to a doctor and, since they have the money, pay his price for an illegal abortion.

Pregnancy and abortion are a never-ending source of crises in the life of a poor working woman, even if she is legally married. Overloaded and exhausted as she is by her numerous tasks in the home, she is forced to try as hard as possible to avoid too frequent and repeated pregnancies. At the same time she might hear that the government is encouraging the use of contraception and the practice of family planning. Yet she does not find it easy to use these methods and faces numerous obstacles as a result of her economic, social, cultural and even religious background. As a result, most wives in Arab countries live under continuous strain of anxiety. They are always in fear of another pregnancy and the burden of a new child to care for.

As is to be expected, the whole weight of practising contraception in Arab societies is thrown on the shoulders of the woman. She is expected to deal, on her own, with such problems as getting the pills, taking them, and suffering their side-effects when they occur. Or she goes to a clinic to have a loop inserted, and then removed if it so happens that colic is severe and bleeding excessive. If any of these methods happen to fail and she becomes pregnant, then the only way out for her, if she cannot face the problems of another child, is to look for an illegal abortion. Then she is exposed to all the dangers of it being done under unsuitable conditions and without adequate medical care. Or if she goes to a good doctor, then she will have to pay the price he asks, which is high because abortion is illegal, and so more money can be made out of it.

The operation of abortion still remains an illegal procedure in most Arab countries, and it is an area which remains in the dark. There are no statistics on the number of operations performed, but only rough estimates calculated in certain hospitals, as a result of the registration of cases of induced and complicated abortion.

However one observation that has been made is that the proportion of operations performed for reasons related to severe ill health due to chronic or other diseases is dropping quite rapidly. On the other hand, the proportion done to preserve the mental and physical health of the mother intact is on the increase. It is clear that this reflects an attempt to fulfil the legal conditions relating to abortion at least from the formal point of view. Usually if mental or psychological reasons are involved, they will have something directly to do with the social or economic circumstances of the patient, which the law is not prepared to recognize as a valid legal excuse for undergoing an abortion. Thus it is that people, and the medical profession, can get around the law, but only if the requisite money is available.

As a result of the above, it has also been observed that the number of abortions done to women of well-to-do families is three times the number done to women from the poorer segments of society, measured in absolute figures. The medical profession is certainly the prime mover behind these statistics, since money is the main vehicle by which an abortion can be obtained by the women who need it.

Professor Ismail Ragab (from Ein Shams University) has divided the medical profession, as far as abortion is concerned, into two main categories:[27] a small minority who agree to perform the operation and dodge the legal provisions in a variety of ways, usually with the aim of making as much money as possible; and a majority who refuse to perform the operation themselves, but are quite willing to refer a patient to one of the doctors who is known for his readiness to do it, despite the fact that such referral is itself an illegal procedure.

Abortion, like most other matters related to women and sex in Arab society, is still one of the issues torn by contradictions, which is another reflection of the double moral standards inherent in a patriarchal class society.

In Egypt estimates indicate that, out of every four cases of pregnancy, one of them ends in an illegal abortion. The result is a host of very serious complications every year, complications to which the poorer class women are much more liable to be victims. Illegal abortion in Egypt today is the single most important cause of death in pregnant mothers.

There is no doubt that the situation of an unmarried mother is even more desperate. This is true not only from the medical point of view, but also from the social and moral aspects. The most frequent cases are poor domestic servant girls, who have been subjected to the advances or assaults of a son or husband in a rich or upper middle class family. A minority are young girls who have believed the vows of the men who were courting them with promises of marriage that did not materialize.

It is a fact that in Egypt the majority of abortion cases are not among unmarried women, since at least 90% of such cases involve married mothers between the ages of 25 and 35 years. Of these, 80% are mothers who have previously had two or more children, but who feel that their families cannot bear the economic and social consequences of an additional child.

The legalization of abortion in Egypt, or in the rest of the Arab countries, will not have a noticeable effect on the frequency of operations, which are spreading like wild fire. But it will have the advantage of bringing out into the open, into the light of day, what is at present an obscure and often criminal procedure performed in great secrecy, a black market operation conducted for high stakes. It will also afford the poorer classes of women in society the possibility, at least in principle, of receiving services similar to their richer counterparts, and will definitely lead quite rapidly to the improvement of whatever services are available, to the avoidance of much negligence and to a reduction in complications. Poor women will be able to obtain abortions under conditions affording a minimum of medical care and cleanliness. This is especially true after the increasing use of the suction apparatus, which is capable of drawing out the embryo in a few minutes, without the use of anaesthesia and without causing any pain.

References

1. The resolution was published in *Al Ahram* — daily newspaper, 18 April 1975, p.11, under the title 'An Old Problem has come up once more. Is birth control "Haram"?'
2. *The Koran*, 'Sourat Al Isra'a', Verse 31.
3. El Ghazali, *Ihy'a Ouloum El Dine*, (Cairo, 1939), p.22.
4. *The Koran*, 'Sourat El Ankabout', Verse 60.
5. *The Koran*, 'Sourat El Ankabout', Verse 62.
6. *The Koran*, 'Sourat El Isra'a', Verse 30.
7. *Hogag El Bokhari*, Vol. 7, p.196.
8. Ahmed El Sharabassi, *Al Islam wa Tanzeem El Osra*, (I.P.P.F., 1974), Vol. 2, p.11. (International Planned Parenthood Federation).
9. *Sahih El Bokhari*, Vol. 7, p.42; *Sahih Mossalam*, 10/12; *Al Tarmazi*, 15/74; *Tarteeb Mousnad Ahmed Ibn Hanbal*, 16/219.
10. *Sahih Mossalam*, 10/14 with explanatory notes by El Nawawi.
11. El Ghazali, *El Ihya'a*, Vol. 2, (El Maktaba El Tougareya Publishers, Egypt), pp.51, 52.
12. *Hashiat El Dessouki wa Sharh Al Darder Ala Matn Khalil*, Vol. 2, p.266.
13. *Kitab El Bahr Al Zakhar*, Matba'at Ansar El Sounna El Mohamediya, 1948, Vol. 3, pp.81-82.
14. *Kitab El Roudah, El Baheya, Sharh El Lama's El Dimishkeya*, Matbaat Dar El Kitab El Arabi, Egypt, Vol. 2, p.68.
15. *Kitab Da'aim El Islam*, Dar El Maaref, Egypt, Vol.2, p.210.
16. *Nazrat Al Islam ila Tanzeem El Nasl*, p.80.
17. Al Ramli, *Nihayat El Mohtag*, Vol. 2, p.416.
18. *The Koran*, 'Sourat El Bakara', Verse 185, The *Azhar Fatwa*, dated 10 February 1953.
19. Abou Bakr El Razi, *Al Hawi*, Ch. 24.
20. Ali Ibn Abbas El Megousi, *Kamel El Sana'a El Tibi* , (The Complete Techniques of Medicine), Ch.28.
21. Ibn Seena, *El Kanoun fil Tib*, Vol. 2, p.375.
22. Dr. Ali Shaaban, 'Mani El Haml fil Islam', article reproduced in the documents: *Al Islam wa Tanzeem El Osra*, (I.P.P.F., 1974), Vol.2, p.211.
23. *El Mahali*, Libn Hazm, Vol.2, pp.35-40.
24. *Daleel El Modaribeen fi Tanzeem El Osra*, Supreme Council for Family Planning, Cairo (Family Planning Board), Vol.1, (First edition, December 1971), p.80.
25. Mohamed El Maki El Nassiri, *Al Islam wa Tanzeem El Osra*, (I.P.P.F., 1974), Vol.2, p.65.
26. *Ibid.*, p.66.
27. Dr. Ismail Ragab in an article under the title: 'Al Ganeen El Moshawah wal Haml El Khata'a,*Health Magazine*, No. 33, 23 January 1973, pp.44-47.

10. Distorted Notions About Femininity, Beauty and Love

One of the most striking shortcomings in Arab societies is that we are not accustomed to examine critically and think over the values that we have inherited from past generations, and particularly those related to women, sex and love. Many people think that these values have descended upon us from the Heavens whereas in fact they are no more than the reflections of patriarchal and class society, where one class rules over another, and where man rules over woman.

One of the first principles of honour and love is that no one should be able to subjugate another. If a rich man oppresses a poor man, this oppression goes against what is considered honourable. If a man owns a woman as though she were his property this relationship cannot, in its essence, be described as honourable. Honour is justice and equality in human rights. Honourable love is love built on such justice and equality.

One of the conditions of true love is an exchange, and a necessary condition for exchange is a balance, an equality between the two partners. Exchange cannot take place between a master and a slave, between something that is higher and something that is lower, just as water cannot flow upwards without special interference. Real love cannot therefore be based on a relationship characterized by exploitation of any kind. It is therefore correct to say that most of the relationships that arise between men and women are not built on true love. The love that seems to exude and well up from Egyptian songs and throb with sighs and crises, is not really love. Nor are the emotions depicted between man and woman in Arabic literature, or the stories of suffering in love — or blind love, or mad passionate love, or romantic love — expressive of feelings that can be called real genuine love.

Love is the greatest experience through which a human being can pass, since by way of such love it is possible for the physical, mental and emotional potentialities of the man or woman to reach their highest point of intensity and to plunge deep down into the self or being.

Action is an essential element of love. Romantic love or *Houb Ozri* is fundamentally a sick emotion, since it is deprived of the quality of action. It is a love that sustains itself through deprivation, and lives on emotional reactions rather than on action.

The Arab woman who is subjected to mental, sexual and psychological suppression has no other alternative than to sacrifice action. For it is man who takes action, and it is the woman's role to await the action of man.

The passivity observed in Arab women is therefore not an inherent or in-born characteristic, but has been imposed upon them by society. Discharging a woman of her natural positive traits is equivalent to discharging her of her responsibilities as a human being, or in other words depriving her of the very core of a human being's personality, and the fundamental nature which differentiates it from that of animals. Woman, thus discharged of her inner core, is left only with her outer skin or envelope. She is emptied of all that counts, and is left only with her exterior physical frame. She, therefore, has no alternative other than to occupy herself with this outer bodily envelope, to massage it, to ensure that it remains smooth to the touch, to remove the rough hair that grows on it from time to time, to sometimes expose its nakedness, and at others to cover it up according to changes in fashion.

Society does everything it can to drum into her head the fact that she is only a body, and that special care must be taken of everything that concerns this purely physical shell. Newspapers, magazines and advertisements, when addressing themselves to woman, speak to her as flesh covered by a layer of skin that requires constant massaging with different kinds of creams, and as lips that have to be painted an appropriate hue.

But even this outer shell in the Arab woman, this external physical appearance, is not hers to deal with as she wishes. It is others who decide for her what she should look like, those who own the industries catering for women in the major capitals of the West. The modern woman in Baghdad, Cairo or Tunis does not wear the clothes she wishes, but rather puts on what a capitalist fashion king in Paris or New York considers suitable for her.

Capitalist production is not governed by any consideration other than that of profit for those who own the industries, or carry on the trade. The essential needs of the vast majority of people are a secondary matter, catered for only to the degree that will ensure the continued working of the profit machine, which avoids public resentment interfering with its functioning. As a result most of the commodities produced specifically for women are not really necessary to the ordinary masses of people in the Arab countries, and are really luxury goods. Is it possible to contend, for example, that the millions of women who toil in the fields and factories of the Arab countries require deodorants to remove the smell of sweat that never dries from their bodies at any time of the working day or night?

This is what makes the chorus of mad screaming advertisements so necessary. These advertisements cover all the areas in a city or town which are easily visible to the eye, with their loud colours, provocative slogans and pictures or drawings of naked or half naked women, lying or sitting or standing, or hugging a man, kissing him, or looking into his eyes. A galaxy of cheap sex is calculated to catch the attention of those who can afford it, thereby promoting luxury goods in countries where the millions are still unable to obtain the bare necessities of life in the form of food, clothing and shelter. The big capitalist fashion houses of the world, of course, speculate on and utilize the psychological and sexual needs of Arab societies, where people are sexually deprived as a result of the moral values that make out of mutual sensual and emotional satisfaction between men and women a sin and a profanation. Thus capitalists also share a substantial responsibility for the double moral standards that govern the life of society. For, on the one hand, they are trying hard to convince the Arab peoples of the need to stand firm by the religious and moral values inculcated and diffused by the Islamic hierarchies, and are spending enormous sums of money to revive religious orthodoxy and fanaticism. And on the other hand, in films, on the television, in magazines, advertisements and books, they utilize women and sex as a principal theme for the commercialization of their production, and completely ignore the values and morals they are trying to instil. This seeming contradiction, however, has a very solid rationale behind it. Religious orthodoxy breeds sexual suppression and therefore tends to make people's minds more preoccupied with matters related to sex. This pent-up sexual energy can best be channelled into commodity consumption with all its sex associations so vividly and subtly portrayed in advertisement campaigns. In addition, psychological and sexual phenomena of another nature, as manifested in violence, aggression, various forms of alcoholic or drug addiction, sexual deviations and all the other by-products of class and male dominant society, are utilized for the further commercialization of industrial production, and to ensure that profits are maintained and increased to the maximum.

It is noticeable that men in Eastern societies concentrate their attention on women's calves or thighs or even buttocks. Whereas in American society during the first half of the 20th Century a woman's breasts were considered that part of her body most worthy of attention in provoking male interest. The actress with big provocative breasts had a very good chance of getting on in the world of films, and of becoming a famous artist. The style and design of fashion, however, changed after the middle of the century, for people had got tired of ogling the ample thighs and breasts of women. Long dresses came in vogue, and very often exposed a large area of the neck, shoulders and breasts. Breasts, therefore, had to shrink in size since they would have looked rather ugly bulging out without any covering. The new fashion which seems to be creeping in is that of exposing a part of the belly or waist, and this is an attempt to copy the East (India, Indonesia and other countries).

The capitalist traders of the world, and those who work for them, however, will never tire of changing. The race for profit must go on, and so different parts of women's bodies must be uncovered, then covered only to be uncovered once again. There are many commodities to be sold, and fortunately the body of woman has many parts that lend themselves to the ingenuity of these modern 'sexologists'. But the pathetic native women who run panting from one place to another in search of the latest models, and who avidly follow the new fashions in clothes and make-up, little know that they are no longer women, but have allowed themselves to be transformed into mere objects, or even parts of an object. They are no longer complete human beings but have become transformed, under the inexorable pressure of capitalist male dominated society, into mere commodities, into a pair of pants or gloves, or a bracelet or a breast, or a thigh or – in the best of cases – into a vagina and a uterus.

All such developments are natural to a society where women have lost the essential constituents of their personality, have been emptied of their human qualities, and have been metamorphosed into an object, a part of the body, or an instrument. Sometimes they are instruments utilized for advertisements, for serving the purposes of buying and consumption, and at others they are instruments of pleasure, passion and sexual satisfaction, or receptacles for bearing children, or commodities to be bought and sold in the marriage market.

As a result what applies to objects, or instruments, or commodities in general applies to a woman. She possesses more value when she is new, or in other words young, a virgin who has not been made use of before. Her value drops with previous use – previous marriage or previous sex. She becomes a second-hand woman. Virtue and moral criteria draw their main features from this distorted and sick attitude towards women. A woman, who has experience of life and men, is not only considered less worthy than a naive and inexperienced girl, but meets with refusal as though experience were a stigma.

Arab men, and for that matter most men, cannot stand an experienced and intelligent woman. It would seem as though the man is afraid of her because of her capacity to understand him and see through his failures, or weaknesses, if necessary. She knows very well that his masculinity is not real, not an essential truth, but only an external shell, built up and imposed on women by societies based on class and sexual discrimination. The experience and intelligence of women are a menace to this patriarchal class structure and, in turn, a menace to the false position in which man is placed, the position of a king or demi-god in his relations with women. That is essentially why most men fear and even hate intelligent and experienced women. Arab men shy away from marrying them, since they are capable of exposing the exploitation inherent in the institution of marriage as practised to this day.

If marriage is to survive as an institution built on exploitation of and discrimination against the woman, and on the alienation of both husband and wife, then the only answer is to continue to bring up and marry stupid, ignorant and naive women. An Arab man, when he decides to marry, will almost invariably choose a young virgin girl with no experience, imbued with a childish simplicity, naive, ignorant, a blind 'pussy cat' who does not have an inkling of her rights, or of her sexual desires as a woman, or of the fact that her mind has its needs and should have its ambitions.

Since the man buys the woman through marriage in order that she might serve him and be an instrument for his pleasures, bear his children, wait on the family members, and care for them in the home, he tends to choose a girl who is many years younger than him, so that she maintains the youth of her body for a long time and can continue to fulfil the functions for which he married her until his old age. A man of forty does not hesitate to marry a young girl of twenty, or even fifteen years of age. This is perfectly natural if the norms of buying and selling are the ones applied to marriage. He who goes to market to buy a slave or hire a servant, will obviously choose a young person who can work hard and continuously without tiring, who is not intelligent and so is easily controllable, and who does not have numerous needs to be satisfied, but will eat little and not ask for many things. Thus the master is ensured that he has somebody who will produce much, and consume as little as possible, and his gains out of the transaction will be maximized.

This explains why Arab men look upon their women as bodies which must remain for ever youthful. The value of a woman deteriorates with age. Attitudes towards the age of women, their youth and their beauty, can be easily understood against this background. Their youth extends in fact over the years during which they are capable of giving the husband sexual pleasure, bearing children for him, and serving the family. It usually extends from the beginning of puberty, that is from the first menstrual period to the menopause. In other words, it encompasses the whole of her fertile age from roughly fifteen to forty-five years.

The life of a woman is therefore less than that of a normal human being, since it only extends over thirty years. Once she no longer has any menstrual periods, her life is considered over, and she is said to have reached *Sin El Ya'as* (the age of despair or of no hope).

Despite the fact that the biological and psychological constitution of women permits them to live longer than men, as has been proved by many recent research studies, society has decreed that the effective life of women is to be only half that of men. Man is considered to reach the optimum of human maturity (physical and mental) between the ages of forty and forty-five years, which is the exact period chosen as the closing chapter for the woman's active life, the chapter 'of no hope'. Thus it is that the very time when she reaches the peak of her intellectual, physical and emotional maturity and activity, is designated by society as the moment of decline, when she is transformed by social and familial pressure into an old barren woman, whose functions in life are over and who is ready to be buried by society while still alive.

Criteria for beauty are also set up against the background of this narrow outlook towards women. A beautiful woman is the young girl with a silvery body, even if her mind is a blank. Her beauty is judged by the shape of her nose and the turn of her lips. She is put to shame if the size of her nose is barely a millimetre longer than it is supposed to be, or if the roundness of her buttocks is a few millimetres less than is considered appropriate. As regards the man, however, nothing counts, except the money he has in his pocket.

Arabic art and literature have played, and continue to play, a crucial role in emphasizing attitudes and concepts like these regarding beauty in women. A never ending stream of songs, poems and novels sing the praises of the girl with the flowing hair, long eyelashes and an appealing fullness of the lips and breasts.

Since beauty is envisaged in a distorted and partial sense, it is natural that concepts of feminity and honour should fall victims to the same logic. Femininity or femaleness means weakness, naivety, negativeness and resignation where girls and women are concerned. These are all qualities that fit in well with the role imposed by society on women, the role of a wife devoted to the service of her husband and her children. Femininity requires a woman to share the same characteristics laudable in obedient and efficient servants, well adapted and resigned to their inferior position. Masculinity, maleness, on the other hand is supposed to be distinguished by qualities that are the absolute opposite, the qualities of a master, of strength, determination, initiative and boldness.

The honour or chastity of a girl is likened to a matchstick that can only burn once and then is over. Once a girl has lost her virginity, therefore, she has irrevocably lost her honour, and can never retrieve it. A man's honour has nothing to do with his chastity. On the contrary, his chastity can be burnt a hundred, nay a thousand times, but he will never lose his honour or consume it.

It is to the merit of the Women's Liberation Movement which has grown in strength, in size and in maturity during recent years, that a new task is already being undertaken, in particular that of formulating new values built on the new science of woman that attempts to penetrate into her real physical, biological, psychological and mental characteristics, and unmask the real causes for the distortion that has affected all aspects of her nature and life. This has necessarily led also to a new science of man and his nature, as a dialectical counterpart completing the two components of human life, man and woman. It has also brought with it new ideas about child rearing, and education, which hitherto were built on a system of suppression and discrimination between the sexes, and served to feed patriarchal class society with the prototypes of men and women which it needs in order to survive.

Undoubtedly the movement for women's emancipation all over the world owes a great deal to Marxist thought and to the writings and struggles of truly socialist men and women, to the battles fought by women against the discrimination suffered by them under different social systems and throughout the thousands of years of human history since man first imposed his domination and tyranny on woman inside and outside the home. This new and vital movement for the liberation of women is the culmination of the long years during which millions of women were oppressed, killed and burned alive, victims of the Dark Ages, the Middle Ages and the Inquisition in Europe unjustly accused of sorcery and devilry, or victims of slave and feudal societies in the countries of the East. It is the culmination of the humiliation and oppression imposed upon Arab women, and on all women in the past, and in the world of today. It is also an indication that a new political and social movement for women will add its tremendous vitality and force to the struggle of all human beings against exploitation.

New areas of knowledge and new sciences are throwing light on the biological and psychological nature of women. These new thoughts are showing their strength, their lucidity and their capacity to counter more and more effectively those outdated concepts and ideas that insist on the fundamental, unchangeable nature of women, a nature which imposes upon them service in the home, and child bearing and rearing, and only allows them to fulfil themselves as mothers and wives, and to find happiness in giving birth to children.

According to modern scientific theories about the economic, social and cultural structure of society and its relation to human nature, it is no longer possible to maintain that there is such a thing as an intrinsic human nature that is stable and unchangeable. Human characteristics are relative qualities that change and adapt themselves to the circumstances and situations under which people are born and live. In other words there is a very important environmental effect on what was once considered as eternal and fundamental human nature. Many scientists now refuse to use the term 'human instincts', preferring 'human motivations' which according to them are picked up mainly in the years of childhood and adolescence.

The tendency towards passivity in women, and the tendency to aggression in men, are therefore not an intrinsic part of their nature, but are time-bound phenomena related to history and civilization, where environmental and socialization processes play a major role. Some scientists also insist that even in animals there is no such thing as an innate nature, but only a set of characteristics which change according to surrounding conditions over a period of time.

There is mounting proof of the fact that the qualities considered as intrinsic to men or women have in fact been acquired from society, the environment and various socialization and educative processes, and that the relationships between the sexes have no fixed or eternal pattern. As a result, sexual morals and values change according to the prevalent social, economic and cultural structures in society. A new research study carried out on the San or 'Bushmen' of the Kalahari desert has brought out very vividly the relationship between sexual behaviour and economic needs. The San live in small family groups around a limited number of wells that are barely sufficient for their needs. As a result, the laws that govern their sexual behaviour are extremely severe, and extra-marital relations between the sexes are strictly forbidden. The reason is that they do not wish to have more children, and in many instances they have been known to commit infanticide with the second child.[1]

The sexual characteristics of human beings are moulded, as is the case with all their characteristics, by society, environmental circumstances and education. Scientists have presumed that natural characteristics are those most prevalent in society and most common among the majority of people. This assumption is incorrect. For example, there are societies like that of Egypt and the Sudan which impose sexual frigidity on the majority of women and girls through the operation of circumcision, involving a total or partial amputation of the clitoris. Is it therefore possible to say that women in these two countries are fundamentally frigid by nature, just because the majority are in fact afflicted with varying degrees of frigidity as a result of this operation? Furthermore, is it possible to maintain that the fundamental nature of women is characterized by sexual frigidity merely because a majority of women, whether in the East or in the West, lack sexual warmth and a positive attitude towards sexual relations, as a result of suppression and the moral atmosphere with which they are surrounded from a very early age?

Would it be accurate to maintain that men are sadistic and women masochistic when we now know these characteristics to be the result of patriarchal family systems and the way in which children and young people are brought up? Male dominant civilization discriminates between male and female children. The male child is taught from the very beginning how to project his personality and how to prepare for a man's life involving strength, responsibility, authority and a positive attitude in the face of difficulties. A girl, on the other hand, is trained and educated right from the start to shrink into a corner, to withdraw and to hide her real self because she is a female and is being prepared for the life of a woman, a life where she must be passive and weak, and must surrender to the domination of the man and be dependent on him.

This discrimination between men and women leads to a distortion of the personality of both, and prevents them from becoming really mature. The tendency to exaggerate a boy's feeling for his own ego and masculinity will usually end in an inferiority complex, since he will always feel that he is unable to rise up to the image expected of him. On the other hand, a tendency to exaggerate the need for a girl to withdraw, and to shrink into an attitude of passivity, (under the guise of feminity and refinement) tends to build up in her a form of superiority complex which results from the feeling of being better than the image that has been created of her.

A superiority complex creates masochistic tendencies in women, and an inferiority complex breeds sadistic and aggressive tendencies in men. Both of these are compensatory mechanisms, and are the two faces of the same coin.

Patriarchal medical science is replete with non-scientific truths and concepts aimed at maintaining discrimination against women, and providing it with a scientific cover to make it more acceptable. Among such 'truths' is the notion that man is aggressive by nature, and that wars can therefore be explained by 'a centre of aggression in the brain' or by aggressive tendencies that are an inbuilt part of his psyche. This is nothing more than an attempt to convince people that wars are in fact a response to biological necessity and an expression of human nature that is unchangeable and will continue to be an inseparable part of man. Similar are the ideas that portray passivity as an integral part of woman's nature, and therefore aim at diverting women's attention from the fact that their passivity is essentially due to social and economic factors that go far back in history.

It is natural that patriarchal society, whether in the East or in the West, should oppose all attempts at change, and fight for its continued existence. The weapons used by patriarchal society vary from era to era and from country to country.

In developed Western societies some of the main weapons are drawn from the arsenal of pseudo-scientific truths that do not take into account the vital role of social and economic factors in the moulding of human characteristics.

Such theories try to explain the revolutionary movements of blacks, youth and women as the result of distortions in the psyche of the people who are involved in them, rather than as the result of the distorted structure of society itself. This is no more than an extension of Freud's theories which explained rebellion against authority or the state as no more than an external expression of people's incapacity to overcome their own inner emotional struggles buried deep in the unconscious.

Yet what can be more satisfying to the ruling classes than to find thinkers and scientists who try to convince the people that their problems and difficulties are the result of the struggles that are going on deep in their subconscious? Or that wars, or discrimination between races and between the sexes, are nothing more than outward manifestations of an aggressiveness and an inborn unconscious instinct for destruction linked to the libido, and not at all the consequences of the capitalist system and all forms of exploitation?

Such pseudo-scientific thoughts lead people to seek the causes of their problems and difficulties within themselves, within their own bodies, and therefore deprives them of a true understanding and awareness of these problems, and of the need to participate in the social movements aimed at changing the structure of society.

In Arab society, cultural and scientific backwardness plays a very important role in holding back the struggles of people and preventing them from being channelled into the right paths. One of the primary weapons used to keep back the revolt of women and youth against the patriarchal system and its values is the misuse of Islam and its doctrines. There is no doubt that the wave of religious fanaticism that has swept many Arab countries in recent years is one of the ways used by the feudal and capitalist ruling classes to hold back the movement towards progress.

The slogan under which the reactionaries operate is that of 'a return to Islamic doctrine'. This slogan is used to mask the real nature of their aims and their desire to maintain the forms of exploitation on which they thrive. They attempt to convince the people that most of the economic and political difficulties and crises that have been faced in recent years are due to the fact that they have strayed from the path of Islam. They take advantage of people's ignorance of the true nature of our problems to proclaim that the only solution to the sufferings of the vast majority of Arab peoples is a return to the fold of Islam. They say that poverty and increasing want for the millions are a manifestation of Allah's wrath against those who have moved away from Islam and its teachings.

Religious associations and organizations have mushroomed rapidly in Arab countries during the past few years. They are busily engaged in propagating such ideas, in spreading false notions about, and advocating false solutions to, the problems of the Arab countries, fully aware of the fact that they can still capitalize on the sympathy evinced by people to those who speak to them in the name of religion and morals.

Every day this religious campaign beats the drums of Islamic morals. Yet, at the same time, parallel commercial campaigns cover the walls and screens of the big cities with bottles of whisky and half exposed women. Any casual stroller in the streets of Cairo, Beirut or Baghdad, or any of the other Arab capitals, can easily perceive that the walls are plastered with advertisements displaying the best wines or liqueurs, scintillating in a fine crystal glass with a woman's fingers around the stem, or film posters with a half naked woman lying full length on a bed. A continuous flow of vulgar, erotic films, built on the most superficial stories, depend for their attraction on belly dances or other forms of sexual provocation that cater for a sexually suppressed young public. The closer the links between the local capitalist or feudal classes and the policies of Western imperialism, the greater the number of advertisements and films based on the commercialization of sex and the female body. In contrast, the further a country moves along the path of socialism and shakes off economic and cultural dependence on the West, the greater the chances are of finding the walls and posters free of such pornographic material. This was true for example of Egypt, the Sudan and Syria some years ago, but now with the shift in policies, and the reinforcement of American influence, commercial sex has once more invaded the main cities and towns of these countries.

International monopoly capital remains on the alert as far as the Arab world is concerned. The rich resources of raw materials, and especially oil, the strategic geographical position and the political importance of the region radiating into Africa, West Asia and the Mediterranean, all tend to make the struggle against foreign exploitation particularly acute. No respite can be expected, for every time one of the Arab countries attempts to escape from the stranglehold of imperialism and international capital, it is immediately surrounded on all sides by continuous attacks on the economic, political and cultural fronts, accompanied by attempts to foment troubles from within, in alliance with reactionary or backward forces. Those who dare to try and break out of the stranglehold must be brought back as soon as possible, lest their example become infectious.

The greater the vigour with which the campaign of sexual and commercial advertisements is pursued, and the more intense the marketing of foreign capitalist production becomes, the stronger the religious pressure that is developed in the form of precepts, teachings, sermons and legislation. For the mass of people must remain sexually and intellectually subjected to the authority of the ruling classes, which draws its support from the authority of God. Not long ago some of the religious leaders in Egypt proclaimed that the power and authority of the ruler is an expression of the power and authority of Allah. 'He who insults or disdains the authority of Allah, will himself be humiliated by Allah. The authority of Allah may be represented by an Emir (Prince) of the Gulf, or a King in a kingdom, or a President of a republic. All such people are no doubt an embodiment of the authority of Allah.'[2]

The more vigorous the campaign of advertisements in the Arab capitals, and the more widespread the display of bottles of liquor accompanied by naked shoulders calculated to ensure that the production of the Western factories is rapidly bought up in the markets, the longer and more vociferous become the columns of newspapers and magazines, the radio broadcasts and the television programmes devoted to campaigning for prohibition. Alcohol in Islam is *Haram* and therefore something must be done to counteract the wide commercialization of hard liquor. Sometimes special laws are promulgated, and are often so contradictory that they become ridiculous, and therefore ineffective. An example is a law punishing the person who drinks alcohol, but not the trader or establishment that sells it. A lot of noise is made so that interest in drink is provoked, so that the glass of wine is held out and yet held back. For the net result is calculated to be an increase in demand and sales, even at the expense of a guilty conscience. In many cases, the law is implemented in a double-handed way. The small liquor shop or cafe in a poor district is closed down or fined, or the proprietor punished, while the big establishments in the more affluent areas of the city continue to sell drink with impunity.

One of the typical examples of what has been happening in this area is the law on prohibition which came into force in Egypt during the year 1976.[3] This law permitted drinking in the big hotels or in furnished apartments, on the assumption that these were places frequented by tourists, whereas in fact the majority, at least of the furnished flats, are not places used by tourists, but rather for the purposes of prostitution. In any case, whether they are frequented by tourists or prostitutes, the fact still remains that they are located on Egyptian territory, that is in an Islamic country, and should therefore be regulated by the same Islamic laws that are applied to dwellings, or cafes, in the poorer districts. It does not seem possible to think that Islam can make exceptions just for the sake of making a few dollars, or earning hard currency or encouraging tourism. It seems obvious that an authentic religious rationale should lead us to activate and reinforce Islam at the expense of tourism, rather than to do the opposite.

However, to be contradictory is the essence of all logic based on exploitation. Thus it is that at the very time when the pictures of half naked women occupy more and more space on our walls, in our films, and in our magazines, an increasing number of women and girls are taking once more to wearing the veil. A growing tendency to impose upon females what is considered the Islamic dress under the guise of feminine modesty or pudicity has become manifest in recent years. Once again the bodies of women must be covered because they are profane and dangerously seductive.

I do not understand how it can be possible for the Arab girl to cover up her hair and her body, and hide her seductiveness, if she is surrounded at every moment of the day by advertisements inciting her to be attractive, to seduce men, to soften her skin with creams and to make her lips red and full, to wear fine elusive stockings that will show off the beauty of her legs, and to wash her hair with lotions that will make it fine, wavy and silky.

Many an Arab girl or woman ends up with some form or other of psychological disorder because of the severe contradictions to which she is exposed. Arab songs and literature unceasingly swamp her senses with association and feelings related to love. Yet if she responds to the call of love, then punishment and reprobation is swift and merciless. The least that will be said of her is that she is a girl without honour and without morals. No man will marry her, even the man with whom she is in love. He will explain to her that he cannot trust a girl who allows herself to love a man before marrying him, even if he is himself that man.

The greater the exploitation imposed upon the Arab peoples, the greater the drain of their resources in oil and other raw materials, the greater the profits pocketed by the multinational and national capitalists, the lower the poor sections of Arab society sink into misery and deprivation, and the more acute the economic crisis and problems faced by the masses. As highly priced goods imported from Western countries invade the markets of Cairo, Damascus, Beirut, Tunis and other cities of the Arab world, the lines of toiling people standing in front of co-operative and fair price shops and popular bakeries grow steadily longer. There they stand for hours, waiting for a loaf of bread, or a cake of soap, or a packet of tea, or a metre of cheap cloth. Walking down the streets of Cairo today, it is impossible not to see the enormous quantitites of highly priced Western imported goods that fill the shopping areas, while hundreds of men and women crowd around the co-operative stores, the bakeries and the popular grocery stores.

The vast majority of people face a severe economic crisis that has considerably affected their standard of living. Corruption, embezzlement, stealing and all forms of violence have become common everyday happenings, and the incidence is so high in the big cities and towns of Egypt that some newspapers have demanded the institution of a new juridical system called the 'night judge' so that immediate action can be taken against the perpetrators of armed aggression, thieves and kidnappers.[4]

The sudden increase in acts of violence, stealing, kidnapping, drug addiction, and in the commercialization of sex, alcohol and narcotics is obvious to all who do not refuse to see. Fathers yield more and more to the temptation of selling their daughters into marriage. Female domestic servants, more often than not, tend to end up as prostitutes, or cheap cabaret dancers, whose job it is to entertain the tourists and rich Arabs or Egyptians. Sexual relations whose aim is money, some kind of material benefit, or security, are the pattern which tends to prevail at the expense of genuine emotions, affection, friendship and love.

These widespread phenomena of moral and sexual corruption are, on the other hand, accompanied by a wave of religious fanaticism which on the surface seems to be contradictory. A chorus of voices is raised, calling for the strict application of Islamic legislation, and the severest punishments such as cutting off the hand of the thief, or stoning an adulterous woman to death. The same voices also demand the banning of sex scenes from all films, of kissing in Arab films, and strict application of regulations prohibiting those under sixteen years of age from seeing certain films. They clamour that exemplary punishment be meted out for open or disguised forms of prostitution or moral corruption, and insist once more that women's rightful place is to be confined to the home. Girls should be strictly supervised and under the continuous control of their families, accompanied wherever they go by a male escort. Some journalists have even suggested that women who tour the Arab countries and are employed in cabarets to perform the belly dance, or other dances of a sexually provocative nature, should be deprived of their Egyptian nationality.[5]

Some Arab writers, however, are opposing this wave of brutal fanaticism. They insist that instead of cutting off the hand of thieves, it would be better to concentrate on cutting out poverty from our lives. That instead of stoning adulterous women to death, it would be preferable to abolish sexual oppression, and allow the young to lead a healthy physical and mental life. Such rational thinking, nevertheless, is like one drop in the ocean of religious bigotry and extremism. For logic and reason are the most dangerous of the enemies that face exploitation and imperialist plunder. The culture, literature and art that is fed to people by newspapers, films, T.V., the theatre and books must therefore aim at drowning the voice of reason and preventing people from becoming aware of the truth. It must refuse to see the reasons why many of the educated youth have chosen a slow mental and moral suicide by indulging in narcotics, sex and crime. If we are once more to speak of honour, whom can we consider less 'honourable', a woman who hires out her body to a man for money with which to buy food, or a state that has bartered logic, reason and morals so that a handful of people with power and capital can continue to earn millions every year? Who is more worthy of punishment, the youth who tries to escape from poverty into a dream world by taking some narcotic pill, or the vested interests that maintain this poverty so that they may thrive?

In any society whose structure is built on exploitation, it is natural that economic and commercial values should clash with moral and religious ones. As a result, patriarchal class societies are riddled with deep-seated contradictions and a double morality which runs through every aspect of life. However, it is always those who are ruled over by others, rather than those who rule, women rather than men, and the toiling classes rather than the upper classes, who are made to suffer the consequences and pay the price for these contradictions which become more acute in backward and poor countries. The Arab region, by virtue of its agricultural and oil resources, may be considered economically rich, yet these riches are not shared by its peoples, rather they are siphoned off by the multinational corporations and a handful of capitalist or semi-feudal Arabs. That is why the vast majority still live in a situation characterized by dire poverty, and by an economic and social backwardness which is itself reflected in an intellectual, mental and moral backwardness rampant in many spheres.

The economic, sexual and moral oppression of women is accentuated by the backwardness of a society. A poor woman is always more severely punished for any 'mistakes' she makes. Riches can help in forgiving a woman, even if she is morally corrupt, indeed very often they may even convert sins into virtues. Money can protect a divorced woman from being homeless, or becoming a beggar, or a legal or illegal prostitute. Money can help a woman to get rid of an unwanted foetus in a doctor's clinic, even though abortion may still be considered a crime.

Arab women are the victims of oppression because of the double moral standards that govern their societies. The economic exploitation imposed on the Arab countries not only leads to a systematic plunder of their resources, but also imposes upon them the double moral standards resulting from the contradiction between the commercial values of capitalism and the religious values inherited from the past.

Woman is made to suffer, as a result of these double moral standards, more than anyone else in society. Her body has to be undressed to draw the attention of people and provoke them sexually through advertisements, films, etc. so that commodities may be more rapidly disposed of on the market. Sex must be instilled into every song, dance or play so that it can be sold, and be more and more attuned to the game where women are the pawn, and their naked bodies the prize. Nakedness in women is therefore a daily requirement. Yet the religious morals which are propagated just as widely insist that her body is profane and must be covered completely, so as to ensure that only the face and hands are showing.

Women are tools, objects, mere instruments, They are objects used for commercial advertising, or for work without pay at home and in the field, or for work with pay outside the home coupled with work for no pay inside it, or they are used to give birth to children for the reproductive purposes of society, or they are sex objects used to satisfy the wants and desires of men.

Perhaps one of the greatest distortions from which the history of the human race suffers is the fact that it has been written from the point of view of the rulers and not of the peoples who have been ruled. As a result it is mainly a reflection of the interests of the ruling class, as against the toiling people over whom they dominate, and a reflection of the interests of men over those of women. History has therefore falsely depicted many of the facts related to women. Arab women are not deficient in their mental capacities, as men and the history they have written tend to assert, neither are they weak or passive. On the contrary, Arab women resisted the patri-archal system and class exploitation hundreds of years before women in America and Europe started fighting the same battles. American women did not begin to realize that they were in fact dancing to the tune played by men until the second half of the 20th Century, nor did they understand until then that, when the word 'man' was used, it referred to the whole of the human race, so that the masculine gender referred not only to men but also to women. That is why some of the Women's Liberation Movements in America are trying to change the English vocabulary. Arab women, on the other hand, made the necessary changes fourteen hundred years ago with the beginning of Islam. The masculine gender was used by the Koran in the early stages to indicate both men and women. The Arab women objected to this, saying: 'We have become Muslims just as you have, and we have done just what you did. Yet you are mentioned in the Koran and we are not.' For people in those days were all called Muslims (masculine). Whereupon Allah started to mention in the Koran, *'Inna Al Mouslimeena* [masculine] *Wal Mouslimat* [feminine] *Wal Mou'mineena* [masculine] *Wat Mouminat* [feminine].'[6]

The history of the Arabs provides many examples of the resistance put up by women which bears witness to the strength and initiative they were capable of showing at different periods of their struggle. It is necessary to delve more deeply into this history, and to understand the real reasons for the unusual boldness and forwardness displayed by women at certain periods in the development of Arab society. If this is done, it will also allow us to penetrate more deeply into the factors that led to the distortion of concepts related to femininity and beauty, and that transformed woman from a human being with a mind, a body and a self, into an empty clown who paints her face with the colours of Christian Dior and Revlon, shows her thighs or breasts under the mini-skirt, swings on her high heels from side to side like somebody affected with a strange malady, binds her breasts and buttocks with strange contraptions, and ruins her eyes with the black of mascara, eyeliners and artificial lashes. This clown then completes the masquerade by putting on a stupid look, an air of naivete and an appearance of frailness to become the 'perfect female'.

True beauty is that of a woman who is herself, who does not forge another personality in order to please her husband lest he divorce her or abandon her for another woman, who does not put on an appearance which is not really hers in order to catch a husband, and who refuses to distort her behaviour, her desires and her conception of happiness to satisfy the norms of society in the hope that people will not fight her, or accuse her of being abnormal. Beauty comes, above all, from the mind, from the health of the body and the completeness of the self. It does not draw its existence from the size of the buttocks, or the deposits of fat beneath curves, or the layers of cosmetics, that cover an underlying anxiety and a lack of self-confidence.

So far, it is only a very small minority of educated women and girls in Arab society who pay more attention to their minds than to their fingernails or eyelashes. However this does not indicate that women have an inferior brain, but is rather a reflection of the upbringing to which girls are exposed from a very early age, and which leads to the moulding of women into superficial and shallow beings. The Arab girl is taught from childhood to give exaggerated attention to her clothes, her body and her looks, rather than to worry about the development of her capacity to think.

Many are the girls who become afflicted with one or other anxiety neurosis, or psychological disorder, because of their desperate desire to fulfil the norms of beauty and femininity imposed upon them. A girl feels that her life and her future depends on the length of her nose, or the curl of her lashes. Any shortfall of less than a millimetre in the length of her lashes can become an acute problem, a veritable crisis in her life.

For society and the family, intelligence in a girl distorts her feminine character. A disposition towards sports and strong bodily development spoils her beauty; a tall stature, a head carried high on the shoulders, and bold wide-open eyes show leanings towards masculinity. The perfect female is submissive walks with lowered head and half closed sleepy eyes, and is short.

Tallness in girls is considered unbecoming according to some of the text-books used in secondary schools. One of the textbooks used in the final year of high school, for both girls and boys, maintains that in the period of growth related to adolescence, it is preferable for boys to be tall and well built, whereas a girl should not be tall.[7] It is not difficult to realize the feeling of inferiority that can take hold of a girl who happens to be tall when she reads this passage in a textbook taught to High School students in Egypt. It is also not difficult to foresee how a boy whose stature is short, or whose shoulders are narrow, would react to the same passage.

Thus we see how it is that education distorts the personality of both males and females at an early age, irrespective of whether the educational process takes place in schools, at home, or through the mass media and cultural institutions.

It is not possible to realize the extent of the harm done, and of the distortion caused, until we begin to study the mental, psychological and organic disorders with which the vast majority of our adolescents are afflicted.

However the problems which affect girls and women are much more widespread, acute and severe. This is particularly true in Arab societies, which are passing through a transitional stage, and shifting over from cultural and social backwardness to a modernism copied without real understanding from the West. This modernization process does not prevent such societies from hanging on to many out-worn traditions in the name of Islam and of Eastern moral values.

Egyptian society is an example of these trends, where much has been copied or taken from Western countries and their experience, and yet where many traditional ways of thinking, and behaving, are maintained. Sometimes the aspects and manifestations of 'modernization' are in their essence more backward than the old traditions. An example is that of the wives in the upper or middle classes of society, who take their husband's name when they marry, contrary to the local custom where the wife keeps her maiden name. For one of the remaining aspects of women's ancient status in Arab countries is the fact that a woman does not lose her name just because she has become a wife.

There has been many a time when I could not prevent myself from reacting with sarcasm, during a reception or party where men and women of the more affluent sections of Egyptian society were gathered, on overhearing women address one another by the names of their husbands. They would pronounce these names with such pride, and even conceit, as though they felt that their value depended upon the worth of their husbands, and that in imitating the women of Europe or the United States, they were producing irrefutable proof of their culture, understanding and modernism. My sarcasm would grow even more barbed on discovering that the women using their husband's names were leading figures in the official women's organizations and made speeches in public about the rights and freedom of women.

In many Arab societies the 'modern, europeanized' woman, who thinks that progress is manifested by a tendency to show more and more of her thighs from under shorter and shorter mini-skirts, to smoke longer and longer cigarettes protruding from cigarette holders, to down glasses of whisky 'on the rocks' or to shake vigorously and insidiously to the mad beat of modern dances, is becoming a common phenomenon in cities and even towns.

However under the shivering, shimmering surface wriggles the female, suppressed mentally, emotionally and sexually. The female who covers her mind with a thick, almost impenetrable veil, even though her thighs and shoulders are naked, the female who still believes that the most noble pursuit for her in life is to marry a man, to serve him, to obey him and to bear him children — preferably male.

References

1. Elizabeth Thomas, *The Harmless People,* (Sackur and Warburg, 1959).
2. *Al Ahram,* Cairo, 24 July 1975. An extract from the speech of his Holiness the Sheikh El Bakouri at the National Congress of the Arab Socialist Union in Egypt, held on 23rd July 1975.
3. *Al Ahram,* Cairo, 17-18 May 1976.
4. *El Akhbar,* Cairo, 25 August 1975.
5. *Al Ahram,* Cairo, 14 May 1976 and 17 May 1976, under the title 'Mofakirat', Usiph Idris and Naguib Mahfouz.
6. Mohamed Ebn Saad, *El Tabakat el Koubra,* Vol. 3, p.145; and the *Koran;* 'Sourat Al Ahzab', Verse 35.
7. See the *Textbook of Psychology for the third year students of High School (Arts and Literature)* by Abdel Aziz El Kousy and Sayed Ghoneim, (Ministry of Education, Cairo, 1976-77), Ch.2, p.132.

PART 2
Women in History

11. The Thirteenth Rib of Adam

To this very day, many people in Arab countries, and even all over the world, literally think that Eve was the first woman to appear on the face of the Earth. They also believe that she was born of Adam and grew out of one of his ribs, as the story goes in the sacred books first of Judaism, then Christianity, and finally Islam. They are not aware of the fact that women trod our planet before these monotheistic religions descended upon men and long before the human race came to know anything about Adam and Eve. If we return to ancient history, many important facts related to the position of woman at home and in society will be revealed. We will also discover that the changes affecting her status and role were intimately related to the way in which the social and economic structure of society evolved. The unveiling of this relationship between the economic and social infrastructure of society and the position occupied by woman constitutes the key to understanding the reasons for the downward path that finally led her at the time of Judaism to a situation where she became a mere rib in the body of man.

The ancient Egyptian civilization is more than 5,000 years old and historically precedes the advent of Judaism, the first of the three monotheistic religions. We have been able to study it in the remains of cities, temples, and other constructions left behind, in the writings inscribed on papyrus and in numerous sculptures, drawings and engravings, remarkably preserved to the present day.

The ancient Egyptians had their own religions, and their own religious practices and rituals, before the monotheistic religions made their entry on the scene. Judaism was influenced in many ways by the religion of the Pharaohs and in particular the monotheistic leanings of Akhnatoun's sun worship. In the successive dynasties of the Pharaonic era, periods were known when the women of Egypt occupied a high place both in the affairs of their country and in the realm of religion. Almost throughout the thousands of years during which ancient Egypt flourished on the banks of the Nile, female gods reigned side by side with male gods over the destinies of human beings.

The concept of religion developed in the human mind long before the monotheistic religions came to be known. Primitive human beings created the idea of gods in the world, or at least of some obscure forces beyond their understanding, endowed with capacities that they did not possess. These forces influenced, or even controlled the lives of people, since they could be generous and bestow rain, good harvests, and sufficient food upon them if they so wished. On the other hand, much harm and evil might be the fate of people at their hands, which were also capable of sowing storms, disease and death,

Historical studies indicate that the most ancient of all gods were female. In Pharaonic Egypt goddesses ruled over many areas and participated with male gods in deciding human destinies. We may cite as examples: Maait, the Goddess of Truth; and Naiyet, the Goddess of War and Floods, Isis, Sikhmet, Hathour and many others.

The elevation of women to the heights occupied by goddesses was a reflection of their status within society before the systems characterized by the patriarchal family, land ownership and division into social classes came into being. With the advent of these systems the status of women gradually dropped over a period of time, but vestiges of the matriarchal system, more or less important, continued to survive in feudal or slave societies such as that of the Pharaohs.

The patrilineal system, which identifies children according to the father and ensures that they carry his name and inherit his property, only evolved at these later stages. Earlier societies tended to follow matrilineal patterns where the mother was the head of the family, and where children were linked in descent to the woman who had given birth to them. These societies were therefore governed by what is known as the matriarchal system.[1]

In the early periods of ancient Egyptian civilization, a legitimate son carried his mother's name and inheritance was often matrilineal (through the mother's line), since it was the eldest daughter and not the son who inherited.[2] The Greek historian, Herodotus, mentions that the Lukians named the son after his mother. Tacitus, the Roman historian, points out that the Germanic tribes used to give primary importance to the sister. In the pre-Islamic era, some of the Arab tribes also followed matrilineal practices.[3] In Asia and Africa a few tribes remain who still follow the same pattern.

It is a well-known fact of human history that the elevated status of woman in society, and in religion, was related to the fact that children carried her name. Under the matriarchal system women occupied a high social position and even ascended the throne of the gods. The monopoly established by male gods was related to the patriarchal system, and the naming of children after the father instead of the mother.

The legal systems related to family structures, inheritance and the naming of children are also a reflection of socio-economic relationships in a society. Economic life in the early stages of human history was dependent on very simple and restricted activities such as picking fruits and nuts, digging or pulling up roots from the earth, catching lizards and rats, or hunting certain animals. These primitive activities obliged humans to migrate continuously from one place to the other in search of food and suitable hunting grounds. The forms of subsistence left no room for a surplus and the continued nomadic life made private property out of the question. In the absence of private property people were not divided into classes, into rulers and ruled. They were all equal members of the community. Simultaneously no division of labour had yet arisen between individuals, or between men and women. It was a society without classes, without differentiation, without masters and slaves.[4]

Letourneau maintains that in all probability it was woman who first discovered the new technology of agriculture, due to her long experience in picking fruits and nuts, and extracting roots from the ground.[5] It was also women who first took over the functions of agriculture and thus maintained, and even reinforced, their favourable economic status, reflected in social status, matrilineal parental relations and a matriarchal system, all of which were prevalent in the early stages of the agricultural era.

In these primitive agricultural societies women played an important role in the social economy, were equal to men within the political structures and occupied a front-line position in so far as the family system and marriage were concerned. Clans were matriarchal, children were named after the mother and were enrolled in the mother's clan and exogamy, that is marriage outside the clan, was the rule. In view of the role of women in the social economy, the man after marriage moved over to his wife's house, worked in the communal fields there and became an additional member of the labour force in her clan. The need for an expanding labour force also explains the practice of adoption in these tribes. Any clan had the right to adopt as many prisoners of war as required. They became a part of the clan and worked in its fields.[6]

The economic importance of woman is manifest in the fact that she was free to separate from her husband by a personal decision on her part without mutual agreement. The husband was then obliged to leave his wife's household and clan and return to his own family and people. The children, however, were left behind with the mother. Women were also equal with men as far as leadership roles within the political structures were concerned and also headed religious rituals, ceremonies and forms of worship. Religious customs and practices did not differentiate between men and women in any way.[7]

However, after some time, it became possible for men and women to settle down in one place. Agriculture became a steady source of food. When methods and techniques improved, it began to yield a surplus and the exploitation of other people's labour became a possibility. The idea of private property, especially in land, spread and replaced the communal ownership of the clan and with it the right to remain on the land generation after generation in order to cultivate it.[8] Private property led man to deprive women of their prerogative in naming their children after themselves. His aim was to identify his children and hand down his property to them after his death. Property and inheritance therefore destroyed the foundation of matriarchal and matrilineal systems and led to the division of society into social classes.

With the expansion of private property these ancient societies became sharply differentiated into two main social classes: the landowners and masters of slaves on the one hand, who constituted a minority; and the vast majority of slaves, who owned nothing not even themselves, on the other. These developments were accompanied by a parallel degradation in the status and position of women, who first in the ruling classes of landowners and concomitantly in the rest of society passed under the economic, social and religious domination of men. Women lost their previous religious prestige and ceased to oversee and head religious rituals and ceremonies. Man monopolized religion for his own purposes and male gods prevailed, whereas women slid down to the lowest rungs of religious status. This process ran parallel to the development of private property. The old structures were replaced by systems based on exploitation and women were relegated to the bottom orders of society. With increasing male domination the patriarchal system started to hold sway as an accompaniment to the division of society into landowners (or masters) and slaves who were the property of masters.[9]

The father became the head of the family, the paterfamilias, and its religious head. He presided over religious rituals and ceremonies. With the patriarchal family the worship of ancestors became finally established as a means of reinforcing the position of the father.[10] The father after his death thus rose to the level of the gods, whereas women were placed on the same level as herds of cattle whose master holds their life and death in his hands. The mother and her children became akin to the property, land and slaves owned by the father. The word *familia* among the ancient Romans in fact meant the fields, houses, money and slaves which constituted a man's riches and property, and which he passed down the line as an inheritance. The woman was part of this *familia,* that is, part of his possessions.

To elaborate in detail on the history of women in ancient societies or on the cult of female worship and goddesses would be a deviation from the main theme of this book, which is the situation of contemporary women in Arab and Islamic society. Nevertheless an approach which seeks to deal with the present without throwing any light on the past is in grave danger of missing, or misinterpreting, some of the fundamental truths relating to women in the Arab world. The present has its roots in the past, just as the future develops from the present. In this sense our knowledge, our understanding of society and our destiny are all influenced to an important extent by what has preceded in history. It is not possible to grasp why women live as they do in the Arab countries, nor to show the way out of their predicament, if we do not go back in history to religion. Just as it is not possible to know why women were relegated to an inferior position in religion if we know nothing about their status and situation in the societies and civilizations that preceded the three main monotheistic religions. To take this argument further, it is therefore wrong to attempt a study of women in Arab and Islamic society without referring to Christianity and Judaism, both of which preceded Islam and influenced it to a very marked extent in many aspects related to its fundamental concepts and teachings. It is equally erroneous to deal with the monotheistic religions and the position occupied by women therein, if we do not trace the paths that connect them with the religions belonging to a still more distant and misty past.

The story of Adam and Eve was born in Judaism, and through Judaism arose the idea that woman was sinful and that sin was sex. With this idea the separation between spirit (or soul) and body was consecrated and canonized for all time. Christianity followed in the wake of Judaism, and went even further in smelting and moulding the iron fetters of prejudice and rigidity in the attitudes and values related to women and sex. To reinforce these fetters and ensure their eternity Jesus Christ the Messiah was made to be born a sacred male, a lord so chaste that women were forbidden to him and sexual relations with them were an experience that he was never to know, or even to seek. Furthermore he was made to be born asexually from the womb of the Virgin Mary who had never known the embrace of a man. God filled her with the breath of his spirit and the embryo of the Messiah developed quietly in the silence of her womb.

These religious concepts and thoughts lead inevitably to the separation of human beings from their bodies and from real life. Thus arose the phenomenon which was to be called the 'alienated experience of reality' as an expression indicating the splitting of human life into two. Henceforward two fundamentally contradictory notions of life were to be locked in struggle all through the ages up to the present day.

First, was the ancient or primitive humanistic notion which believes in the essential goodness of the human body and its functions, and which derives its roots from the religions of Ancient Egypt that gave great emphasis to the vitality, generosity and richness embodied in the physical qualities of both men and women.

A second notion which spread its influence widely after Judaism and Christianity, and which leads to the alienation of the body from reality, encourages an escapist attitude towards the objective material world. Here the alienation is in relation to the material world, whether subjective or objective, where the term 'material' is used in its philosophical sense and not in the mundane sense usually attached to it. Human beings escape into the world of spirits, souls, ideas and illusions divorced from reality, and base their conception of the world and themselves on an 'idealist' approach. 'Idealism' — again in a philosophical sense — has very often been wilfully confused with 'ideals' or 'noble motives' whereas in fact there is no necessary relation between the two.

The woman in Christianity was once again sacrificed at the altar. A victim of the Judaic Jehovah and of the highly patriarchal religious practices related to Judaism, she now fell a victim to the cult of the Virgin Mary and the chastity of a Christ raised above the human level of desires and physical needs. She was caught and crushed between the two millstones of this struggle between the body and the spirit or soul, or, to express it differently, between good as emanating from the spirit and evil with its roots and sustenance in the body. God had created man in his own image, and God was spirit. Woman on the other hand was the body, and the body was sex. Man alone was a complete portrayal of the God of the Heavens, on earth, but woman could never become complete until espoused to a man, for through marriage woman's body was at least endowed with a head. This head was her husband. In the Old Testament it is possible to trace the origin of this beheaded and distorted image of woman. Man was allowed to pray before God without covering his head since he resembled the Creator and was akin to Him. A woman, however, was enjoined to cover her head when praying because, according to a common religious interpretation, she — unlike man — was found lacking in something essential. She was a body without a head. Since the main difference between a human being and an animal lies in the head, or in other words the brain, only man could be considered a complete human being. Woman was only an animal body dominated by passion, sensuality and an insatiable lust, carrying within herself evil as an integral part of her nature, a consecration of God's will and an embodiment of Satan in the human being. All the prophets known in history, all the high priests, and monks and friars and frocked servitors of religion were men, dedicated to serving God and required to shun women for all life since women were descended from Satan.

Artists of the Middle Ages have left behind many paintings and drawings depicting women kneeling on the ground behind Satan and trying to kiss his posterior. In the 13th Century Saint Thomas Aquinas and Albertos Magnus, who were considered the most prominent theologians of the time, propounded the idea that women were capable of having sexual relations with Satan. The Inquisition and its tribunals searched diligently for the women who had slept with Satan so that they could be burnt alive. There were certain signs and symptoms carefully defined by these conscientious dispensers of justice. They were called the signs of Satan and, once discerned in the victim, constituted irrefutable evidence of Satan's imprint.

Arab men both in the pre-Islamic and Islamic eras enjoyed a great degree of sexual freedom whether within the family through multiple marriages and divorce, or outside it through sexual relations with concubines and women slaves.

This was not an exclusive characteristic of the life of Arab men but holds true for other societies as well. Men have accorded themselves this wide degree of sexual freedom ever since the patriarchal system and patriarchal relations were established in society. The special privileges of men are not related to their geographical distribution, or to the country from which they came, or to the cultures of the East or the West, but rather to the socio-economic structures of society. Therefore when a society remains patriarchal and characterized by class distinctions and divisions, men are accorded rights and freedoms of which women are deprived.

Yet those who have written about the Arabs, and in particular the schools of imperialist and orientalist thought, have chosen to gloss over this fundamental truth. In so doing they have shown either an incomplete understanding of the factors that govern the relations between man and woman, or a conscious and premeditated bias which makes them portray the East and the Arabs in an unfavourable light. To them the sexual freedom practised by Arab men is a unique phenomenon unknown in other parts of the world, and Islam the only religion that has made of women the objects of sexual pleasure for

men. To them the Arab male is exceptional in the fact that he practises polygamy or extra-marital relations as a normal part of his life. And yet all men,
in all corners of the earth, and in all the known periods of history since the
world first witnessed the ascendancy of the patriarchal system over the more
ancient matriarchal society, have practised sex with women other than their
wives, either openly or in secret, sometimes slipping under a dark doorway,
and at other times flaunting their mistresses for all to see. Christianity
viewed sexual laxity with greater severity than any other religion, and
imposed virginity not only on Jesus Christ and his mother, Mary, but also on
the men who donned the vestments or the robes of religion to become priests
or monks or friars in the service of God. Yet despite the orthodoxy and
sexual strictness inherent in Christianity's teachings, history is an uncompro-
mising witness to the fact that the 'holy men of God' had recourse to diverse
and varied ways of expressing and satisfying their sexual needs, and that
prostitution flared up as never before in the periods known for the predominance of puritanical attitudes and values. Luther's Reformation was partly
an attempt to correct the abuses that had become rampant within the
church.[11] One of his observations was that a large part of the revenue of the
Catholic Church was drawn from the dues paid by brothels. To him it
appeared that the Church was working hand in hand with Satan since its very
sustenance seemed to come from one of his favourite occupations. From the
money of these brothels, from the sweat of women's thighs, were built the
'beautiful houses of God' where people came to worship and pray. Revenues
largely drawn from subscriptions and charity came from men who dipped
their hands into their pockets and dropped a few pieces of silver or bronze
into the wooden boxes of the church before continuing on their way to the
brothel. For was it not understandable that they should seek God's mercy and
forgiveness before sinning with a fellow woman?

Prostitution was unknown until the patriarchal family established itself in
society.[12] It was the only possible solution to a situation in which a single
husband was imposed on every married woman whereas the man was free to
have sexual relations with women other than his wife. The need arose for a
category of women with whom the men could practise extra-marital intercourse whenever they felt the desire, and with it was born one of the oldest
occupations in the world,an occupation assigned exclusively to women, and
for which there was no alternative since, in its absence, with whom could the
male practise his sexual licence?

Thus it was that the patriarchal system established the social institution
which came to be known as prostitution, and side by side with it a new social
category, the 'illegitimate child' — the fruit of sexual relations between man
and the prostitute.

The prostitute and the illegitimate child became the sacrificial victims
slaughtered at the altar of the patriarchal god. It was they who were made to
pay the price for the birth of the patriarchal family, its survival and its
reinforcement. Men on the other hand were exempt, exonerated. No price was
paid by them, no reputation sullied, no suffering incurred for the privilege of

an unshackled sexual freedom and a free, or almost free, ticket to pleasure. Nothing — except the process of dehumanization and alienation which was to be the common lot of both men and women throughout the long centuries, since the people of the earth were first divided into classes, and once divided into classes experienced what it meant to be differentiated according to sex, race, creed and colour, and the sum of their worldly possessions. The common lot of men and women, fragmented into body and mind, matter and spirit, belief and action, and torn asunder by the double standards that cut like a sword through the personality.

To my mind the Arab men were perhaps more straightforward and honest than other men have been. They did not try to conceal their sexual life behind heavy curtains, or a smoke-screen of puritanical values. They reflected their relationships with women creatively and without inhibitions in literature and poetry.

I do not belong to the category of people who believe that to seek sexual pleasure is a sin, nor do I think it possible to consider men and women who insist on attaining sexual satisfaction and fulfilment as afflicted with some form of deviation or depravity. On the contrary, it is Christian and Victorian puritanism and orthodoxy which consider sexual pleasure and desire to be the work of the devil, which are at fault and are a deviation from what is natural to the human being. Such attitudes were taken so far that there came a time when a new-born child was considered impure until it received a Christian baptism. They were also the basis on which grew up the asexual rigidity of the Church characterized by a set of cold, severe Calvinistic values related to 'renunciation of the world', chastity, virginity and 'sexual sin'.

These values, however, were applied in real life and practice not to the ruling classes but only to the ruled, not to men but only to women, and not to the rich but only to the poor. They acted as shackles upon the mind and fetters around the body, making it all the more easy for the forces of reaction, oppression, and dictatorship to dominate and domesticate the vast masses of men and women living under their yoke. The patriarchal family was one of the important social changes that paved the way for the division of society into masters and slaves, and a corner stone in the structure of the ancient empires built on colonization. In the same way, the puritanical values of the Christian Church at different stages of its development were utilized to enforce systems built on oppression and are still part of the arsenal of heavy weapons which maintain a continuous barrage in the war against the revolutionary struggles of women, coloured races, and the exploited classes living under semi-feudal or capitalist systems which have drawn their main support from imperialism and neo-colonialism.

History has shown the close link that exists between economics and religion, between economic relationships (and needs) and the moral and sexual values that predominate in a given society. These values change in different periods, under different social systems, and with the historical evolution of countries. Economic necessities and needs, which are in turn reflected in political changes and imperatives, act as a crucial factor in moulding the values that govern our lives and influence our sexual ethics.

As an example of economic necessity engendered by the growth of European capitalism at the beginning of the industrial era finding its expression and legitimisation in the sphere of high morality, we may cite the concept of *sublimation,* which became a scientific theory cherished as one of the achievements of the Freudian school of psycho-analysis. The basic solid facts behind this 'noble' idea, however, are probably very different to what its propagators and disciples thought them to be. Society at that time, and with it the rising capitalist class, was in urgent need of the greatest possible physical effort on the part of the workers in the mushrooming factories and industrial areas. This physical effort, the source of profit and capital accumulation, was particularly necessary at a stage where sophisticated technology and machinery were still to be discovered and invented. It was imperative that every drop of sweat and every ounce of energy be extracted from the bodies of workers, and this was only possible through maximising the degree of material, social and religious oppression. An important weapon in the armoury of exploitation was the creation of sacred values which made out of toil a supreme virtue. As an inevitable corollary to a life of toil, life's pleasures and sex had to be sacrificed, and the only way was to depict them as unworthy, degrading, lower forms of human activity, which were more suited to the world of animals than to that of men and women.

Thus it was that capitalist accumulation was accompanied during this period by puritanical values, morals and norms of behaviour which found their origin in a rigid Calvinistic Protestantism. At a later stage, however, when industrial societies witnessed a rapid advance in technology and machinery, when human physical effort was no longer so much in demand, when standards of living had risen and hours of work had dropped, when production had been multiplied a hundred fold and consumption had made rapid strides, the puritanical values and moral codes which taught renunciation and abstention to the working man and woman lost their significance and their function. In an era when the cry for more consumption became the order of the day, to preach the bible of sacrifice and the ethics of non-consumption became out of place. From then onwards, men and women had actively to be exhorted to follow the path of worldly desire and pleasure, to give free rein to their physical needs, and to worship the fetish of consumption. It was also necessary to divert the human race, which unfortunately was learning and understanding more rapidly than ever before, from pondering too deeply on the reasons for its woes, lest people discover what and who was responsible for the hunger and deprivation from which they suffered.

It is easy to understand why segregation and the veil were imposed upon women at a later stage of Islam, whereas in the earlier stages women were allowed to move about freely and expose their faces for all to see. Even today, some of the Arab countries still maintain the customs that developed in later Islamic society. Segregation and the veil were not meant to ensure the protection of women, but essentially that of men. And the Arab woman was not imprisoned in the home to safeguard her body, her honour and her morals, but rather to keep intact the honour and the morals of men.

In addition, the fact that men felt the need to prescribe such customs, and to keep the women away from participation in normal life seems to explode the myth of the powerful male and the defenceless and weak female. The tyranny exerted by men over women indicates that they had taken the measure of the female's innate strength, and needed heavy fortifications to protect themselves against it.

To my mind, Islamic culture rests on the above premises, namely that woman is powerful and not weak, positive and not passive, capable of destroying and not easily destructible, and that if anyone needs protection it is the man rather than the woman.

However, this is only one aspect of the situation, for truth is many-sided. On the other side lies the fact that this innate resilience and strength of the woman bred fear in the heart of primitive man. And it was this fear, or even terror, that led him to oppress and subjugate her with all means at his disposal, be they economic, social, legal or moral. All these means had to be mobilized and synchronized to place at his disposal an overbearing and formidable armoury, used exclusively to conquer the indomitable vitality and strength that lay within women, ready to burst out at any moment. The building up of this armoury was a logical consequence of a specific situation. For the potential force that lies within a being itself decides the counter-force required to hold him or her down and to suppress their capacity for resistance. It is not difficult to understand, therefore, why the severest and most violent of laws were those that governed the sexual life of women, and decided what was permissible and what was impermissible for her. Burning alive and assassination were sometimes a merciful penalty for disobedience to these laws. There are men of science and anthropologists who believe that primitive woman was too powerful to be subdued by the laws laid down by men, and that she put up a violent and long drawn our resistance against the establishment of the patriarchal system during its early stages, and in defence of the wide freedoms and possibilities of natural expression she had enjoyed until then. Mary Jane Scherfey believes that one of the factors that delayed the onward march of male patriarchal civilization for more than 6,000 years, was the powerful sexual nature of primitive woman.[13]

It is also not difficult to understand why, even today, there are men who will kill a woman if she oversteps the limits of the prescribed sexual laws or moral codes imposed upon her. We often hear about the father, brother or uncle in Upper Egypt who killed the daughter because, on the night of her marriage, defloration did not yield the expected patches of red blood on a white cloth, or about a husband shooting his wife because he saw her with another man.

References

1. For a description of the matriarchal system see the writings of Bachofen, Frederich Engels, Morgan, E. Sidney Harfland, W.H.R. Rivers and Robert Briffault.

2. See *El Mar'a El Arabia fi Misr El Kadeema (Women in Ancient Egyptian History)*, by William Nazir, (Dar El Kalam Publications, 1965), p.34.

3. *Tarikh El Arab Kabl El Islam (History of the Arabs before Islam)*, Vol.5, Gawad Ali, (Religious Publications of the Iraqi Scientific Council, 1955), p.258 ff.

4. See Frazer, Shapiro, Spencer and Gillen, Thomas, Diamond, Letourneau, *Property — Its Origin and Development* (London, 1892) for an account of the lives of 'Bushmen' in Southern Africa and Aborigines in Australia.

5. See the writings of Letourneau, Crossland, Robert Loy, *Introduction to Anthropological Civilizations*, (New York, 1947).

6. See Louis Morgan, Frazer, Gross and others.

7. See Sarwat El Assiyuti, *The Family System in relation to Economy and Religion*, (Arab Renaissance Publications, Cairo, 1966), p.110.

8. Letourneau, *Property — Its Origin and Development*, pp.49, 366-7. Also Sarwat El Assiyuti, *op. cit.*, p.112.

9. Frederich Engels, *Origin of the Family, Private Property and the State*.

10. Crossi; and Ali Badawi, *Abhas fi tarikh El Shara'i (Studies in the History of Religious Laws)*, (Legal and Economic Review, 1931), pp.731, 746. Also Sarwat El Assiyuti, *op. cit.*, p.115.

11. *Enarationes in imose wa*, pp.43, 344, 25-35.

12. T.E. James, *Prostitution and the Law*, (W. Heinemann), Ellis, Prost, and Shurtz.

13. Mary Jane Sherfey, *The Nature and Evolution of Female Sexuality*, (Vintage Books, 1973), pp.137-140.

12. Man the God, Woman the Sinful

Akhnatoun the Egyptian King, social reformer and philosopher, was the first to formulate a monotheistic religion worshipping one god — Raa, or Harakhni, who scintillates and shines and burns at the horizon in the form of a great light (*Shu*) and is enveloped within the sun.[1] The thought of Akhnatoun had a great influence on Moses, the prophet of Israel, and this can be followed in the close similarity which exists between verses of the Old Testament and the writings of Akhnatoun. Christianity inherited from the legacy of Judaism, and Islam in its turn built up its system of religious thought, values and precepts on the two monotheistic religions which had preceded it.

One of the famous myths shared by all three religions is that of Adam and Eve. This story, which comes as a part of the Genesis of the Earth, occupies in all its beautiful and significant symbolism a prominent part in both the Old Testament and the Koran.

The first man on Earth, Adam, went as far as denying Eve her ability to bear children and bestowed this power on himself since, as the story goes, 'Eve was born of Adam's rib'. This is symbolic and reflects the predominant position that man had annexed for himself in these early stages of history characterized by increasing landownership pursued with lust and greed, slave markets where men and women were sold like cattle, an accentuation of the division of society into classes, accompanied by a ferocious exploitation of unpaid labour and a patriarchal system in its most extreme forms.

The original story of Adam and Eve, as told in the Old Testament and Koran, shows clearly the injustice suffered by woman, and the attempt to mask her situation by religious sanctification aimed at smothering all doubt, all discussion and all resistance. For that which God has ordained no man or woman may question.

My first and therefore vivid recollection of this feeling of injustice goes back to the day when I heard my school teacher reading out to us the story of Adam and Eve. At the time I was still a child attending primary school. I was afraid to express what I felt and kept it to myself.

But, whenever I returned to this story, my child's mind somehow could neither believe nor accept it. For God is assumed to be just and justice requires that there should be no discrimination between Adam and Eve. God is also endowed with an infallible logic, so how can we explain the glaring contradictions that run like red threads through the texture of this religious canvas? God glorifies the mind of man in his sacred books and makes of him the symbol of thought and intelligence, whereas woman personifies the body, a body without a head, a body whose head is the man. Yet in the story Eve is more intelligent than Adam, able to understand what Adam fails to grasp, and to realize that the forbidden tree bears the most delicious and exhilarating of all fruits — knowledge, and with knowledge the capacity to differentiate between good and evil. She was quick and sensitive enough to perceive that God's warnings not to approach the forbidden fruit carried a hidden purpose behind them, an attempt to conceal some truth and the fear that if once their hands had stretched out to the branches, and once their teeth had bitten into the juicy fragrant flesh, their minds would be able to discern between good and evil. From that moment they would rise to the level of their Creator. Man who was created in the image of the God would himself become God.

In my child's mind everything seemed to indicate that Eve was brilliant, whereas Adam was like a sheep following in her wake.

At a later stage when I had started my higher education at the Helwan Secondary School, I was sitting quietly at the back of the class when the Arabic language teacher asked to analyse the grammar of 'Mostapha Praises Allah'. I said that 'Mostapha' was a noun, masculine gender, acting as subject and 'praises' was the present tense of the verb to praise, in the third person singular. 'Allah' was a noun acting as object. The teacher hardly gave me time to complete the last part before he said in a single breath: 'May Allah have mercy on us. You must say "Allah who sits on the throne of all majesty, masculine noun, acting as object." ' I repeated after him: 'Allah who sits on the throne of all majesty, masculine noun, acting as object.' At the adjective, masculine, I hesitated for a moment and then went on. In a flash an idea had occurred to me, 'Why was Allah masculine and not feminine?' and I burst out with my question with all the eagerness that comes from an original thought. The teacher shot to his feet, trembling with wrath and disapproval and shouted out in a loud voice: 'May Allah have mercy on us. How can Allah be feminine, thou girl who hast no shame? How dare you place Allah with the female sex. Allah is masculine! Masculine! And all the sacred verses of the Koran use He and not She when speaking of Allah.'

That day I was given a zero in grammar, accompanied by a warning, or rather a threat, that questions like the one I had asked were sufficient to fail me in the final examination. Nevertheless he was prepared to forgive me for my impious questions if I never reverted to them again.

But I could not stop myself from thinking. When I grew older, it occurred to me that the only difference was that men have a protruding sexual organ. Could that mean that Allah was also like men in this sense. So I asked my father whether Allah possessed a male sexual organ. And because he was broadminded and had accustomed us at an early age to think freely, to question and not to believe in anything that was not convincing, he did not tremble in wrath like my teacher but answered calmly: 'Allah is masculine but has no sexual organ, because He is only a spirit and has no body.'

But the next question was already on the tip of my tongue and our dialogue continued:

'How can a spirit be masculine? Are there masculine spirits and feminine spirits?'

He said: 'A spirit is a spirit, and is neither male nor female.'

'Why did you then say that Allah is masculine?'

'Allah is a spirit and is neither male nor female.'

'Why then do all the verses of the Koran use the male gender when speaking of Allah?'

'Because it is not appropriate to address Allah or speak of him in the female gender.'

'Then you mean that the female or feminine gender is unworthy and suffers from some fault, or failing, or stigma, whereas this is not the case with the male gender?'

'Yes, the superiority of males over females is the real reason behind the fact that prophets have always used the male gender when addressing Allah or speaking of Him. All prophets were themselves males and we have never heard of a woman prophet. The first man on earth, Adam, was placed above Eve since he was at the origin of the human race, was more powerful and gave life to her from one of his ribs. Whereas Eve incited him to eat of the forbidden fruit and to disobey the warnings of Allah.'

I was by now thoroughly bemused but intent on not giving up. 'What you say, father, is rather contradictory. How is it that Eve, who was born of a rib in Adam's body and was much weaker than him, should have suddenly acquired an unusual strength that permitted her to convince Adam, so that he listened to her and disobeyed the orders of Allah. There her role was positive and her personality more powerful than that of Adam who remained passive and followed her word.'

'Yes, but Eve was positive only where evil was concerned.'

* * * *

It is the right of ordinary human beings to ask for and expect prosperity, food, clothing and security, from the female God. On the other hand, philosophers, men of science, and artists seek for knowledge from these Gods, and above all for an understanding of their true nature. The difference between one human being and another lies in knowledge, and the difference between one God and another lies in knowledge also.

I remember having read this passage as a child in one of the old books in my father's library. They were probably the words of Plutarch inscribed in his book on the Egyptian Goddess, Isis. Despite the passing of many years, I still remember it and recall also that Homer considered the God, Zeus, as being superior to Osiris because he had greater knowledge. The woman god Isis was, however, the greatest of gods because she possessed more understanding and knowledge than all other gods. Her name, Isis, itself signifies wisdom and knowledge. The structure in which her status is lodged itself indicates the process of discovering understanding and is called *Izion* which means that he who enters the *Zona* or house of the goddess will attain the truth.[2]

All those who have written about Isis maintain that her true worshippers are not the priest clothed in sacred robes and wearing a flowing beard, but those persons who seek truth and knowledge without respite.

If we read the story of Isis and Osiris, we find that it was Isis who was the source of all action, work and creation. In fact, she it was who re-created and re-built what men such as Touphoun, had destroyed. Touphoun symbolized everything that was superfluous, irrational and chaotic. All that was useful and constructive found its source in Isis's activities and merely took the shape of Osiris. Osiris was no more than the concretized form of Isis's actions.

By virtue of her intelligence and knowledge, Isis was able to overcome the malign force of Touphoun who cut Osiris's body into small pieces and scattered them afar. His sexual organ was devoured by the fish in the waters of the Nile, but Isis was able to reassemble his body and create him anew. She provided him with a renewed sexual organ to replace the one he had lost.

The mythological story of Isis shows clearly that woman in ancient society was the source of creation and action. Man, however, was the object of action, the result of woman's initiative and versatile creativity. That is why the name, Isis, means in fact wisdom, knowledge and rapid action. Osiris, on the other hand, only means the pure (virtuous) or sacred.

Isis created Osiris who was in fact merely the result of one of her actions. She also gave birth to Horus, her son, and imparted life to the greatest of all gods, who is said to have given birth to Isis or Athena through his head.

Iodexus explains that the ancient Egyptians portrayed Zeus as being incapable of movement because his lower limbs were stuck together. He thus remained completely isolated, far away from everything because of his infirmity which paralysed him completely and was a source of shame. It was Isis who cut through a separation between his limbs and endowed him with the capacity to move and walk.[3]

The meaning to be derived from this myth is clear, since it was Isis who gave life, knowledge and the capacity for movement to Zeus, Osiris and Horus. Yet the men who later on explained the meaning of this story did not realize its significance, or perhaps pretended not to understand it, so that they could modify and distort it to suit their own ends, to make out of the male god the Source and the Creator, and out of the woman one of his creations. For did not Zeus give birth to Isis from his head, and did not Adam give birth to Eve from his rib?

Thus it is that the myth of Adam and Eve does not differ in essence from that of Isis and Osiris, except for the enhanced sanctity bestowed upon it by the sacred heavenly books which placed it for many outside the scope of rational discussion.

Eve was also deprived of her capacities for knowledge, movement and creation and thus suffered the same fate as Isis. Yet, if we read the original story as described in the Old Testament, it is easy for us to see clearly that Eve was gifted with knowledge, intelligence and superior mental capacities, whereas Adam was only one of her instruments, utilized by her to increase her knowledge and give shape to her creativity.

Yet, despite the prominent role played by ancient woman and ancient female gods in so far as knowledge, creativity and thought were concerned, these mythological stories were interpreted differently. Truth was made to stand on its head so that man could become the god, the creator, the being that gave birth to woman.

Man usurped the throne of strength to become the source and the origin of all things, and woman was relegated to the position of a weak, passive dependant when in fact, at the early stages of history, she had occupied the predominant position. Adam followed Eve, and Isis was stronger and more powerful than the most tyrannical of all men, Touphoun – Touphoun, the evil and cunning god, was able to overcome his gentle and kind brother, Osiris. It was Isis who came to the rescue of Osiris and triumphed over Touphoun, fighting him with the very same weapons he had used, for she bought the devil with her riches.

Woman's knowledge and capacities went deeper and further back in time than those of men. Woman was stronger in mind and in intelligence than Satan, and was always able to overcome the devils and gods with her wisdom and knowledge. Eve triumphed over the Creator when she was able to make Adam obey her, rather than his God.

In those days, man seemed always to follow after woman, attracted by her intelligence and wisdom. His fate would vary, over time, from a share of knowledge, wisdom and creative action to the opposite extreme of annihilation as happened to Touphoun and other devils.

However, man was almost never objective when it came to interpreting these mythological stories which clearly reflect the high status which woman enjoyed in the pre-historical and pre-monotheistic stages of human life.

Some analysts insist that man, at certain periods related to these stages, was able to overcome woman by the force of arms and so usurp her godly vocation, her creativity and her capacity to reason, and thus attribute all things to himself. In the story of Isis, for example, it is said that her son, Horus, cut off her head or knocked off the kingly or godly crown which she wore because she released Touphoun from his captivity and pardoned him when he was brought to her in chains.

The Old Testament also decapitated woman and made of her a body without a head. The husband therefore became the head of woman. This is the source of a very popular conception which considers that women have no brains, or are endowed with a lesser intelligence than men, despite the fact that, initially, women were the real possessors of knowledge and thought, and men were relegated to the situation of a follower.

History however has seen a fundamental change and, with it, the ancient myths have been interpreted so as to favour the patriarchal and class interests born with the birth of slave societies.

I remember reading somewhere in the ancient stories of Egypt and Greece that the crocodile was the image of god, being the only animal that did not emit any sound.[4] The contention was that the 'reason of god' or the 'work of god' did not need sound to transmit itself. These stories also maintained that Zeus was deaf since he was deprived of ears. It was not fitting that the god that ruled over all things should listen to anyone. In addition, as mentioned before, he was born with an infirmity which deprived him of movement, his two lower limbs being stuck together. Thus it was that he crawled like the crocodile.

It was the woman, Isis, who was destined to bestow on him the ability to walk.

References

1. *Pharaonic Egypt,* Jean Yoyot, Arabic translation by Saad Zahran in the series, 'A Thousand Books', (Ministry of Higher Education, Cairo, 1966) p.1,209.
2. *Zona* is the temple of the idols decorated appropriately. *Al Ifsah fi fikh el Logha,* p.697.
3. *Isis and Osiris,* translated from the Greek by Hassan Sobhy El Bakri, in 'A Thousand Books' series, 235, (Dar El Kalam, Cairo), p.93.
4. Plutarch, *Isis and Osiris,* translated from Ancient Greek, in *ibid.,* p.108.

13. Woman at the Time of the Pharaohs

The earliest and perhaps greatest of all ancient civilizations has been a fertile field for historical research. Scholars and Egyptologists repeatedly registered the fact that, in the preliminary stages of ancient Egyptian society, women were frequently drawn and engraved on the walls, and their size corresponded to that of men, indicating equality in status and prestige. But, later on, the female size started to decrease which meant that women were losing position in relation to men. This change was found to correspond with the appearance of private property extending from the VIIth to the Xth Dynasty (2420-2140 B.C.). Their status remained low throughout the period of the Middle Kingdom from the XIth to the XIIIth Dynasty, and during the period of the Hexus, as a result of the predominance of oppression, injustice and harsh exploitation of slaves accompanied by early feudalistic systems in some areas. It was only with the later Kingdom (1580 B.C.), after the vast uprisings and rebellions which swept the Egyptian people, including women and slaves, into a struggle against the foreign invaders and the landowners, that woman largely regained the position and prestige she had previously lost. Famous queens took over and reigned supreme during the XVIIIth Dynasty. For example Nephertiti, and Hatchipsoot who is well known for her powerful personality and her reign which lasted 22 years (1504-1483 B.C.). Hatchipsoot's statue was sculptured in the form of a sphinx, with a human head and a lion's body as a symbol of strength of mind and physique. Her reign was characterized by prosperity and progress. She proved her qualities as a ruler and a queen, but after she died Tohotmus III replaced her on the throne and gave orders that her statues be destroyed and her portraits and engravings be erased from the walls.

However, on the whole, ancient Egyptian women did not receive prominence except during the Ancient Kingdom, that is before private property and landownership became predominant. In that early period, Pharaonic woman laboured in textile and carpet manufacture, traded in the markets and shared in hunting side by side with her husband. Drawings of the wife on the family tomb were equal in size to those of the husband and showed the esteem and respect accorded to women, as well as their equality, in duties and rights. This practice continued through the IIIrd and IVth Dynasties (around 2780 B.C.) In the Bangam statue engraved on the walls of the Karnak temple, the wife precedes her husband. A memorial stone erected in honour of a woman called Bisisht, who lived during one of the periods of the Ancient Kingdom, indicates that she presided over a group that brought together medical doctors. An Egyptian husband was tried by a judge and punished with a hundred lashes of the whip for having insulted his wife, and was warned that he would be deprived of his share of the money earned jointly by the couple if he reverted to insulting her again.[2]

Ancient Egyptian women were also often highly cultured. A record shows that a man, called Khanoum Reddi, was working as librarian in the service of a great lady known as Nephro Kabith. He mentions that the lady appointed him in the town of Dandara as supervisor of the stores of books belonging to her mother who loved the sciences and arts.[3]

Women in ancient Egypt practised sports, swimming and acrobatics in the same way as men did. They drank wine at gatherings in the company of men and clinked their cups with them. Sometimes they even drank very heavily. A papyrus speaks of one woman who exclaims: 'Give me eighteen cups of wine. I shall drink until the grape lifts me up in the air. Inside I feel as dry as straw.'[4]

There are archaeologists like Armand, Muret and Prested who believe that during this period a child was named after its mother. Women entered into all fields of activity and occupied a wide variety of posts including those of governor of a province, ruler or minister, queen and goddess. The veil was unknown and no segregation between the sexes existed. Husband and wife were equal in all respects until the IIIrd and IVth dynasties of the ancient Kingdom. When big landownership developed parallel to slave society, and imposed its control over the state during the Vth dynasty, men enforced the patriarchal family system in order to ensure that inheritance of property was reserved for their sons.[5] With the rise of the patriarchal system, another parallel system developed, namely polygamy and then concubinage, ending in the birth of the first illegitimate children and the loss of status which afflicted women, bringing them down to the bottom of society.

The first revolutionary uprising by slaves against large landowners and the administration which ruled in their name was recorded in the VIIth Dynasty (2420 B.C.). This historic event is known as the Memph Revolution and was directed against the landowners and reigning monarchs. The Egyptian people, men and women, burnt down the Royal Palace. They expressed their contempt for property and insisted that equal opportunities be provided for all without exception. However, some historians have depicted this revolt as a mere change of property from the hands of some, to the hands of others and have written saying: 'Those that were unable to order a pair of sandals for themselves now took possession of the treasures.'[6]

But big landownership reasserted its position once more, and in the year 2160 B.C. the Egyptian people rose in revolt for the second time against the Pharaohs and their rule. The era of the Xth Dynasty was thus ushered in. Concubinage was abolished and illegitimate children disappeared from the scene since children were named after their mothers. But the big landowners returned to the attack and the second period of their uncontested rule

(1094 B.C.) was announced on the day when Harhour, the High Priest, took control of all power. Concubinage became an integral part of daily life and men enforced their sole right to divorce, and their monopoly of the priesthood as a vocation.

A new onslaught on the system of big landownership was launched by the people in the year 663 B.C. Subsequently the reign of King Bokhoris, who belonged to the XXIVth Dynasty, witnessed fundamental changes. Sons were freed from the father's authority, women regained their rights and the priests no longer exercised any control over marriages as they had done in the past, since marriage lost its religious sanctity. Thus, under the patriarchal system, man becomes invested with religious priestly authority and marriage is submitted to statutes and laws laid down by religion. The patriarchal system is also necessarily accompanied by concubinage and polygamy, and by a rigid and inhuman regulation of women's lives in all aspects, whether religious, social or sexual.

Parallel with the expansion of primitive landownership, an ever increasing number of slaves, interspersed with forms of hired labour in certain crafts, became a necessity if the land was to be cultivated. This new economic era, buttressed by appropriate social and religious values, therefore required a growing progeny to toil on the land and to replace the substantial proportion of deaths linked to the prevalence of high mortality rates. One of the religious values that evolved in support of these needs was the idea that the bigger the number of family members praying to and for the ancestors, the easier it would be for them to make their voices heard. Polygamy was therefore born not only of male sexual appetite linked with male dominance, but also with this striving for extensive progeny. Wives were also a source of wealth since they shouldered many heavy tasks in both field and home, without expecting any payment in return apart from their keep. Their lot was that of unpaid labourers, no better off than slaves, and, to a woman, having more wives in the household was in many ways a boon. Tasks could be shared, heavy loads lifted together and the burdens of life carried on several pairs of shoulders rather than one. Sometimes they might even be a source of human comfort in the face of grief, exploitation and injustice.

Polygamy for the man meant the satisfaction of sexual appetite. To reinforce his right to several wives and to sanctify his economic greed and sexual lust, the support of religion was necessary. On the other hand, since monogamy for women was required to identify and reinforce patrilineal descent and ensure the inheritance of property by the sons of the father, another set of values sanctifying man's ownership of women, both economically and sexually, had to be prescribed and legitimized. Here again religion came to the rescue.

But, in her turn, woman did not feel that a single man could quench the thirst of her sexual desire. She too needed more than one husband, and in a situation where her only man was shared with other women, she was reduced to the vain attempt of finding satisfaction in being married to a fraction of a man. The sexual desire of strong primitive woman was, therefore, out of all proportion to her actual share of sexual life.

As was inevitable, woman resisted the limits within which man tried to confine her natural needs. Man, in his turn, fought against this resistance with all his might in an attempt to enforce his discipline and control by a set of iron laws, precepts and customs. Death for women was the price for adultery, imprisonment was a lighter fate, and a cruel jealousy perhaps the lightest of all, a jealousy which later became the emotion depicted by modern man as the highest expression of love, a noble feeling described with warmth by men of letters and poets in both East and West. Shakespeare's Othello, and Othello's jealousy which led to the murder of his beloved Desdemona, are a vivid portrayal of the evil discharge pent up in man ever since private property and possession of women began to spin the web that imprisons his soul and alienates him from his own humanity.

An array of laws and regulations descended from heaven and rose up from the solid earth to enforce chastity, virginity, marital fidelity and obedience on women alone, lest a pale cold beam of doubt cross the mind of man that some outsider might have slipped into his children's pen under cover of darkness and become a candidate for his inheritance.

Yet, despite the heavy guns pointed at women, despite the tabernacles, wise whisperings, values and customs and a merciless legal and moral code, doubt in the fidelity of woman has always lain like a shadow over the mind and heart of man. This doubt, which has accompanied man ceaselessly from the early primitive days to the most modern of contemporary societies, is so strong, so deep-rooted, that it cannot be misplaced, cannot be a mere illusion. Behind it lies objective reality, and a logical and inexorable rationale, a reality and a rationale which nevertheless remain contradictory, absurd and unreal because they are based on and derived from the age-long double standard which has so governed the lives of men and women: a set of free standards for the male and an authoritarian, enslaving code of chastity and sexual rectitude for the female.

This double moral standard has its roots deep in the past, embedded in the fundamental upheaval in social relations when man first learnt that he could own and that, if he owned, he could exploit both slave and woman. From that moment the fate of woman was decided for thousands of years. She was destined to lose her equality with man in society, at home and even in the sacred realms of religion.

This degradation in the status of women reached its lowest point in ancient Rome where women were entirely in the grasp (*manus*) and at the mercy of men.[7] The Dark Ages had begun for her with the first civilizations, with the dawn of a new era which ushered in the promises and the reality of human progress. For history and the division of society into classes had ordained that, in order that some might have the leisure to administer and to think, to imagine and to invent, the vast majority, composed of slaves and labourers and women, had to toil and suffer.

Thus it was that woman was dethroned from her position as head of tribes and clans, deprived of her right to name the children born of her own womb, and transformed into an unpaid slave. She was imprisoned behind walls like an animal in a cage, and sold or bought openly in a slave auction or under the guise of marriage to a man. Divested of her freedom to choose or make decisions, it was the father or one of the male elders who decided on the man she would marry, and on the price that they could obtain in the bargain. The Roman father of the *familia* thus disposed of the womenfolk for they were his possessions and one of the sources of his wealth.[8]

In Roman law, the domination of man over woman was consecrated in its most extreme forms. The father not only enjoyed the prerogative of selling his daughter into marriage, but also had the pleasure of putting an end to her life if in his view the necessity arose. After marriage these patriarchal rights were transferred to the husband who then legally owned the mother of his future children.[9]

During a trip to India in 1974, I visited a region in the tea plantation areas near the town of Conoor in the southern state of Tamil Nadu. The region is inhabited by a number of tribes whose life is very different from that of the usual urban or even rural inhabitants. The men have rather original functions in life. They do no work but merely supervise the premises and activities of the temple, and dance at religious festivals. Their faces are painted with special white and carmine powders, their hair grows long and flowing, and they wear ornaments and rings hanging from their ears, very similar to those with which an Egyptian peasant woman would adorn herself. The women, however, after working all day on the tea plantations or in the potato fields, return to their homes to cook, wash and feed their husbands and children. I was invited to attend a religious festival organized by one of these tribes, called the Kothas, in the village of Drichijadi. I witnessed the men with long hair, painted faces and elaborate earrings dancing around the temple, while the women and young girls sat at a distance in the area prescribed to them and looked on.

I asked the head of the tribe why this was so, and he explained that the ground encircling the temple was sacred and therefore women and girls were not allowed to tread on it with their feet. Women, young girls and even female children were also not allowed in the temple.

Within the boundaries of this village there were two temples. The first, called the Shiva temple, housed a small statue of the god Shiva hewn in black stone. The second had been built for the goddess Parvathi, wife of Shiva, also widely worshipped in India. I was astounded to learn that the men had not only forbidden the women from entering Shiva's temple, but also prevented them from visiting the goddess Parvathi, despite the fact that the statue before which the villagers prayed was that of a woman. In answer to my questions, the head of the tribe argued that the realm of religion is reserved for males, whereas the earth is woman's domain. Elaborating on this idea, he went on to say that women possess everything in life. They work in the fields and at home, and feed all the members of the family. Even the children are theirs, since it is they who give life and birth to them. Men can never be sure of their fatherhood. They have nothing left in life except the gods and the temples. They must therefore exercise their exclusive right to these gods and temples, lest they fall under women's domination.

Children in these tribes are named after the mother since polyandry is common and the women marry more than one man. The father of the child is, therefore, unknown in many cases. In addition, despite the fact that the woman is the bread winner of the family since she alone is the source of all work and income whether in cash or kind, the tribe is governed by a system of traditions and customs enforced by the elders and prescribed, according to them, by the god Shiva. In this system man rules, makes the decisions, and distributes the earnings to the members of the tribe. In the name of Shiva and his precepts, men take possession of the women's income and preside over the life of the family. The women are thus relegated to the position of mere labourers, or even slaves, under the control of the men. As a further development of this male authority, children were beginning to take their descent from the father's line, and monogamy was gradually being enforced on women to ensure that the father could identify his children.

These tribes may be considered as being in an intermediate stage between the matriarchal system which still prevails in small pockets of Southern India and the highly patriarchal societies of the North. It is one of the numerous patterns which intervene between the two opposing poles of the family structure. However, in this huge country, covering a wide spectrum of historical phases, very diverse situations may be found. For example, about 40 miles from Delhi, there are tribes in rural areas who practise a surreptitious form of polyandry. When one man is with the woman, his *chappals* (sandals) are left outside the door to alert the household that she has a visitor.

All the evidence shows that man was only enabled to assert his predominance through ownership of the means of production and control of both economic activity and religion. His ascendancy in religion was attained by a kind of self-nomination that permitted him to frame the laws of conduct and morals, to interpret them and to enforce them in the name of the gods whom he represented. Man always feared woman as the source of life, endowed with mysterious and awesome capacities, strong, patient, resilient, hard working in forest, field or home. When individual production could yield a surplus, exploitation became possible and some people were able to live on the labour of others.

Why was it that man gained the upper hand over women? There are diverse theories which try to explain this change. Perhaps a plausible explanation is the fact that women were more involved in child bearing and rearing than men, especially as a numerous progeny was required to balance the high incidence of death and the need for labour on the land.

I always remember my visit to the village of Drichijadi like a sudden opening into the past, vivid, captivating but painful. Here were the descendants of ancient woman, strong, enduring, her labouring hands thickened, coarse and with a firm grip. Around the houses of the village sprawled the men, basking in the sunshine, smoking, drinking, playing games with little stones held lightly in their smooth, delicate palms and fingers, while the women toiled away, naked feet planted in the earth, heads bent, the sun tracing the long hours of their labour across the sky from horizon to horizon.

References

1. See William Nazeer, *Women in Ancient Egyptian History*, (Dar El Kalam Publishing House, 1965). Also Adil Ahmed Sarkiss, *Dar El Kitab El Arabi* (1967) and Jean Yoyot, *Pharaonic Egypt*, translated into Arabic by Saad Zahran (1966).
2. William Nazeer, *op. cit.*, p.28.
3. *Ibid.*, p.16.
4. *Ibid.*, p. 68.
5. Adil Ahmed Sarkiss, *op. cit.*, and Jean Yoyot, *op. cit.*
6. *Ibid.*, p.66.
7. Fouchelle de Collange, *The Ancient City*, (Hachette Publications, Paris, 1948), p.98.
8. Sarwat El Assiyuti, *The Family System as related to the Economy and Religion*, p.119.
9. V. Girard, *Roman Law*, (French edn.), p.180 ff. and V. Glatz, *The Solidarity of the Family in Greece*, (French edn.), p.31 ff.

14. Liberty to the Slave, But Not for the Woman

The monotheistic religions, in enunciating the principles relating to the role and position of women in life, as we have seen, drew inspiration and guidance from the values of the patriarchal and class societies prevalent at the time. These class societies were built on the division mainly into landowners and slaves, whether men or women.

The messages that were carried to their peoples by the Prophets Moses, Jesus and Mahomet in their essence were a call to revolt against the injustices of the slave system. True, there were differences in the content and the form of their revolutionary teachings due to the fact that each was born at a different time and in a different society with its own social and economic characteristics. But they all had in common this rebellion against the evils and injustices of slavery. It varied in extent and depth, yet was always there.

As a result, since the position of women was closely related to the social and economic relationships predominant at the time, it was natural, that any attempt to resist the injustices suffered by people, and to change the structure that was the basis of society, would overflow and encompass the position of women to a greater or lesser degree. This was particularly true in the earlier stages of the transformations resulting from Judaism, Christianity and Islam. Nevertheless the position of women remained inferior to that of men, in all three religions, but especially in Judaism.

A Hebrew household was embodied in the patriarchal family, under the uncontested and undivided authority of the father who was very much like the Roman head of the *familia*. Each household among the 'Sons of Israel' was composed of a number of wives and concubines, their children and the wives of the male sons, the grandchildren, and the slaves.[1] The head of this large household was the father who was known as the *roshe*.[2] He enjoyed absolute juridical and legal authority,[3] chose his heir according to his sole wishes[4] and disposed of his daughters in complete freedom since it was his right to sell any of them to whoever would pay the price he wanted.[5] The life of a child depended on his will since he could put an end to it whenever he so desired,[6] or offer the child as a sacrifice to God.[7] The biblical story of Isaac, the son who yielded to Abraham his father when the latter decided to sacrifice him to Jehovah, is well known. This right over life and death extended to all those who lived in the household and over whom the father wielded his absolute authority. For example he could kill the widow of his son by burning her if she committed adultery after having lost her husband.

The woman in a Jewish household was part of the *familia* as in Rome, that is an integral part of the father's inheritance composed of money, property and slaves. The household comprised the women, the male slaves, the female slaves, the bulls, the donkeys and other things.[8] The husband was called the lord or master of the women[9] and they addressed him as 'my lord'.[10] The birth of a son was an occasion for rejoicing whereas the birth of a daughter brought sadness and lamentation.[11]

Yet despite the tight fetters to which a woman had to submit, the man was free to have as many wives and concubines as he desired sexually and could even have intercourse with his daughters. The two daughters of Lot took turns in sleeping with their father until they both became pregnant and bore sons. Moab and Bennami Jacob 'took unto himself' two sisters.[12] A man could divorce his woman at any time and the Old Testament recounts how Abraham expelled his slave Hagir the Egyptian and her son from his household and left them in the desert with nothing but some bread and a goatskin of water. They wandered over the burning sands until they were lost; they were never heard of again.[13]

Polygamy was widely practised by the 'Sons of Israel', especially among the richer families and kings. David is known to have married many women and in addition to have kept a retinue of slaves and concubines.[14] Rehoboam married 18 women and owned 60 concubines and through them had 28 sons and 60 daughters.[15] And Abigah waxed mighty and married 14 wives and begat 22 sons and 16 daughters.[16] But Solomon excelled and surpassed all the other kings for he married 700 women, and kept 300 concubines.[17] He began his kingly life with the murder of his elder brother because the latter tried to compete with him in the inheritance of their father's harem.[18]

In opposition to the almost unlimited sexual freedom accorded to men, women were severely restricted. Virginity was an essential condition before a man would marry a woman, and if she was unable to prove her virginity he would immediately divorce her. However, when corruption and immorality became rife at the end of the 7th Century B.C., the man's right to divorce was no longer allowed in certain cases. Firstly, if the husband accused his wife unjustly of not being a virgin before marriage, the father and mother could arrange to display the marks of her virginity on a cloth before the elders of the city, upon which these elders would undertake to punish the husband and impose upon him a fine of 100 pieces of silver, to be paid to the father of the girl in recompense for having spoilt the reputation of a 'virgin of Israel'. The man was then obliged to accept her as his wife and forbidden to divorce her for the rest of his days.[19] Secondly, if the girl was a virgin and the man had indulged in premarital sexual relations with her, he would have to agree to pay the father 50 pieces of silver, to marry the girl and not to divorce her for the 'rest of his days'.[20] If a woman divorced by her husband married a second man, who in his turn divorced her, or died, leaving her a widow, her first husband was not allowed to remarry her since 'she has been defiled'.[21]

The people of Israel in those days groaned under the burdens and oppression of a slave society, ruled by landowners who monopolized the land, the cattle and the labour of the men and women. The family was highly autocratic and patriarchal, ruled by the iron hand of the father. In addition, a third category of oppressors had arisen: the priests who had annexed to themselves wide social powers which they used to enhance their authority and material position. One of the practices that was common was that of the 'bitter water'. A woman suspected of infidelity by her husband was dragged to the priest and submitted to gruesome torture which was supposed to prove her culpability or innocence. She was stripped of her clothes up to the belly, divested of all ornaments, and the tresses of her hair were let loose. She was then covered in a heavy black cloth tied by a rope to her breasts, and made to undergo the test of the 'bitter water'.[22] This consisted of a mixture prepared by the priest and composed of sacred water, the sweepings of the temple and the ink dissolved from a piece of cloth on which, he invoked, in writing, everlasting damnation upon her were she proved to be guilty. She was made to drink this loathsome and nauseating potion from an earthenware pot and if any signs or symptoms of illness appeared (swelling of the belly and rotting of the thigh) she was considered guilty and eligible to any of the forms of punishment used against adulterers.

The attitude of society towards adultery has varied according to the economic and social conditions prevalent at the different stages of human development. Primitive tribes and matriarchal societies used to accord sexual freedom to both men and women. However, with the development of private property which reinforced the 'passion of acquisitiveness and ownership' and the development of the patriarchal system, the husband began to demand complete fidelity of his wife, which meant that no other man was to come anywhere near her. Men also expected chastity and virginity in the girls they were to marry. The patriarchal societies of the early days established a system of procedures for dealing with adulterous women which were inspired by, and drawn from, their autocratic oppressive social structures and the cruel tyranny of male dominance. The men who ruled the destinies of the people of Israel decided that a woman who committed adultery should be done to death either by burning her alive as Jehovah tried to do with his son's wife, Thamar, or by hurling stones at her until the last breath of life had fled from her crushed and bleeding body.[23] This was the rule ordained in the Book of Deuteronomy.[24] The man, however, could fornicate with as many wives, concubines and slave girls as he wished, and commit a thousand adulteries with impunity. Roman law differed little from Judaic customs since it also gave the man the right of life and death over his woman if she committed adultery.

Islamic society, in its turn, was characterized by a patriarchal system built on private property and a class structure composed of a minority who owned the herds of sheep, camels and horses and who as traders travelled far and wide over the commercial routes of the Arab peninsula, and a majority who were slaves interspersed with a few independent plebians. Authority in Islam belonged to the man as head of the family, to the supreme ruler, or the Khalifa (political leader), or Imam (religious leader), or the Wali (governor of a province), or a witness. All these positions could only be occupied by men. Islam inherited from Judaism the penalty meted out to adulterous women, namely that of being stoned to death. In fact women were known to have been subjected to this savage and merciless death during the life of the Prophet Mahomet and later on in the early stages of Islamic expansion. The Koran stipulates that both partners in adultery, the man and the woman, should be stoned to death. However, the fact that a man could have any number of wives, concubines and women slaves at his beck and call meant that the richer or more powerful men did not need to have recourse to illegal adultery. The owner of numerous herds or of the camel caravans, the men with influence and power over others, could change their wives at will and marry new women whenever they set their eyes on a beautiful face, or a young girl, or a shapely slave waiting to be sold in the market. Why should a man commit adultery if it is his right to divorce his wife at any moment and marry another woman, and to keep up to a total of four wives at one time and any number of concubines or girl slaves his right hand could afford? The religious laws or *sharia,* therefore, were meant to be applied only to women when they dared to challenge the patriarchal system which only allowed a woman one husband, a family and a roof, or alternatively left her a virgin and spinster to the end of her days should no man decide to purchase or marry her. The religious laws were also meant to punish poorer men (who owned only a few sheep or were small artisans and traders), and hired labourers and slaves, all of whom often found it difficult to marry, or whose limited resources imposed a fidelity that lacked conviction and prevented them from changing wives, or marrying up to four, or owning the slaves and concubines whom they would watch, with envy in their eyes, being bought and sold in the market place.

Christianity, however, differs from Judaism and Islam in that it was more severe in restricting the sexual freedom not only of women, but also of men. Jesus Christ started by applying the rules to himself, and is said to have practised complete abstinence throughout his short but stormy, eventful and fascinating life. He therefore never married, like his mother the Virgin Mary who never knew what it was to lie in a man's embrace as the story goes in the New Testament. Jesus Christ went as far as to say: 'Ye have heard that it was said by them of old times, thou shalt not commit adultery. But I say unto you that whosoever looketh on a woman to lust after her hath committed adultery with her already in his heart.'![25]

Until the advent of Christianity, Jewish men used to apply the precepts of Judaism as embodied in the Old Testament and which permitted a husband to divorce his wife without having to give reasons for such a step. The New Testament, as the Book of Matthew tells us, disavows this practice as being contrary to the wishes of God: 'The Pharisees also came unto him, tempting him, and saying unto him: Is it lawful for a man to put away his wife for every cause? And he answered and said unto them: Have ye not read that he which made them at the beginning made them male and female? And said, for this cause a man shall leave father and mother and shall cleave to his wife, and they twain shall be one flesh? Wherefore they are not twain but one flesh. What therefore God hath joined together let no man put asunder.'[26]

Jesus Christ, however, opposed the stoning to death of a woman who committed adultery and prevented the Pharisees from enforcing this punishment in a saying that has become famous: 'Let him who is without fault throw the first stone at her.'

Christianity, like Judaism and Islam, was born in the womb of a patriarchal slave society where Rome had the upper hand and extended her empire to distant lands, including Palestine. Christ was, no doubt, a revolutionary leader who expressed the aspirations and hopes of the slaves and poorer sections of society. He opposed the wealthy elements of the Jewish people who were hand in glove with the Roman authorities. He stood up against the injustices and oppression of the Roman overlords and fought stubbornly for his progressive ideas which, at the time, meant a radical change in society. He attempted to build up resistance in his own way against the exploitation and corruption of all those who were in power, whether they were Romans or belonged to his own community. But rather than depending on a revolutionary struggle against the slave system, he remained a proponent of non-violence and a propagator of human purity, human pity, and a strict moral code. The dawn of Christianity, therefore, emphasized the spiritual and moral aspects of its teachings, and castigated those who lost themselves in the material and sensual pleasures of life, including sex. Male slaves and their womenfolk were the victims of the sexual freedom and licence practised by the Romans and the Pharisees of the Jewish community. Jesus Christ, by vigorously and uncompromisingly attacking adulterous practices, not only in women but also in men, was in fact giving voice to the interests of the slaves and poorer sections of society whose women were prey, waylaid at every corner by human wolves.

The spiritual values of Christianity led to the outlawing of polygamy and shed doubt on those who indulged in repeated marriages. However, at a later stage, the religious hierarchies that grew and fattened on the teachings of Christ allowed the system of concubinage to creep in once more. Despite the limitations placed by Christianity on man's sexual freedom, woman was maintained in her inferior underprivileged situation as compared with him. The patriarchal system still reigned supreme and grew even more ferocious with the gradual shift to a feudal system in the last years of survival of the Roman Empire. This change first took place at the outer reaches of the Empire where the authority of the Roman State was difficult to maintain, especially in the face of the continued incursions of barbarian tribes.

The Christian, or rather Catholic, Church drifted away more or less rapidly from the original teachings of Jesus Christ. The Catholic Church was itself the biggest landowner in Europe, and its estates and pasturages occupied one-fifth of all cultivated land. It was therefore natural for the cardinals, high priests and monks to link their interests very closely with those of the feudal landlords, and to ensure that their religious teachings served the feudal system and kept the serfs from revolting against their masters.

With the reinforcement of this feudal patriarchal system, the women inevitably continued to suffer grievously. The weight of oppression weighed heavily on their lives, and the accusations of being Satan's ally and a source of evil and catastrophe to all men followed them mercilessly everywhere. Men exercised complete control over women through the social customs and laws that were applied in the home and outside it, and found no difficulty in killing or burning a woman alive for the flimsiest of reasons. Torture was commonly used on women in Europe.[27]

In the 14th Century the Catholic Church proclaimed that, if a woman dared to treat an illness or disease for which she had no special training, she would immediately be branded as a sorceress, the penalty for which was death.[28] For the cure of body and soul is God's exclusive domain, and he alone has the right to delegate these powers to his representatives on earth, the male priests. Death is therefore a just punishment for the woman sorcerer.[29] During the period we are describing, the priests maintained that a few drops of sacred water were enough to cure any disease, and that they alone had the secret of this knowledge and the right to use it.

Woman was also the victim of the male philosophers and thinkers who moulded public opinion. We have already mentioned Tertullian, who insisted on the relationship between women and Satan. Men, like Thomas Aquinas, supported this outlook which originated at a much earlier stage with Socrates, who is known to have said that man was created for noble pursuits, for knowledge and the pleasures of the mind, whereas women were created for sex, reproduction and the preservation of the human species.

As mentioned earlier, Christianity was against polygamy at the outset. But with the establishment of the feudal system, accompanied as it was by wars and famines and a heavy death toll, the head of the family, apart from satisfying his sexual desires, wished to have numerous children on whom he could depend to supervise and run his estates and participate in labour. As a result, polygamy and concubinage crept back on the scene. Among others, Saint Augustine, the Christian philosopher, made a spirited defence of men, saying that such a practice did not aim at the satiation of sexual appetite but rather at ensuring sufficient reproduction and a multiplication of people on the earth in conformity with God's will and in obedience to what he had ordained. For did not God say to the Sons of Israel from whom the long awaited Messiah would arise 'Increase and multiply'?

Monogamy, therefore, remained in practice a moral code only for women, lest the patriarchal system be eroded and collapse. Glorification of virginity and the virgin led the Church to elevate the Virgin Mary to a higher place, and she came to be known as the Goddess of Heaven and Earth, a description that had hitherto been reserved for the ancient female goddess who had been worshipped before the era of Judaism. Above the head of the Virgin Mary were now placed the moon and stars of Isis, and in her lap lay the sacred child. This was nothing but a modified version of an old drawing of Isis and Horus. With this promotion of Mary to the level of a goddess went the cult of virginity upheld with cold rigidity until the present day.

Islam started its early career around 700 years after Christ, when Christianity was already a well established religion. The Prophet Mahomet was profoundly influenced by the two other great monotheistic religions. In the journeys he undertook for commercial purposes outside the Hedjaz, he often met people who recited verses of the Old and New Testaments to him. Mahomet at the beginning of his life was a poor shepherd boy, living in a society of masters and slaves which seethed with passion, lust and the quest for lucre, cruel to man and above all women, licentious, idolatrous, eroded by vice and obscurantism. The Prophet's early teachings were directed against the class system based on slavery, and defended the rights of the poor and of women. But the patriarchal system was strongly entrenched in most of the tribes, except for a very few who still exhibited one or other form of matriarchal relations, and the structure built around the unquestioned predominance of man therefore remained as firm and as unshaken as ever. The continual tribal wars, in which many men were killed, the need to build up the new Islamic order, the large numbers of women prisoners of war and slaves, all tended to make out of polygamy a practice responding to social needs. Islam, therefore, put its religious stamp on sexual freedom for men and their right to have several wives, as well as concubines and women slaves. In actual fact, once again it was the big slave owners, heads of tribes and rich men who were able to enjoy the benefits of such rights, since they alone had the means to buy or keep so many women.

Pre-Islamic society, or what was later called *El Gahelia* (The Age of Ignorance), was a tribal structure built upon slavery. Prisoners of war were considered the property of the victors, and each man would take into his household a number which corresponded to his power and means. Islam brought no changes in this area and permitted a man to share his home and bed with these women, and yet be under no obligation to marry them. Furthermore, this system of concubinage did not oblige him to recognise the children born of these relations. However, if the man did agree to this recognition, the child was immediately considered free, that is no longer a slave, and the woman, in her turn, was set free after the death of her master.

The owning of concubines was also allowed in Christianity after the first heat of Christ's teachings had died down, and in Christian Ethiopia to this day the presence of concubines in some households is a common occurrence. Egypt, however, abolished this extreme form of legalized prostitution at the end of the 10th Century (during the era of the High Priest, Abraham, who lost his life in 970 A.D. due to this decision).

The history and literature of the Arabs are literally teeming with stories about the lives of these women slaves and concubines who were exposed to different forms of economic, social and sexual oppression. They were used by their masters to carry out household chores, such as cleaning, washing, cooking, collecting firewood etc., but also in home duties of another kind, namely singing, dancing and catering to their masters' sexual needs. In some cases the master would transform them into prostitutes as a means of making capital out of their bodies.[30]

Ibn Habib has written that, among the customs rampant in the (pre-Islamic) *Gahelia* society, was for men to make profit out of the opening between the thighs of women slaves, some of whom displayed a white flag in the market to draw the attention of those who desired to fornicate.[31] And Ibn Abbas describes how: 'In the time of the *Gahelia* they used to force their women slaves into committing adultery and then pocket the price that was paid by the man. That is why a verse of the sacred Koran was sent: "Do not force your daughters into prostitution if they wish to keep their purity intact, because you pine after the ephemeral things of life. But for those who continue to do so, when what is done has been done, God remains forgiving and compassionate." '[32]

The father married his daughters, very often against their will, to the men who made the highest bid. When a woman's husband died, the uncle or brother of the deceased visited the woman and threw his cloak over her uttering the words 'I have first right over her', after which he was free either to keep her with him, or to sell her at a price on the marriage market, with or without her approval, or to prevent her from ever marrying again, or to strip her of whatever inheritance and money her late husband might have left.

In some of the Arab tribes, a woman could be ravished by force if the man was strong enough to overcome the resistance put up by the men of her tribe. Once he had taken her to his household, it was his right to make her live with him as his wife. The ravishing could take place either during a war, or by a surprise attack or conspiracy. The poet Hatem El Tai proudly describes this practice in a line which says: 'We do not marry their daughters with their consent, but take them at the point of our swords.'

Women very often fought desperately to avoid this fate even if death were the penalty. One of the well known phrases conned by these women was '*el mania wala el dania*' which means 'rather death than degradation'. Fatima Bint El Khorshib (Fatima, daughter of Khorshib), when ravished by Gamal Ibn Badr, threw herself headfirst from the palanquin in which she was being transported and died on the spot, of a broken neck.[33]

History tells of the sufferings and torture, often ending in death, which were the inexorable fate of women slaves bold enough to rebel against their masters or even just to disobey them, or to sing songs directed against those who held power or were heads of their tribes. Some of these women slaves even mustered enough courage to attack the Moslems and insult Mahomet, the Prophet of Allah. Sarah was a famous slave singer who aimed her barbed words against the Moslems. She was among those whom Mahomet ordered to be executed on the day of his victorious entry into Mecca.[34] In the region of El Nagir, it was recounted that some women had rejoiced when the Prophet died and Abu Bakr, the first of the Caliphs, ordered their hands and feet to be cut off.[35] Thus women who dared to give voice to their protest or opposition could be exposed to cruel punishment. Their hands might be cut off, or their teeth pulled out, or their tongues torn from their mouths. This last form of punishment was usually reserved for those who were singers. It was said of these women that they used to dye their hands with henna, brazenly display the seductions of their beauty, and beat time with their fingers on tambourines and drums in defiance of God, and in derision towards the rights of God and his Prophet. It was therefore necessary to cut off their hands and tear out their tongues.[36]

However, there is no doubt that under Islam men and women slaves were given rights which they did not enjoy in the preceding period. Islam fought against the oppression of slaves and the poor, opposed injustice and corruption, and called upon the Arab tribes to cease their habits of alcoholism and gambling and to give up the practice of usury. But the pre-eminent position of man as compared to woman was not shaken. Man remained the master and the mentor. Marriage in essence was a property right or contract, the husband owning his wife by virtue of the dowry and of the fact that he supported her. The duty of the wife was to obey, whereas the husband could divorce her whenever he wished and marry more than one woman at a time.

Thus it was that the Moslem Arab woman remained part of the man's property. Even today in the Arab countries, including Egypt, women are still subjected to marriage laws that have not changed radically since those early days. Whatever improvement there has been in the personal status of women, as wives or mothers, is not so much due to the law, still supported by powerful religious and conservative forces, but rather to the socio-economic changes that have taken place in some countries like Egypt, Iraq, Syria, etc.

One of our famous contemporary writers, the late Abbas Mahmoud El Akkad, has often sung the praises of the patriarchal tribal system which emphasizes that women are the property of men. Since security is a necessity in the life of those who inhabit the desert, it was essential that they should be known among their enemies and their fellow men for their capacity to defend and secure their property. Among all the forms of property protected by man, woman comes first.[37]

References

1. Levi, *The Family*, p.79; and Duffaut, *Systems and Organizations in the Old Testament.*
2. See Chronicles I (Old Testament), Ch.7, Verse 7.
3. See Genesis, Ch.38, Verse 24.
4. See Genesis, Ch.48, Verses 14ff.
5. Genesis, Ch.21, Verses 7 ff.
6. Genesis Ch.42, Verse 37.
7. Genesis, Ch.22, Verse 10.
8. Exodus, Ch.20, Verse 17.
9. Exodus, Ch.21, Verse 3.
10. Exodus, Ch.18, Verse 12.
11. Genesis, Ch.35, Verse 17.
12. Genesis, Ch.29, Verses 15 ff.

13. Genesis, Ch.21, Verse 14.
14. Samuel I, Ch.18, Verse 27, Ch.25, Verses 39 and 43. Samuel II, Ch.3, Verses 3 and 4, and Ch.5, Verse 13.
15. Chronicles II, Ch.11, Verse 21.
16. Chronicles II, Ch.13, Verse 21.
17. Kings I, Ch.11, Verse 3.
18. Kings I, Ch.7, Verses 13-25.
19. Deuteronomy, Ch.22, Verses 13-19.
20. Deuteronomy, Ch.22, Verses 28-29.
21. Deuteronomy, Ch.24, Verses 1-4.
22. See Numbers Ch.5, Verses 11-18.
23. Genesis, Ch.38, Verse 24; and Deuteronomy Ch.22, Verse 21.
24. Deuteronomy, Ch.38, Verse 24; and Ch.22, Verse 21.
25. Matthew (New Testament), Ch.5, Verses 27-28.
26. Matthew, Ch.19, Verses 3-6.
27. In the face of the inhuman suffering inflicted by torture a woman had to admit her guilt before the priest as the only way out and had to concur that her body was inhabited by evil spirits and devils. See Jules Michelet, Christina Holi, Thomas Zsass and others.
28. Jules Michelet, *Satanism and Witchcraft*, p.19.
29. Quoted in Christina Holi, *Witchcraft in England*, p.130.
30. *El Mehbar*, 240.
31. Nasser El Din El Assad, *El Keyan Wal Aghani fi Asr El Gaheleya*, 1960, pp.43-4.
32. *Tafsir El Tabri* (Maimanieh), Ch.18, pp.92-3.
33. Abu Farag El Asfahani, *El Aghani*, Vol.16, p.21.
34. Nasser El Din El Assad, *op. cit.*, p.91.
35. El Balathiri, *Fetouh El Boldan*, 1966, 1:102.
36. *Tarikh El Tabari*, Vol.4, pp.2014-5.
37. Abbas Mahmoud El Akkad, *Gamil Boussaina*, p.18.

PART 3
The Arab Woman

15. The Role of Women in Arab History

Whenever my readings have taken me back to the pre-Islamic period, I have always been amazed at the number of 'women personalities' who played an important role in the tribal society of those days, and at the prominent place they occupied in literature, culture, the arts, love and sex, and in the social and economic life of their people. There were even women who became famous for their active, important participation in political struggles, wars, and well-known battles. This was the case in both the pre-Islamic and Islamic eras and even during the lifetime of Mahomet the Prophet.

The history of the Arabs, like a rich and ornamented tapestry, is studded with the brilliant names of these women. To mention only a few, we can remember Nessiba Bint Kaab who fought with her sword by the side of Mahomet in the Battle of Ahad and did not abandon the fight until she had been wounded thirteen times. Mahomet held her in great respect and said 'the position due to her is higher than that of men.'[1] Another woman Om Solayem Bint Malhan, tied a dagger around her waist above her pregnant belly and also fought in the ranks of Mahomet and his followers. On the other side, there were again women who took part in the fighting and in battles against Mahomet. Among them was Hind Bint Rabia, the wife of Abou Suffian. She wore armour and a warrior's mask in the Battle of Ahad and brandished her sword before plunging it with a mortal thrust into enemy after enemy.[2] Hind was an Arab woman who insisted on her freedom and on making her own decisions in personal life. She said to her father: 'I am a woman who holds her life in her own hands and knows what she wants.' And her father answered: 'So it shall be.'[3] Hind was well known for her logic and quick wittedness, even in answering the Prophet. Together with other women she stood before him and proclaimed their conversion to Islam. Mahomet spent

some time going over the principles of Islam for their benefit. When he came
to God's directive 'do not kill your children', which refers especially to the
practice of burying new born female babies alive in order to get rid of them,
she said 'It is you who have killed our children.'⁴ In the Battle of Badr, fought
between the Muslims and the Koraishites (members of the tribe of Koraish
who bitterly opposed Mahomet for a long time), Hind lost three men from
her family: her father Ataba Ibn Rabia, his brother Shiba and his son Walid
Ibn Ataba, the brother of Hind. After this battle Hind swore to avenge them
and took an oath not to perfume herself or go near her husband until this
was done. She kept her promise during the Battle of Ahad in which the
Koraishites were victorious over the Muslims.

Another very prominent woman among the Arabs at that time was
Khadija, first wife of the Prophet. She was known for her imposing personality, her independence, both socially and economically since she earned her
own living through trade, and the freedom which she insisted upon in her
choice of husband. She exercised this freedom in choosing to marry Mahomet,
who was fifteen years younger than her. She sent a woman, called Nefissa, as
her emissary to him. In the book *El Tabakat El Kobra* which contains the first
comprehensive history of the Arab nation, the author, Mohammed Ibn Saad,
reports Nefissa the emissary as having said: 'She sent me to him secretly and
told me to propose that he marry her. And he did.'⁵ Khadija had for some
years employed Mahomet to take care of her trading interests and manage
her affairs. It was thus that she came to know him well.

Pre-Islamic society was composed of numerous tribes which lived in the
desert and in towns under varying economic circumstances. Some were more
or less matriarchal in structure like those of Khanda and Gadila.⁶ Kings before
the period of Islam were sometimes named after their mothers as in the case
of Omar Ibn Hind. The Prophet himself was proud of his descent from the
women of his tribe and was wont to say of himself: 'I am the son of the El
Awatek from the tribe of Solayem [Atika Bint Hilal, Atika Bint Mora, and
Atika Bint El Awkass, all women of this tribe] .'

Arab society in this Gahelia period represented a cross between the patriarchal and matriarchal systems where, however, man had the upper hand. In
it was reflected the gradual disappearance of matriarchal characteristics
within a society that had passed over to the patriarchal stage as a result of the
control exercised by men over the economy and over religion. Women in the
desert areas and oases enjoyed a greater degree of liberty than women in the
towns because they were involved in obtaining the means of livelihood. These
desert women also mixed freely with men and did not carry the veil.

Both male and female goddesses were known in the pre-Islamic era, and
the Arabs believed that the god or goddess of each tribe played an active role
in war, and fought to ensure victory for its people. The tribes, therefore, used
to go into battle carrying paintings or statues of their gods or goddesses. Abou
Suffian, one of the tribal leaders of Koraish, had his standard bearers carry
El Lat and Ozza in the battle against the Muslims at Ahad. El Lat and Ozza
were both goddesses and, together with Hind, constituted a female force which

brought victory over the Muslims and reinforced the faith of the tribe in their own power! However, if defeated, a tribe would often renounce its weak god and adopt the god of the conquering tribe, or of a tribe that was known for its martial prowess. The result was that the worship of certain gods became preponderant and their number diminished over time.[7] The important position occupied by some goddesses was symbolic of the relatively higher prestige enjoyed by women in Arab tribal society, and a reflection of the vestiges of matriarchal society that still lived on and were prominent in some of the tribes.[8]

These aspects of matriarchy may possibly be the reason explaining the relatively important role played by women in both pre-Islamic and early Islamic society, and manifest in a number of women characterized by their strong personalities, their ability to reason and convince, and their positive attitude towards the problems of personal and social life. Many of them were also active in the fields of production, commerce and trade. As a result of this participation in economic activity side by side with men, the women acquired independent personalities both inside and outside the home, and were often free to choose their husbands.

Before Islam it even used to happen that a woman would practise polyandry and marry more than one man. This form of marital arrangement was called *zawag el mosharaka* or 'the marriage of sharing'. The woman was not allowed to exceed ten husbands, and if she overstepped this limit society branded her as a prostitute. Aisha, the wife of the Prophet, in describing the Gahelia period says: 'The group could reach up to ten. They would enter into the woman and penetrate her. When she became pregnant she would send for them, and no one could refuse to come. They would gather around her and she would say to them: "You know what has happened. Now I have given birth to a child. He is your son", and she would name the man she desired as father and guardian to the child. And the man could not refuse.'[9]

Asfahani mentions in his writings that 'when a bedouin woman divorced her husband, she changed the door of her tent to the opposite side so that if it was East it became West, and if it was South it became North. Once she had made this change, divorce was immediate.'[10]

Before the advent of Islam, the Arabs practised a form of marriage called *istibdaa*. Once more we have a graphic description of what this actually was in the words of Aisha. The woman, once relieved of her menstrual period and therefore pure, was asked by her husband to 'send for X [the name of a man] and lie with him'. The husband would then keep away from her until the signs, indicating that she had become pregnant from the man with whom she had lain, grew evident. Usually the man chosen would be one of the important figures in society, the aim being to have a child who might inherit his superior qualities. But once the proof of her pregnancy was beyond doubt, the husband would in all probability resume his sexual relations with her. The child when born was considered the offspring of the legal father and not of the 'great man' who had lain with his wife.

Istibdaa was one form of polyandric relations among the Arabs, and is still practised in some societies where a sterile woman may have extramarital relations in order to become pregnant.[11]

When I was still a child I used to hear the women in my village, Kafr Tahla, talking about sterile women who visited the sheikh (the religious mullah) and asked him for a special charm that, once worn by them, would lead to pregnancy. At a later stage I learned that this charm was sometimes a piece of wool which the woman was told to push up into her vagina. When I tried to find out the secret hidden in this piece of wool which made it capable of turning a sterile woman into a fertile one, I came across something very interesting. Apparently some of these sheikhs used to moisten the piece of wool in fresh semen and ask the woman to push it up the vagina immediately. The meeting between the woman and the sheikh always took place in a dark room and she therefore did not notice what he was doing, or sometimes pretended not to notice. Her desire to have a child and to erase the stigma attached to her infertility and childlessness was enough to make her close her eyes to whatever the sheikh might do, even if he went as far as impregnating her directly instead of using the piece of wool. The sheikhs followed these practices, as they said, in order to cure the barren woman,[12] but it was also a way of satisfying their own sexual desires. In most cases, however, it served both purposes since often it was the husband of the woman who was infertile and who blamed his wife unjustly in order to cover up his own weakness.

Marriage, carried out according to the practice of *istibdaa* or the use of a piece of wool impregnated with sperm, are both methods akin to the idea of artificial insemination which in its essence is the replacement of the father's sperm by sperm from another man.

In the West the idea of artificial insemination has been looked upon as an important innovation and an indication of the broadmindedness with which people in the developed countries face these problems. Yet way back in history, almost 1,300 years ago, the same idea was being practised, perhaps in a more human way since the husband in *istibdaa* freed himself of all jealousy in the hope of getting a healthy and brilliant child. The other man was only used as a fertilizer. This reminds us of Lester Ward who maintained that the role of man in the early stages of human development was simply that of a fertilizer in relation to woman.[13] The early drawings on the walls of the Cogul caves in Spain where women were depicted in a complete form, whereas the male was reduced to his sexual organ, are consistent with Lester Ward's contention.

In the pre-Islamic era the Arabs also practised other original forms of marriage. One of them was called *zawag el mutaa*, or 'marriage of pleasure', which aimed at no more than providing a legalized opportunity for both partners to enjoy sex together. The man marries the woman for a certain number of days, usually three, but they might be more or less, and pays her a sum of money which is fixed by mutual agreement. He is not obliged to recognize any child born as a result of this short-lived wedlock.

A second form was *zawag el hiba*, or 'marriage of sacrifice', in which the woman would say to the man: 'I give myself to you', meaning that no conditions were attached to this marriage and that she did not enjoy any rights over the man. Here, again, the father was not held responsible for any child that might be born of this relationship with the woman.

In both these marital arrangements, if there was a child, it would be named after the mother. Islam, however, abolished such practices, at an early stage.

Arab women did not lose their independence and positive personality traits suddenly. It was a gradual, slow process related to the socio-economic changes taking place in society, and they struggled hard not to lose their ancient rights. Sometimes they were successful, but it was mostly a losing battle, ending in the complete predominance of the patriarchal system.

But women, even in the early phases of Islam, continued to exercise their right to choose their husbands, and this free choice was not an infrequent occurrence. One of the well-known stories in this connection is that of Leila Bint El Khatim who went to Mahomet, the Prophet of the Moslems, and said to him: 'I am Leila Bint El Khatim. I have come to show myself to you. Marry me. And Mahomet said: 'I hereby marry you.' But when she went back to her relatives, they told her that she had made a big mistake. She was of a jealous nature and would not be able to stand the other wives of Mahomet, for it was his right to marry as many as he wished. So she went back to Mahomet and said: 'I am a woman with a sharp tongue and cannot bear your other wives. So let me free.' So he said to her: 'I have let you free.'[14]

The Arab woman of these societies before the Middle Ages not only enjoyed the right to choose her own husband, but could also contradict her man, turn away from him in anger, and refuse to share his bed, no matter how important he was, even if he were the Prophet himself, when they felt there was reason enough. Most Muslims today would be surprised to know that, in some of Mahomet's sayings, he explains the importance of sexual play in ensuring sexual fulfilment as a physical need.

El Ghazali, one of the most eminent Moslem philosophers, was in some areas profound and advanced enough to reflect Mahomet's insistence that one of the factors that can lead to the weakening of a man's personality is to practise sex without play and to neglect the necessity of ensuring that the woman is also satisfied. He quotes the Prophet as having said: ' "No one amongst you should throw himself on his wife, as beasts do. Before you join with your wife in intercourse, let there be a message running backwards and forwards between you and her." So people asked him: "And what should the message be?" Upon which he answered: "A message of kisses and tender words." '[15]

Mahomet, as a Prophet and leader of his people, could easily have yielded to the temptation of pretence and hypocrisy which so many men in situations only vaguely akin to his have done. He could have put on a mask of sublime contempt or righteousness towards all matters related to women, love and sex. But that was not his way, nor did it fit in with the characteristics of a man who was self-confident and sure of himself as a complete, normal human being. For him it was easy to treat himself as a person capable of loving women and the good things in life. He experienced no reservations in expressing his love for woman as something natural. When Amr Ibn El Aas (later conqueror of Egypt) asked him, who was the closest person to his heart, he answered: 'Aisha' (his young wife). But Amr Ibn El Aas said: 'I mean among men.' Back came the reply: 'Her father . . .'[16]

One of the striking differences between Western and Islamic thought in relation to sex was in the diametrically opposed attitude of each to the question of sexual satisfaction. In Islam sexual satisfaction, and not sublimation or suppression was considered more conducive to liberating men and women's full capacity to work, to concentrate and to create in the fields of human endeavour, whether related to the affairs of the earth or those of the heavens. Islam considers that the mind, the brain and the reason of human beings is the most important gift bestowed upon them by Allah. The brain or the mind was given to the peoples of the earth in order that they might use it to gain knowledge, knowledge about life and the earth and people and science and Allah. Knowledge is the highest form of worship for a Muslim believer. And in order that the mind might devote itself to acquiring knowledge, and be able to concentrate all its powers of thought, it is necessary to expend and let out pent-up sexual energy, and to satisfy sexual desire, thus avoiding weighing down the soul and occupying the mind with matters that might lead it to stray from the path of knowledge and the worship of Allah.

Here Islam is in agreement with the modern schools of psychology which maintain that sexual satisfaction is a necessity for intellectual and cultural activity and creation. This approach is also far more scientific than that of Freud and his school, where sexual sublimation or suppression is considered essential for cultural progress and for the very existence of civilization.

Recent advances in psychology have shown that unsatisfied sexual energy is not transformed into productive, cultural or intellectual creation, but rather tends to be diverted away from its normal course, leading to all sorts of blocks and inhibitions resulting from the storage of internal energy and ending up causing sexual deviations and nervous and other psychological disorders.

It is not difficult to see that the greater recognition, accorded by Islam and its Prophet Mahomet to the rights of women in life and in sex, was the direct result of the comparatively high position occupied by Arab woman in those days, her more active participation in various aspects of life, whether within or outside the precincts of the home, and the prominent role played by a number of outstanding Arab women.

It is time for the modern Arab woman to remember these other women who lived in the same region 1,300 years ago, who walked the same earth and breathed the same air and had the courage to refuse and to protest. Women like Zeinab Bint Gahsh, wife of Mahomet, who in anger could say 'No' to a gift from the Prophet sent by Allah and 'No' again when its value was increased threefold. Once more it is Aisha, a valuable chronicler of Mahomet's life, who describes the incident as follows: 'The Prophet of Allah slaughtered for meat and instructed me to divide it up among his wives. He sent Zeinab Bint Gahsh her share but she returned it. He said: "Increase her share." But once again she met his offer with refusal. I said to him: "Her refusal means that she now hates you." '[17]

Aisha herself, despite her young age, was a living example of how prominent Arab women stood firm on many issues in those days. She was well known for her strong will, versatile and incisive logic and eloquence. She wielded a powerful intelligence which sometimes was even a match for the inspired and gifted Prophet of Allah. She had no hesitation in opposing or contradicting him whose word was all powerful among the Muslims. Hafsa, another of Mahomet's wives, saw fit to draw her example from Aisha, upon which one of the Prophet's close followers commented: 'You wish to criticise the Prophet like Aisha does.'[18] Aisha not only sometimes pulled up the Prophet but was wont to do the same thing with other men. She expressed her thoughts with a forthright and incisive logic and one day Mahomet, while seated in the midst of other men, pointed towards her and said: 'Draw half of your religion from this red one.'[19] She fought in several wars and battles, and was actively involved in politics and cultural and literary activities to such a degree that the theologian of the Muslims, Orwa Ebn El Zobeir, said: 'I have not seen anyone who is more knowledgeable in theology, in medicine and in poetry than Aisha.'[20] This, despite the fact that she did not reach the age of eighteen until after Mahomet's death.

Aisha was capable of discussing any subject with Mahomet. She would differ with him and give vent to her anger whenever he married another wife. She would rebel against him and sometimes even incite his other wives to rebellion. She even went as far as to challenge him in relation to some of the Koranic verses which descended upon him from Heaven. When, in one of these verses, Allah permitted Mahomet to marry as many women as he wished, she commented with heat: 'Allah always responds immediately to your needs.' The story, in the words of Mohammed Ibn Omar Ibn Ali Ibn Abi Talib, runs as follows: 'The Prophet of Allah, Allah's blessings and peace be upon him, did not die before Allah had bestowed upon him the right to have as many wives as he desired, and said unto him "Take to yourself as many as you wish of them [women] ." And when this verse descended, Aisha said: "Indeed Allah responds immediately to your needs." '[21]

Many Arab women of today have inherited the tradition of Aisha and of those who stood up for themselves and for their rights. However, most women in our region have succumbed to the heavy load of a patriarchal class society and have ended up prisoners of the home, of the veil and of a system which prevents them from participating in the economic and social life of their society.

References

1. Mohammed Ibn Saad, *El Tabakat El Kobra*, Vol.8, (Dar El Tahrir Publishers, Cairo, 1970), p.302.
2. Abdel Rahman El Sharkawi, *Mohammed the Prophet of Freedom*, (Kitab El Hilal, Cairo, 1967), p.171.
3. Mohammed Ibn Saad, *op. cit.*, p.171.
4. *Ibid.*, p.172.
5. *Ibid.*, Vol.8, p.9.
6. Abdallah Afifi, *El Maraa El Arabia fi Gaheleyatiha wa Islamiha, (The Arab Woman in the pre-Islamic and Islamic Periods)*, (Dar Ihya El Kotob El Arabia Publishing House, Egypt, 1921), p.1950.
7. Gawad Ali, *History of the Arabs before Islam*, Vol.5, Section of Religious books, (Magma El Ilmy El Iraqi Publishing House, 1955), p.67.
8. For the meaning of the word *Ousa*, see *Lisan El Arab*, Vol.2, p.416.
9. Aboul Farrag El Asfahani, *El Aghani*, Vol.16, p.2.
10. *Ibid.*, Vol.16, p.102.
11. Adel Ahmed Sarkiss, *Al Zawag Wa Tatawir El Mogtama, (Marriage and the Evolution of Society)*, (Arab Book Publishing House, Cairo, 1967) p.108.
12. Similar practices occur in some parts of India within the precincts of Hindu temples. The women address themselves to the priest and request him to cure them of their infertility. The writer Amrita Pritam, in one of her well known novels entitled *That Man*, describes how such happenings occur in secrecy so that only the woman and the priest know the real parentage of the child which might eventually be born.
13. Lester F. Ward, *Pure Sociology*, (Macmillan, 1914), p.353.
14. Mohammed Ibn Saad, *op. cit.*, p.107.
15. El Ghazali, *Ihya'a Oloum El Din*, (Dar El Shaab, Cairo, 1970), Ch.3,p.734.
16. Mohammed Ibn Saad, *op. cit.*, p.137.
17. *Ibid.*
18. *Ibid.*
19. Aisha was called the 'red one' because of the colour of her face. See Ahmed Kharat, *The Status of Women in Islam*, (Dar El Maarif, Egypt, 1975), p.64.
20. El Sheikh Abdallah El Afifi, *Al Maraa El Arabia Fi Gaheleyatiha was Islamiha*, Vol.2, p.139.
21. Mohammed Ibn Saad, *op. cit.*, pp.140-1.

16. Love and Sex in the Life of the Arab

A famous work of art, *A Thousand and One Nights*, has been used by many Western researchers and authors, who describe themselves as 'orientalists', as a source of material and information for studying the life of the Arab. They consider that these stories especially those dealing with love and sexual intrigues, afford an insight into the understanding of the Arab character, seeing them as keys with which to open the doors to the 'Arab Soul', and as valuable means towards penetrating the depths, or rather the shallow waters, of the Arab mind and heart.

Yet anyone with the slightest knowledge of Arab literature knows that the stories related in *A Thousand and One Nights* are only a partial and one-sided reflection of a very narrow section of Arab society, as it lived and dreamed, loved and fornicated, intrigued and plundered, more than ten centuries ago. I do not know very much about the level reached by European civilization at the time, the state of human affairs in society there, in the sciences and in the arts, but I at least know enough to be able to say that Arab society had undoubtedly advanced much further. Many are the scholars, writers and researchers who have made comparisons between the West and the Arab World, only drawing their examples from a period in our history, now more than a thousand years old. One would have to have a very bad memory to forget, in one gigantic leap, what is in terms of time half the number of years which have elapsed since the birth of Christ. How can we depict the contrasts between the Arab character at the time when the people of *A Thousand and One Nights* flew on their magic carpets, and the Western mind of the Victorian era when purity floated like a thick veil over the corrupt and bloated features of a hypocritical society.[1] How much more true and scientific would a comparative study have been of the lifestyles of Arab and European men from the same period, or at least from the Middles Ages when the clergy, who were the male intelligentsia of the time, were busy prompting women accused of sorcery to utter the most obscene sexual epithets, and, under insufferable torture, forcing them to admit to the very crimes which they had been taught to describe?[2]

This picture of the sex-mad Arab fawning on an extensive harem is maintained with dubious insistence even today. Without exception the films, magazines and newspapers that roll out from the reels of Western producers and the dark-rooms of Western monopolies, depict Arab men as trotting behind the skirts of women, ogling the ample bosoms of seductive blondes, and squandering their money, or quenching their thirst for alcohol or sex. Arab women, in their turn, are depicted as twisting and turning in snake-like dances, flaunting their naked bellies and quivering hips, seducing men with the promise of dark passion, playful, secretive and intriguing, a picture drawn from the palaces of *A Thousand and One Nights* and the slave women of the Caliph, Haroun El Rachid.

Is it possible to believe that this distorted image of Arab men and women is representative of their true life and character in the Arab world of today? Personally, I am sure that it is not even representative of men and women living at the time of Haroun El Raschid. Perhaps it has some authenticity as a reflection of certain aspects of the life led by palace rulers and their concubines in those bygone days, but these were only an infinitesimal minority compared to the vast mass of Arabs, who led a harsh and difficult existence with no room for, nor possibility of ever experiencing, the silken cushions, soft flesh and fiery liquids of dissipation. The sexual life of kings and princely rulers, whether in the past or present, in the modern West or more archaic East, to the South of the Earth's equator or to the North, has maintained the same essential pattern, embroidered with a greater or lesser degree of sophistication or refinement, sadism or depravity.

Sweeping judgements, which depict the nature of Arabs in general, and the men of the Arab world in particular, as being obsessed with sex and more inclined to pursue the pleasures of the body than men from other regions or countries, are therefore unfounded and incorrect. Their aim is to contribute to and maintain a distorted image of the Arabs in the minds of people all over the world, to falsify the true colours of their struggle for independence, progress and control over their destinies, and to facilitate the task of conservative, reactionary and imperialist forces that continue to survive and prosper by such means.

I believe that freedom in all its forms, whether sexual, intellectual, social or economic, is a necessity for every man and woman, and for all societies. Nevertheless, I feel that the sexual freedom that has accompanied the evolution of modern capitalist society has been developed very much in a unilateral direction and has not been linked with, or been related to, a parallel development of social and economic freedoms. This sheds some doubt on the real motives behind the consistent and ever increasing campaign calling upon men and women to throw their sexual inhibitions and beliefs overboard. It also jeopardizes the chances of human progress and fulfilment, since a one-sided development that does not take into consideration the totality of life can only lead to new distortions and monstrosities.

This is why there is a growing realization that sexual freedom, as it is preached today in modern capitalist society, has no valid answers or solutions to many of the problems of personal life and human happiness, and that it is only another and perhaps more ingenuous way of making people pay the price of ever expanding consumption, of accumulating profits and of feeding the appetites of monopolistic giants. Another opium to be inhaled and imbibed so that mobilized energies may be dissipated rather than built up into a force of resistance and revolt against all forms of exploitation.

In this respect, Eastern and Arab societies have not differed from the West. Here again it is mainly economic necessity which governs the direction in which values, human morals and norms of sexual behaviour move. The economic imperatives of Arab society required a wide degree of sexual freedom to ensure the provision of large numbers of offspring. Polygamy, as against polyandry, tends to be more prolific as far as children are concerned. Arab society, still primitive and badly equipped to face the vicissitudes and harshness of desert life, suffered from a very high mortality rate, especially among infants and children, which had to be compensated for by correspondingly high birth rates. The economic and military strength of tribes and clans in a society which possessed neither modern tools or machines, nor modern weapons, depended very much on their numbers. In addition, the simple crude existence of desert life and the extreme poverty of nomadic tribes meant that, while the cost of maintaining a child was minimal, the child could play useful roles in meeting the productive needs of the time, being capable of running errands or looking after the camels and sheep.

Wars and battles were an integral part of tribal life and flared up at frequent intervals, and death took a heavy toll of the men. This was particularly the case after Islam started to establish itself and expand. It was natural that this new threat should meet with the resistance of the neighbouring rulers and the older religions entrenched in the surrounding regions, and that the Muslims should be obliged to fight numerous battles before they could succeed in establishing and stabilizing their new State. The result was heavy losses in men and a marked imbalance characterized by a much higher number of women, accentuated by the throngs of women slave prisoners brought back from victorious battles.

The easiest and most natural solution to such a situation was to allow men to marry more than one woman, and in addition to choose from among the women brought back from the wars, or sold in the markets, those whom they considered suitable to be wives, concubines or slaves in their households. Each man did so according to his means, and these means of course varied widely from one man to another. With a superfluity of women, a man would take pride in the number of women he could maintain, and the bigger this number, the more occasion for him to boast about the extensiveness of his female retinue, and about his powers over women, whether in marriage or in love. On the other hand, women would compete for the favours of men and excel in subtle allurements to attract men towards marriage, love and sex.

This was perhaps an additional factor which tended to make Arab women more forward and positive in love and sex, characteristics in clear contrast to the passive attitudes assumed by the vast majority of women living in our modern era. The other factors, mentioned previously, were the matriarchal vestiges which at the time were still strong in Arab society, and the naturalistic attitudes of Islamic teachings which prevented love and sex from being

135

considered sinful as they were by Christianity, On the contrary, Islam described sexual pleasure as one of the attractions of life, one of the delights for those who go to Paradise after death. As a result, Arab women had no hesitation in being positive towards sex, in expressing their desire for men, in exercising their charms, and weaving their net around whoever might be the object of their attentions. Perhaps they were following in the footsteps of their mother, Eve, who had so ably enticed Adam to comply with her wishes and fall victim to *fitna*,[3] with the result that he dropped from the high heavens in which he was confined and landed with his two feet on the solid, rough, but warm and living earth.

For the Arabs the word 'woman' invariably evokes the word *fitna*. Arab women combined the qualities of a positive personality and *fitna*, or seductivene to such an extent that they became an integral part of the Islamic ethos which has, as one of its cornerstones, the sexual powers of women, and which maintains that their seductiveness can lead to a *fitna* within society. Here the word is used in a related but different sense to mean an uprising, rebellion, conspiracy or anarchy which would upset the existing order of things established by Allah (and which, therefore, is not to be changed), From this arose the conception that life could only follow its normal steady and uninterrupted course, and society could only avoid any potential menace to its stability and structure, or any disruption of the social order, if men continued to satisfy the sexual needs of their women, kept them happy, and protected their honour. If this was not ensured a *fitna* could easily be let loose, since the honour of women would be in doubt, and as a result uneasiness and trouble could erupt at any moment. The virtue of women had to be ensured if peace was to reign among men, not an easy task in view of the *fitna* (seductiveness) of women.

Islam's contribution to the understanding of love, sex and the relations between the sexes has never to my knowledge been correctly assessed and given the consideration it deserves. However, the contradictory aspects inherent in Islamic society are reflected in another dramatically opposed tendency which runs through the body of Islamic teaching, and is a continuation of the rigid, reactionary and conservative reasoning that dominated the concepts and practices of Judaism and Christianity in matters related to sex.

Islam inherited the old image of Eve and of women that depicts them as the close followers and instruments of Satan, the body of women being his abode. A well-known Arab saying maintains that: 'Whenever a man and a woman meet together, their third is always Satan'.Mahomet the Prophet, despite his love for and understanding of women, warns that: 'After I have gone, there will be no greater danger menacing my nation and more liable to create anarchy and trouble than women.'[4]

This attitude towards woman was prominent throughout Islamic thought and she always remained a source of danger to man and to society on account of her power of attraction or *fitna*. Man in the face of such seduction was portrayed as helpless, drained of all his capacities to be positive or to resist. Although this was not a new idea, it assumed big proportions in Islamic theology and was buttressed by many *Ahadith* (proverbs and sayings).

Woman was therefore considered by the Arabs as a menace to man and society, and the only way to avoid the harm she could do was to isolate her in the home, where she could have no contact with either one or the other. If for any reason she had to move outside the walls of her prison, all necessary precautions had to be taken so that no one could get a glimpse of her seductiveness. She was therefore enveloped in veils and flowing robes like explosive material which has to be well packed. In some Arab societies, this concern to conceal the body of women went so far that the split-second uncovering of a finger or a toe was considered a potential source of *fitna* in society which might therefore lead to anarchy, uprisings, rebellions and the total destruction of the established order!

Thus it is that Islam confronted its philosophers and theologians with two contradictory, and in terms of logic, mutually exclusive conceptions: 1) Sex is one of the pleasures and attractions of life; 2) To succumb to sex will lead to *fitna* in society — that is crisis, disruption and anarchy.

The only way out of this dilemma, the only path that could reconcile these two conflicting views, was to lay down a system or framework for sex which on the one hand had to avoid *fitna* while on the other would permit abundant reproduction and a good deal of pleasure within the limits of Allah's prescriptions.

The Imam, El Ghazali, explains how the will of Allah and his wisdom are manifested in the fact that he created sexual desire in both men and women. This is expressed in the words of his Prophet when he said: 'Marry and multiply.' 'Since Allah has revealed his secret to us, and has instructed us clearly what to do, refraining from marriage is like refusing to plough the earth, and wasting the seed. It means leaving the useful tools which Allah has created for us idle, and is a crime against the self-evident reasons and obvious aims of the phenomenon of creation, aims written on the sexual organs in Divine handwriting.'[5]

For El Ghazali, apart from reproduction, marriage aims at immunity from the Devil, breaking the sharp point of desire, avoiding the dangers of passion, keeping our eyes away from what they should not see, safeguarding the female sexual organs, and following the directives of our Prophet when he said: 'He who marries has ensured for himself the fulfilment of half his religion. Let him therefore fear Allah for the other half.'[6]

Islamic thought admits the strength and power of sexual desire in women, and in men also. Fayad Ibn Nageeh said that, 'if the sexual organ of the man rises up, a third of his religion is lost'. One of the rare explanations given to the Prophets' words by Ibn Abbas, Allah's blessing be upon both of them, is that 'he who enters into a woman is lost in a twilight' and that 'if the male organ rises up, it is an overwhelming catastrophe for once provoked it cannot be resisted by either reason or religion. For this organ is more powerful than all the instruments used by Satan against man.' That is why the Prophet, Allah's peace be upon him, said, 'I have not seen creatures lacking in mind and religion more capable of overcoming men of reason and wisdom than you [women].'[7] He also warned men: 'Do not enter the house of those who have

absent ones' — meaning those women whose husbands are away — 'for
Satan will run out from one of you, like hot blood'. And we said, 'From you
also, O Prophet!' He answered, 'And from me also, but Allah has given me his
support and so Satan has been subdued.'[8]

From the above, it is clear that the Arabs were accustomed to discuss freely
with Mahomet and treated him as an ordinary human being like themselves. If
he said that Satan ran in their blood, they would riposte that Satan also ran
in his blood. Upon which, Mahomet admitted that he was no different from
them except in the fact that Allah has come to his rescue and subdued Satan
within him. The Arabic word which has been translated into 'subdued' is
aslam, which means 'to become a Muslim' (to know peace, to be saved). The
meaning of Mahomet's words, therefore, is that his Satan has become a
Muslim. Mahomet emphasized the same point when he said: 'I have been
preferred to Adam in two ways. His wife incited him to disobedience, whereas
my wives have helped me to obey. His Satan was a heretic, whereas mine was
a Muslim inviting me always to do good.'[9]

Islam, therefore, inherited the attitude of Judaism towards Eve, the sinful
woman who disobeyed God, and towards sex as related essentially to women,
and to Satan. Man, on the other hand, though endowed with an overpowering
sexual passion, does not commit sin except if incited to do so by the seductiveness and devilry of woman. He is therefore enjoined to marry and thereby is
able to beat back the evils of Satan and the bewitching temptations of women.

Islam encourages men to marry. Mahomet the Prophet of the Muslims, says
to them:'Marriage is my law. He who loves my way of life, let him therefore
follow my law.'[10]

Despite the fact that Islam recognized the existence of sexual passion in
both women and men, it placed all its constraints on women, thus forgetting
that their sexual desire also was extremely strong. Islam never ignored the
deep-seated sexual passion that lies in men, and therefore suggested the
solutions that would ensure its satisfaction.

Islamic history, therefore, witnessed men who married hundreds of women.
In this connection we may once more quote El Ghazali: 'And it was said of
Hassan Ibn Ali that he was a great marrier of women, and that he had more
than two hundred wives. Sometimes he would marry four at a time, or
divorce four at a time and replace them by others. The Prophet Mahomet,
Allah's blessings and Peace be upon him, said of Hassan Ibn Ali: 'You resemble
me, and my creativity.'[11] The Prophet had once said of himself that he had
been given the power of forty men in sex.'[12] Ghazali admits that sexual desire
in men is very strong and that: 'Some natures are overwhelmed by passion and
cannot be protected by only one woman. Such men should therefore preferably marry more than one woman and may go up to four.'[13]

Some of the close followers of Mahomet (El Sahaba) who led an ascetic
life would break their fast by having sexual intercourse before food. At other
times they would share a woman's bed before the evening prayer, then do their
ablutions and pray. This was in order to empty the heart of everything and so
concentrate on the worship of Allah. Thus it was that the secretions of Satan

were expelled from the body.

Ghazali carries his thoughts further and says: 'Since among Arabs passion is an overpowering aspect of their nature, they have been allowed to marry women slaves if at some time they should fear that this passion will become too heavy a burden for their belief and lead to its destruction. Though it is true that such a marriage could lead to the birth of a child that will be a slave, yet enslaving the child is a lighter offence than the destruction of religious belief.' Ghazali evidently believes that religion cannot be preserved from destruction unless men are allowed to marry as many women as they wish, even though in so doing they would be harming the interests of the children.

It is clear that Islam has been very lenient with men in so far as the satisfaction of their sexual desires is concerned. This was true even if it led to the enslavement of children and injustice to innocent creatures or if sought at the expense of a woman slave completely deprived of a wife's normal rights and whose children were destined never to enjoy the rights of a free child born of a free mother.

The inevitable question which arises in the face of these facts is: Why has religion been so lenient towards man? Why did it not demand that he control his sexual passions and limit himself to one wife, just as it demanded of the woman that she limit herself to one husband, even though it had recognized that women's sexual desire was just as powerful, if not more so, as that of men? Why is it that religion was so understanding and helpful where men were concerned, to the extent of sacrificing the interests of the family, the women and even the children, in order to satisfy their desires? Why, in contrast, was it so severe with woman that death could be her penalty if she so much as looked at a man other than her husband?

Islam made marriage the only institution within which sexual intercourse could be morally practised between men and women. Sexual relations, if practised outside this framework, were immediately transformed into an act of sin and corruption. A young man whom society had not endowed with the possibilities of getting married, or buying a woman slave from the market, or providing himself with a concubine, had no way of expending or releasing his pent-up sexual energies. Not even masturbation was permissible.

Ibn Abbas was once asked what he thought of masturbation? He exclaimed: 'Ouph, it is indeed bad. I spit on it. To marry a slave woman is better. And to marry a slave woman is preferable to committing adultery.' Thus it is that an unmarried youth is torn between three evils. The least of them is to marry a slave woman and have a slave child. The next is masturbation, and the most sinful of all is adultery.[14]

Of these three evils, only the first two were considered permissible. However, the institution of marriage remained very different for men to what it was for women, and the rights accorded to husbands were distinct from those accorded to wives. In fact, it is probably not accurate to use the term 'rights of the woman' since a woman under the Islamic system of marriage has no human rights unless we consider that a slave has rights under a slave system. Marriage, in so far as women are concerned, is just like slavery to the slave, or the chains of serfdom to the serf. Ghazali expressed this fact clearly and succinctly when speaking of the rights enjoyed by a husband over his wife: 'Perhaps the real answer is that marriage is a form of serfdom. The woman is man's serf and her duty therefore is absolute obedience to the husband in all that he asks of her person.'[15] Mahomet himself said: 'A woman, who at the moment of death enjoys the full approval of her husband, will find her place in Paradise.'[16]

The right enjoyed by a wife in Islam is to receive the same treatment as her husband's other wives. Yet such 'justice' is impossible, as the Koran itself has stated: 'You will not be able to treat your women equally even if you exert much effort.' The Prophet himself preferred some of his wives to others. Some Muslim thinkers opposed polygamous marriage for this reason, and maintained that marriage to more than one woman in Islam was tied to a condition which itself was impossible to fulfil, namely to treat the different wives in exactly the same way and avoid any injustice to one or other of them. A man obviously desires his new wife more than the preceding one(s), otherwise he would not seek to marry her. Justice in this context should mean equality in love, or at least the absence of any tendency to like one wife more and so prefer her to the other(s).[18]

Some Muslim thinkers interpret the two relevant verses of the Koran differently: 'Marry as many women as you like, two, three, or four. If you fear not to treat them equally, then marry only one' and 'You will not succeed in being just with your women, no matter how careful you are.'[19] They consider that justice in this context simply implies providing the women with an equal share of material means for the satisfaction of their needs and that it does not refer to equality in the love and affection borne by the husband for his women.[20]

The question, however, is: What is more important to a woman, or to any human being who respects her dignity and her human qualities, justice in the apportioning of a few piastres,[21] or justice in true love and human treatment? Is marriage a mere commercial transaction by which a woman obtains some money from her husband, or is it a profound exchange of feelings and emotions between a man and a woman?

Even if we were to assume the impossible, and arrive at a situation where the man treats his wives equally, it would not be possible to call this a 'right', since the first and foremost criterion of any right is that it should be enjoyed equally by all individuals without distinction or discrimination. If a man marries four wives, even if he treats them equally, it still means that each woman among them has only a quarter of a man, whereas the man has four women. The women here are only equal in the sense that they suffer an equal injustice, just as in bygone days all slaves were 'equal' in that sense under the system of slavery. This can in no way be considered equality or justice or rights for women.

The slave and feudal systems came into being in order to serve the interests of the slave and feudal landowners. In the same way, the system of marriage was created to serve the interests of the man against those of the woman and the children.

El Ghazali when speaking of the benefits of marriage for men expresses himself in these words:

> Marriage relieves the mind and heart of the man from the burden of looking after the home, and of being occupied with cooking, sweeping, cleaning utensils and arranging for the necessities of life. If the human being did not possess a passion for living with a mate, he would find it very difficult to have a home to himself, since if obliged to undertake all the tasks of looking after the home, he would find most of his time wasted and would not be able to devote himself to work and to knowledge. A good woman, capable of setting things to rights in the home, is an invaluable aid to religious holiness. If however things go wrong in this area, the heart becomes the seat of anxieties and disturbances, and life is seized with things that chase away its calm. For these reasons Soleiman El Darani has said: "A good wife is not a creation of this world, for in fact she permits you to be occupied with the life of the hereafter, and this is so because she looks after the affairs of your home and in addition assuages your passions."[22]

Thus it is that a man cannot devote himself to his religious life, or to knowledge, unless he has a wife who is completely preoccupied with the affairs of his home, with serving him, and feeding him, cleaning his clothes and looking after all his needs. But are we not justified in asking: What about the wife? How can she in turn devote herself to her religious life and the search for knowledge? It is clear that no one has ever thought of the problem from this angle, as if it were a foregone conclusion that women have nothing to do with either religion or knowledge. That their sole function in life is sweeping, cooking, washing clothes and cleaning utensils, and undertaking those tasks that Ghazali has described as a source of trouble and disturbance to the heart, and that chase away the calm of life.

How clear it is that the mind of women and their ambitions, whether in science or in culture, have been completely dropped from all consideration, so that man can consecrate himself completely to such fields of human activity. He furthermore imposes on woman the troubles and disturbances of the heart and mind that result from being occupied with such domestic tasks, after which she is accused of being stupid and lacking in religious conviction. Woman shoulders all these burdens without receiving any remuneration except the food, clothing and shelter required to keep her alive. Man not only exploits her mind for his own ends by abolishing it, or at least preventing it from developing any potential through science, culture and knowledge, not only does he plunge her whole life into working for him without reward, but he also uses her to satisfy his sexual desires to the extent required by him. It is considered one of her duties, and she must respond to his desires at any time. If she fails to do so, falls ill, refuses, or is prevented by her parents, it is his right to divorce her, and in addition deprive her of alimony.

Among the sacred duties of the wife is complete obedience to the husband. She is not allowed to differ with him, to ask questions, or even to argue certain points. The man on the other hand is not expected to obey his wife. On the contrary, it is considered unworthy of a man to do what his wife suggests or asks of him. Omar Ibn El Khattab once said: 'Differ with your women and do not do what they ask. Thus you will be blessed. For it is said: Consult them and then act differently.' The Prophet advises: 'Do not live a slave to your wife.' The Muslim religious leader, El Hassan, goes even further when he maintains that: 'Whenever a man has started to obey the desires and wishes of his woman, it has ended by Allah throwing him into the fires of Purgatory.'[23]

One of the rights of a woman is to be paid a sum of money in the form of a dowry when she is married, and to receive another sum of money as alimony if her husband divorces her. In addition, he is supposed to feed and clothe her, to give her shelter in a home. However, the woman cannot specify any conditions as far as the home she is expected to live in is concerned. It might be a hut made of wood or mud, or a beautiful brick house, depending on the means of the husband. She cannot determine the size of the dowry, or the sum paid to her as alimony, or the food which she is supposed to eat and the clothes she will wear. All these things are decided by the husband according to his assessment of the financial means at his disposal, and how he should spend them.

According to Islamic rules, a woman can ask to be paid for breastfeeding her child.[24] The husband is obliged to pay her for this from his earnings, if the child itself has not some financial resources laid aside for it. If these exist, the payment is made to the mother out of them. The mother is not forced to breastfeed the child if she does not want to, even if pay is offered to her. She can ask to be paid as long as there is no other woman who has voluntarily agreed to breastfeed the child, and to whom the father has no objection. However, if such a woman does exist, the wife no longer has the right to ask for any nursing payment.

Here again it is the husband's will that is crucial, since he can prevent the mother from being paid for nursing her child by finding another woman for this purpose, either on a voluntary basis or for a lower wage.

The mother is also eligible for payment for the rearing of her children, but here again it is the father's prerogative to choose another woman who can offer her services either on a voluntary basis or for less pay.

Such limited rights are almost insignificant, surrounded as they are by impossible conditions and cannot be considered of any real value. On the contrary, they afford the man a possibility of dispensing with the services of the children's mother immediately she makes a request to be paid, thereby in fact obliging her to forego her right to payment for nursing or child-rearing. The vast majority of women, unable to be immune to the tendency for society and families to exaggerate and sanctify the functions of motherhood, cannot but sacrifice themselves for their children and give them everything, including their lives. To sacrifice some minor sum of money is therefore a matter of no consequence.

The exploitation to which a wife and a mother is exposed is evident from the fact that she carries out a number of vital functions without being paid. She is cook, sweeper, cleaner, washerwoman, domestic servant, nurse, governess and teacher to the children, in addition to being an instrument of sexual satisfaction and pleasure to her husband. All this she does free of charge, except for the expenses of her upkeep, in the form of food, clothing and shelter. She is therefore the lowest paid labourer in existence.

The exploitation of woman is built upon the fact that man pays her the lowest wage known for any category of human beasts of burden. It is he who decides what she is paid, be it in the form of a few piastres, some food, a dress, or simply a roof over her head. With this meagre compensation, he can justify the authority he exercises over her. Men exercise their tutelage over women because, as stated in the Koran, they provide them with the means of livelihood.

Man's lordship over woman is therefore enforced through the meagre piastres he pays her and also through imposing a single husband upon her to ensure that the piastres he owns are not inherited by the child of another man. Preserving this inheritance is the motive force behind the severe and rigid laws which seek to maintain a woman's loyalty to her husband so that no confusion can affect the line of descent. It is not love between husband and wife which is sought to be nurtured and cherished by these rules. If it were love between the couple that was the basis of this search for loyalty between husband and wife, such loyalty would be required equally from both the woman and the man. However, since loyalty is sought in the woman alone, by imposing monogamy on her, whereas the man is permitted to multiply and diversify his sexual relations, it becomes self-evident that conjugal devotion is not a human moral value, but one of the instruments of social oppression exercised against the woman to make sure that the succession and inheritance is kept intact. The line of descent which is sought to be preserved is, of course, that of the man. Thus adultery on the part of the woman, her betrayal of the nuptial vows sworn to on the day of marriage, means the immediate destruction of patrilineal descent and inheritance.

Money is therefore the foundation of morals, or at least of the morals prevalent where property, exploitation and inheritance are the essence of the economic system. Yet in religion it is assumed that true morals are dependent rather on human values. The Koran clearly says: 'Neither your wealth, nor your children can, even if you tread the path of humiliation, bring you close to me.' 'The highest esteem is given by Allah to those who are the purest.'[25]

We have mentioned before that society realized early on the powerful biological and sexual nature of women, which power it compared to that of Satan. It was therefore inevitable that her loyalty and chastity could only be ensured by preventing her from having relations with any males apart from her husband and the men with whom she was forbidden to have sex such as the father, brother, and paternal or maternal uncles. This is the reason behind the segregation that arose between men and women, and the outlawing of free intermixing between them, a segregation put into effect by imprisoning the women within the four walls of the home. This confinement of women to the home permits the attainment of three inter-related aims: 1) It ensures the loyalty of the woman and prevents her from mixing with strange men;

2) It permits her to devote herself entirely to the care of her home, husband and children and the aged members of the family; and 3) It protects men from the dangers inherent in women and their powers of seduction, which are so potent that when faced by them 'men lose two-thirds of their reason and become incapable of thinking about Allah, science and knowledge.'

The Muslim philosophers who so oft proclaim such opinions borrow most of their ideas from the myth of Adam and Eve, seeing woman as a replica of Eve, endowed with powers that are dangerous and destructive to society, to man, and to religion. They believe that civilization has been gradually built up in the struggle against these 'female powers', in an attempt to control and suppress them, so as to protect the men and to avoid their minds from being preoccupied with women to the detriment of their duties towards Allah and society.

In order to preserve society and religion from such evils, it was essential to segregate the sexes, and subjugate women by fire and steel when necessary for fire and steel alone can force slaves to submit to unjust laws and systems built on exploitation. Woman's status within marriage is even worse than that of the slave, for woman is exploited both economically and sexually. This apart from the moral, religious and social oppression exercised over her to ensure the maintenance of her double exploitation. Slaves, at least, are partially compensated for the efforts they make in the form of some material reward. But a woman is an unpaid servant to the husband, children and elderly people within the home. And a slave may be liberated by his master to become a free man, and thus enjoy the rights of free men, foremost amongst which is the recognition that he has a brain and religious conviction. But a woman, as long as she remains a woman, has no chance or hope of ever possessing the brain and religious conviction of a man. For women are 'lacking in their minds and in their religious faith.'

Since men possess more reason and wisdom than women it has become their right, and not that of women, to occupy the positions of ruler, legislator, governor etc. One of the primary conditions in Islam to become a religious or political leader (Imam) or governor (Wali) is to be a 'male'.[26] Then follow piety, knowledge and competence.

The major ideas on which Islam has based itself in dealing with the question of women and sex can thus be listed as follows:

1) Men should exercise their tutelage over women because they provide for them economically. They are also superior to women as far as reason, wisdom, piety, knowledge and religious conviction are concerned. Authority is the right of men, and obedience the duty of women.

2) Men's energies should be expended in worship, religious activities and in the search for knowledge. This is to be attained by making women devote themselves to serving their men in the home, preparing food and drink, washing, cleaning and caring for the children and elderly.

3) The sexual desires of men should be duly satisfied so that they can concentrate with a clear mind and heart on religious activities, the worship of Allah, the search for knowledge, and the service of society. This also aims to ensure

that religion is safeguarded and society preserved from being undermined, or even collapsing. Sexual desire is to be satisfield through marriage, the aims of which are reproduction and also experience of one of the pleasures promised in Paradise, so that men may be motivated to do good and so be rewarded in the after-life. It is men's uncontested right to fully satisfy their sexual needs by marrying several women, or by taking unto themselves women slaves and concubines. Masturbation however is an evil, and adultery an even greater sin. 'Let those who cannot marry remain chaste so that Allah may bestow upon them of His riches. Let he who can marry a woman, who has matured without marriage, take her as a wife. If he cannot, then abstinence is the path.'[27]

4) The seduction of women and their powers of temptation are a danger and a source of destruction. Men must be protected from their seductive powers, and this is ensured by confining them to the home. Man is exposed to annihilation if he succumbs to the temptations of women. In the words of Ibrahim Ebn Adham, 'he who is accustomed to the thighs of women will never be a source of anything.'[28]

5) Women are forbidden to leave the home and enter the outside world of men except if an urgent necessity to do this arises, as in illness or death. If a woman goes outside her home she must cover her body completely and not expose her attractions or anything that is liable to seduce a man. Her ornaments should be hidden and her external genital organs preserved intact.

Islam encouraged men to marry and went as far as considering it a religious duty. A familiar Arab saying goes as follows: 'Marriage is half of religion.' Men were not only asked to marry, but permitted to take several wives, and to have extramarital sexual relations almost at will, by living with concubines or women slaves. They were thus led to boast of the number of women they owned, and to speak with pride of their sexual powers.

The sexual powers of man became a part of the Arab ethos, and within this ethos, were related to manliness and virility. It became a matter for shame if a man was known to be impotent or sexually weak. Obviously, it could only be a woman who would be able to know, and therefore judge, if a man was sexually deficient, and in this resided another source of woman's hidden strength enhancing the dangers she represented. Men therefore had to be protected from her, and society did this by ensuring that her eyes were prevented from seeing anything outside the home — like an animal that becomes blind from being kept in the dark — by covering her face with the thickest of veils, and by obscuring her mind so she would become incapable of discerning the weak from the strong. This is the origin of the greater value attached to a virgin as compared with a woman, when the time comes for her to marry. The virgin knows little or nothing about men and sex, whereas a woman has experience drawn from her past relations with men and from her knowledge of the arts of sex. She can easily discern where lie the weaknesses of a man and where lies his strength. Hence the reduced value attached to a widow or a divorced woman.

Mahomet the Prophet, however, did not comply with these general rules of male conduct in Arab society. He was married fourteen times to women who had been divorced or widowed. The only virgin he married was Aisha. In this respect he was also much more progressive, and much more open-minded than most of the men of today, who still prefer to marry a virgin and look for the usual bloodstains on the nuptial sheet or cloth. That is why, especially in rural areas, the custom of defloration by the husband's or *daya's* finger is still widespread, and is meant to demonstrate the red evidence of virginity on a white cloth symbolic of purity and an   intact family honour.

As we have seen, the status of women and the attitudes towards them changed rapidly after the death of Mahomet. In the very essence of Islam, and in its teachings as practised in the life of the Prophet, women occupied a comparatively high position. But once they were segregated from men and made to live within the precincts of the home, the values of honour, self-respect and pride characteristic of Arab tribal society became closely and almost indissolubly linked to virginity, and to preventing the womenfolk of the family from moving into the outside world. A popular saying among the Palestinians, very common until the middle of the 20th century, goes: 'My woman never left our home until the day she was carried out.'[29] I remember my mother describing my grandmother and saying that she had only ever moved through the streets on two occasions. The first was when she left her father's house and went to her husband after marriage. And the second when she was carried out of her husband's house to be buried. Both times no part of her body remained uncovered.[30]

Segregation between the world of men and that of women was so strict that a woman who dared to go outside the door of her home was liable to be maltreated at the hands of men. They might limit themselves to a few rude and insolent glances, or resort to coarse sexual remarks and insults, but very often things would go even further. A man or a boy might stretch out his hand and seize her by the arm or the breast. Sometimes young boys would throw stones at her in the lanes and by-roads of cities and towns, and follow in her footsteps with jeering remarks or sexual insults, in which the organs of her body would be villified in a chorus of loud voices. As a girl I used to be scared of going out into the streets in some of the districts of Cairo during my secondary school days (1943-48). I remember how boys sometimes threw stones at me, or shouted out crude insults as I passed by, such as 'Accursed be the cunt of your mother' or 'Daughter of the bitch fucked by men'. In some Arab countries women have been exposed to physical or moral aggression in the streets simply because their fingers were seen protruding from the sleeves of their dress.[31]

This tendency among males to harm any woman caught crossing the boundaries of her home, and therefore the outer limits of the world prescribed for her by men, or who dares break into and walk through domains reserved for men, proves that they cannot consider her as merely weak and passive. On the contrary, they look upon her as a dangerous aggressor the moment she steps over the frontiers, an aggressor to be punished and made to return immediately to the restrictions of her abode. This attitude bears within itself the proof of woman's strength, a strength from which man seeks to protect himself by all possible means. Not only does he imprison woman within the house, but he also surrounds the male world with all sorts of barricades, stretches of barbed wire, fortifications and even heavy guns.

The female world, on the other hand, is looked upon by men as an area surrounded by, and peopled with, obscure and puzzling secrets, filled with all the dark mystery of sorcery, devilry and the works of Satan. It is a world that a man may only enter with the greatest caution, and a prayer for Allah's help, Allah who alone can give us strength and show us the way. Thus it is that the Arab man in the rural areas of Egypt mutters a string of Allah's names through pursed, fast moving lips, on entering a house in which there are women: *'Ya Hafez, ya Hafes, ya Lateef, ya Sattar, ya Rab, ya Satir, ya Karim.'* ('O great preserver, almighty one, God the compassionate, who art alone shielder from all harm, protector from evil, bountiful and generous') In some Arab societies the man might add *destour,* which is the same word used by peasants to chase away evil spirits or devils.[32]

Here again we can observe the commonly held idea of a close link between women and devils or evil spirits. It goes back to the story of Eve, and the belief that she was positive and active where evil is concerned, an instrument of Satan's machinations. The development of a Sufi theology in Islam, characterized by renunciation of the world, and meditation and love for Allah — which became a cult of love in general — allowed women to rise to the level of saints. However, the number of women saints remained extremely small as compared with men. On the other hand, where it came to evil spirits 80% of them were popularly considered to be female.[33]

The history of the Arabs shows that the women were undoubtedly much less afraid of the men than the men were of the women. The tragedy of Arab men however, or rather of most men all over the world, is that they fear woman and yet desire her. But I think it can be said that Arab men in some periods, especially in the pre-Islamic and early Islamic eras, were able to overcome their fear of women to a much greater degree than men in the West. Or perhaps, more precisely, the men's desire for their women was stronger than the inhibitions built from fear. This is due to the difference in the objective conditions prevailing in Arab societies as compared to the West, and to the fact, discussed earlier, that Islam (contrary to Christianity) recognized the validity and legitimacy of sexual desire.

As a result, sex and love occupied a much more important place in the life of the Arabs, and in their literature and arts. But parallel to this flowering in the passions which bind men and women together, there was an opposite and almost equally strong tendency in the teachings of philosophers and men of wisdom, and in the literary works of writers and poets, that warned against indulging in the pleasures of sex. Men were abjured not to become 'impassioned' with women or to fall victims to their seductions. One of the famous injunctions of the prominent Arab thinker, Ibn El Mokafa, says: 'Know well that one of the things that can cause the worst of disasters in religion, the greatest exhaustion to the body, the heaviest strain on the purse, the highest harm to the mind and reason, the deepest fall in man's chivalry, and the fastest dissipation of his majesty and poise, is a passion for women.[34]

Ibn Mokafa was no doubt directing his remarks exclusively to those men who possessed 'majesty', 'poise', and a well garnished purse, since only those who possessed these trappings could possibly lose them through love of women. Other men, those that constituted the vast majority among the people and who possessed neither majesty, nor poise, nor purse of any kind could not benefit from his advice, or even be in the least concerned with it. They were completely, or almost completely, stripped of all worldly possessions and therefore sometimes even of the means to have just one lawful wife, pay her dowry and keep her children. Such men could not be expected to strut back and forth on the scenes of love and passion.

In Arab society, as in all societies governed by a patriarchal class system where enormous differences exist between various social levels, sex and love, sexual freedom and licence and a life of pleasure were only the lot of a very small minority. The vast majority of men and women were destined to toss and turn on a bed of nails, to be consumed by the flames of sacrifice and to be subjugated by a load of traditions, laws and codes which forbid sex to all except those who can pay its price.

The Arabs, exposed as they were to the shortages and harshness of desert life, to the difficulties and perils of obtaining the bare necessities in a backward and rather savage society, and to the burden of exploitation by their own and surrounding ruling classes, were known for their fortitude, patience, and capacity to stand all kinds of deprivation, whether from food, sex or even water. Yet they were capable, like people in all lands, and at all stages in human development, of finding compensation in other things. This might explain to us why the Arab people were so fond of listening to the stories of *A Thousand and One Nights,* pulsating as they were with the passions of beautiful women and the seductions of sex. This eagerness to listen to, and repeat, what had been told over a thousand nights, aroused a fiery imagination and substituted illusions for what life could not give them in fact. These stories, as Sadek El Azm describes them, 'have as their theme incidents and happenings that have been built around an intricate web of passion and love, which appeared all the more fascinating in that it did not conform with the moral codes and religious laws that held sway in the life of society, nor with the way in which good and evil, legitimate and illegitimate, permissible and impermissible were conceived of.' Thus it is that wives are made to betray their husbands with lovers and male slaves, virgins to meet with their handsome favourites in secret, and men to abandon their wives and seek out their mistresses in the rapture of soft summer nights. All those with whom these stories deal are engaged in the sole occupation of giving free rein to their voluptuous and hotly flowing desires, with all the means at their disposal, even if this should entail lying, deceiving, betraying people's confidence and running away from facing the consequences of one's acts. The predominance of these themes in the popular stories of this book echoes the yearnings that lie buried in the hidden depths of every man and woman condemned to live through the daily grind of a routine life, and dreaming of a chance to experience the throbbings of a violent passion. Yet where is the way out when everything around them stands like a vigilant sentinel intent on keeping their footsteps away from the exciting, sinuous and dangerous paths? The only door that remains open is that of tales and stories where people can live in imagination what is forbidden to them in fact by custom and tradition.[35]

For the traditions and customs prevalent in Arab society imposed limitations on sex which in actual practice were much stricter than the sexual freedom they accorded. They tended to create a sharp separation between love and sex, and between the body and the soul, a heritage which the human race carried down from Judaism, and which was the direct result of damning sex eternally with the stigma of sin and viewing it as something defiling and degraded. The Arab, therefore, related love to the soul and believed that it was a pure emanation of the spirit, just like the love of Allah, or of one's country, or the feeling and affection reserved for a mother. Sex and the body, however, were dragged down to the level of earthly animal desires that should not defile the noble feeling of love.

Romantic love in the West, therefore, had its counterpart in *el hob el ozri* among the Arabs. The separation between sex and love was carried so far that the Arab also carved out a deep ravine between love and marriage. A man was not allowed to marry the woman he loved. Numerous are the famous Arab stories of *hob ozri*, such as that of Gamil who fell passionately in love with Boussaina. In order to stand between her and Gamil, her parents obliged the girl to be betrothed to a hideous looking one-eyed man. Another very famous story is that of Keiss, the well-known Arab poet, who filled the heavens and the earth with poems which he composed to sing his love for Laila. She was also prevented from marrying him and given to another man. And again, the young girl, Afra, was to remain for ever separated from Orwa Ibn Hizam, the man who had loved her so deeply and passionately.

The tragedy of *hob ozri* is a very common theme in Arab literature and poetry. The Arabs throughout the ages have expressed in song and verse the tortures of love, and the pleasurable pain of separation and yearning between lovers deprived of one another. As an example, let us quote Ibn Hazm who says: 'Love is a fatal disease, a state of ecstasy, an infirmity for which we yearn. He who is not afflicted searches for its woes, and he is seized with its malady no longer seeks to be cured.'[36] He goes on to say in verse: 'The suffering that has befallen me through you, my hope in life, is the source of my ecstasy. I will never turn away from you till the end of my days.'

This masochistic tendency to take pleasure in pain is not limited to the Arab alone, but is peculiar to the whole of the human race ever since body was separated from mind, and sex equated with sin. The human being as a species has been differentiated from animals by the relatively greater size and importance of his or her brain, and by the continuous development and evolution which took place in this higher organ of the body which was necessary in overcoming the dangers that stalked the earth,the storms of nature, and the catastrophes of life. I think that perhaps one of the greatest afflictions to descend upon the human race in all its history has been the separation between body and soul, and the inescapable development arising from this separation, namely the equating of sex with sin. These ideas had a much greater destructive power than all the wild beasts of the forest, and human beings could have been crushed by them, were it not for the wonderful capacity of the brain to adapt itself and to undergo continuous evolution. Any animal without a brain faced with these ideas would have had only one of two alternatives. Either complete abstention from sexual relations − which would inevitably have led to the disappearance of the species. Or the continued practice of sex − leading to death engendered by a terrible feeling of guilt and unhappiness at the repetition of an act which was equivalent to the worst of crimes. Both alternatives had to end in death.

But the brain of the human being, which for all practical purposes is the only weapon he or she possesses in life, had this wonderful capacity to adapt and develop which enabled them to overcome this idea, just as they overcame the lions and tigers of the forests. They did not do it by wrestling with these dangerous wild beasts, but overcame them by cunning and intelligence, and by running away or escaping into the trees whenever cornered. Similarly, they did not overcome these destructive ideas by a face to face encounter and by open resistance, but followed the same tactics of escaping, outflanking and disappearing in search of protection and ways out of the trap. Masochism, or the pleasure of pain, was thus a protective device, by which the human being tried to rid her or himself of an over powering feeling of guilt, saying in effect, 'Yes. By practising sex I am guilty of sin, but I make atones for my sin by experiencing this almost intolerable pain, in which I even discover some pleasure.'

Freud made a grievous mistake when he expounded his theories on the psychology of women, and when he described masochism as an essential cornerstone of the nature with which woman was born. For woman is not alone in being masochistic. Man also shares the same characteristic and both of them are victims of the thinking which lead to the separation of body and soul. However, since the evils of the body and of sex were attributed to women much more than to men, it is natural that the feeling of guilt in woman should be much stronger and deeper than it is in man. She is in greater need of experiencing pain and suffering, so that she can expiate her sin. The Old Testament inspired women with the idea of such suffering when it said, 'thou shalt give birth to children in sorrow and pain.' Freud made the mistake of seeking the causes of masochism in the biological and psychological nature of women, rather than in history and the development of society.

Some Arab thinkers have opposed the concepts which create an artificial chasm between body and soul, and have tried to make peace between them. One of these thinkers is El Sheikh Abou Ali El Hassan Ibn Ali Ibn Seena (well known as Avicenna) who died in the year 1027 A.D. Ibn Seena was ahead of the philosophers and thinkers of the West in his scientific approach to man as a total human being, and in his appreciation of the importance of the body and its sensual perceptions. He was one of the very first men of science and knowledge in the world to insist on overcoming the separation between body and soul and to reconstitute the original and intimate link that exists between sex and love. Man is a total being for Ibn Seena, and cannot be fragmented or divided up into separate parts.

In his famous book *Al Kanoun Fil Tib* Ibn Seena writes that the psyche or soul, just as is the case with sex, is composed of two forces, a conscious force and a motive force. The conscious force is also like sex and in turn is composed of two forces, an unconcealed conscious force appearing on the surface, and a hidden conscious force buried in the depths. The unconcealed conscious force appearing on the surface is sensual or related to the senses.[37]

Ibn Seena perceived with a degree of clarity remarkable for his time, and certainly ahead of Western science, the bridges that related psyche to body and the fact that the former was divided into conscious and subconscious. Freud was, therefore, not the first to conceptualize this division of the human psyche claimed as a discovery of Western science.

Another of the most important contributions of Ibn Seena was his essay on love.[38] In this essay, perhaps for the first time, love between man and woman was considered to play a positive role. Ibn Seena here again bridges the gap between the activity of the animal psyche (as it was then described) and the expressive psyche in man (conscious, related to speech), and between the two poles of natural physical or bodily love (sex) and spiritual love. He assigned to the lower self (the body) a role, and upheld that it participates with this role side by side with the higher rational expressive self (expressive here in the sense of speech). Love of human beauty, or in other words sexual love, is considered a vehicle by which man can approach closer to God. Thus Ibn Seena in this essay upheld his essential thinking about the self or psyche, and its components, and accorded it a rightful place in the totality of his philosophical thinking. He surpassed his predecessors and was the first man of knowledge and science to build up a concept of graduated harmony between the body and the self (the soul, psyche or mind). Thus he differed from all those whom he had superseded and who were intent on seeing the body and self as locked in a continuous and unabating struggle.

Ibn Seena, however, repeated the mistakes that other men had made before, or were to make later. Like Sigmund Freud he considered that a man was one thing and a woman another. He considered that the urine of woman had less shine to it than that of men because of her innate curiosity.[39] From his book *El Kanoun fil Tib* we quote the following passage: 'The urine of women in any case is thicker, and whiter, and has less shine to it than the urine of men. This is due to their active curiosity, the weakness of their digestion, the greater width of the openings through which it flows, and the fact that the secretions of the uterus mix with the urine.'

Ibn Seena was nevertheless an exceptionally brilliant philosopher, thinker and man of science. He has not been given his due in the Western world and lesser men by far have been given much greater prominence. The reason for this is not difficult to discover. We do not live in a neutral world and our civilization has been biased in favour of the minds and contributions of white

Westerners, rather than those of more dark-skinned Easterners, just as it has had an age-long bias towards men as against women. This bias cannot be explained by the natural superiority claimed by some 'scientists' for the Western brain and its alleged qualities of greater intelligence and creativeness, but rather by a deliberate attempt to erase the cultural heritage of peoples who were once colonized, to sever the continuity between their past, present and future, and thus to render easier the attempts at imperialist and reactionary subjugation for those who still dream of maintaining more modern versions of old colonial empires.

Ibn Seena's prejudice in favour of men's urine is in no way more remarkable and ridiculous than Freud's leanings in favour of the male penis, leanings which he carried so far that his whole analysis of the psychology of women was built on the fact, so crucial for him, that they had been, poor creatures, deprived of the signal privilege of possessing a male protrusion at the lower end of their bellies. Freud believes that women are not as they are, women, but rather males who lack a man's penis; they do not wish to admit this fact, the fact that they are castrated males, and live in the hope of being able to get a male sexual organ at some time or another in spite of everything.[40]

References

1. P.H. Newby, *A Selection from the Arabian Nights,* translated by Sir Richard Burton, Introduction from p.vii-xvii (Pocket Books, N.T.,1954).
2. Franz G. Alexander and Sheldon T. Selesnick, *The History of Psychiatry,* p.68.
3. *Fitna,*in Arabic means woman's overpowering seductiveness. It combines the qualities of attraction and mischievousness.
4. Abou Abdallah Mohammed Ismail El Bokhary, *Kitab El Gami El Sahib,* (1868), p.419.
5. Abou Hamid El Ghazali, *Ihya Ouloum El Dine,* Dar El Shaab Publishers, (Cairo, 1970), p.689.
6. *Ibid.,* p.693.
7. *Ibid.,* p.695.
8. *Ibid.,* p.696.
9. *Ibid.,* p.700.
10. *Ibid.,* p.683.
11. *Ibid.,* p.697.
12. Mohammed Ibn Saad, *El Tabakat El Kobra,* Vol.8, Dar El Tahrir, (Cairo, 1970), p.139.
13. *Ibid.*
14. Abou Hamid, El Ghazali, *Ihy'a Ouloum El Dine,* Dar El Shaab Publishers, (Cairo, 1970), p.697.
15. *Ibid.,* p.746.
16. *The Koran: Sourat El Nissa'a,* Verse 129.
17. *Ibid.*
18. *El Zamakhshari,* Vol.I, p.143 and *El Kourtoubi,* Vol.5, pp.407-8.
19. *The Koran: Sourat El Nissa'a,* Verses 3 and 129.

20. *El Kourtoubi,* Vol.5, pp.20-2; *El Galadine,* Vol.I, p.27; El Hassas, *Ahkam El Koran.*

21. Egyptian unit of money. One hundred piastres equal one Egyptian pound.

22. Abou Hamid El Ghazali, *Ihya Ouloum El Dine,* p.699.

23. *Ibid.,* p.706.

24. Sheikh Mohammed Mahdi Shams El Dine, *Al Islam wa Tanzeem El Waledeya,* Al Ittihad El Aalami Litanzeem El Waledeya. El Maktab El Iklimi Lilshark El Awsat wa Shamal Afrikia 1974, Vol.2, p.84.

25. *The Koran: Sourat Sab'a,* Verse 37.

26. *Al Imam Abou Hamid El Ghazali,* Dar El Shaab Publishers, (Cairo, 1970), Chapter 3, p.202.

27. *The Koran: Sourat El Nour,* Verse 33.

28. Abou Hamid El Ghazali, *Ihy'a Ouloum El Dine,* Dar El Shaab Publishers, (Cairo, 1970), p.706.

29. Tewfih Canaan, *Kawaneen Gheir Maktouba Tatahakam fi Makanat El Mara'a El Filistineya (Magalat El Torath, Wal Mogtam'a)* El Takadoum Publishers Al Kouds (Jerusalem), No.2, 1974, p.39.

30. My maternal grandmother lived in Cairo (1898-1948). She spent her whole life doing the chores at home and looking after her husband and children. She belonged to a middle class or rather higher middle class family. On the other hand, my paternal grandmother who lived during almost the same period in our village, Kafr Tahla, never knew what it was to wear a veil and used to go out to work in the fields or to buy and sell in the market every day, just as other poor peasant women did.

31. Tewfik Canaan, *Kawaneen Gheir Maktouba Tatahakam fi Makanat El Mara'a,* p.40.

32. I very often heard the word *destour* repeated by villagers, whether men or women, in gatherings for *zar* (exhortational sessions) when mention was made of evil spirits or devils. One of those present would shout *destour* which means 'O God, chase away the evil spirits from our way'. The same word is used to clear the way for a man, especially when women are present, and are required to withdraw or to be warned by him that he is about to come in. The world also means the established order, constitution, or constitutional laws.

33. Tewfik Canaan, *El Yanabi'i El Maskouna Wa Shayatin El Ma'a (fi filistine) Magalat El Torath Wal Mogtama,* El Takadam Press, (Jerusalem), No.2, July 1974, p.38.

34. Ibn El Mokafa, *El Adab El Saghir, Wal Adab El Kebir,* Maktabat El Bayan, (Beirut, 1960), p.127.

35. Sadek El Azm, *Fil Houb Wal Houb El Ozri,* Manshourat Nizar El Kabbani, (Beirut, 1968), p.69.

36. Ibn Hazm, *Tok El Hamama, p.11.*

37. *El Kanoun Fil Tib,* El Sheikh Abou Ali El Hassan Ibn Ali Ibn Seena, Vol.I, p.71.

38. Gustav Von Grebenaum, *Studies in Arabic Literature,* p.83. Ibn Seena's essay on Love has been translated into Arabic by Dr. Ihsan Abbas. A.J. Denomy, *An inquiry into the origins of courtly love in Medaevial studies,* (1945), Vol.6.

39. *El Kanoun Fil Tib,* Libn Seena, p.146, (Tabit El Halabi), Moassasset El Halabi Wa Shorakah, Cairo.

40. Sigmund Freud, *Some Psychological Consequences of the Anatomical Distinction Between Sexes,* Selected Papers, Vol. 5, (Hogarth Press, 1959).

17. The Heroine in Arab Literature

The image drawn of women by Arab writers and poets in more ancient times, but also in contemporary literature, does not differ except in details from that which has been depicted in the West. Whatever differences exist are mainly due to the changes in place and time, or some writers being more forwardlooking than others. Variations are superficial and in no way influence the essential picture of women who remain subjugated to men by the patriarchal system, whether in the context of an industrial society, or in that of an agricultural setting, whether feudal or capitalist, retrograde or advanced, Eastern or Western, Christian or Muslim.

The content of art and literature essentially depends on a struggle intrinsic to the work. This struggle may end in success or in failure, but it is always a type of drama or tragedy that deserves to be told, to be described, and to be registered whether it be humorous or conducive to sadness, tragic or comic. Many are the incidents and strange situations in life that inspire tears and laughter at the same time.

One of the most important of these struggles is that which has gone on, and continues without respite, between man and woman, ever since the day when she was stripped of her natural and reasonable right to name her children and decide their descent. The tracing of a child's lineage and its name with reference to the father, though it has lasted for many thousands of years, has not become any the more natural or reasonable as a result. An established and time honoured injustice can never acquire the quality of justice simply because of the long passage of time or its ancient heritage. The struggle between man and woman began with the establishment of the patriarchal system, and went on right through the ages to the present day. The male of the human species never lost his fear that one day woman would be victorious and regain the rights she had lost. The proof of his fear lies in the fetters and chains with which he has surrounded her body and mind, fetters and chains that take the form of strict and sanctified laws, or scientific theories about her 'self' and her psychology, or certain moral codes, or even emotions that take on the form of love and nobility and protection but whose real substance is made up of jealousy, acquisitiveness, domination and possessiveness. The proof of this almost obsessive fear is the fact that man has never given up the attempt to limit her freedom and to control every aspect

155

of her life, sometimes in full consciousness of what he is doing and at others without even realizing his own motives. As though the moment he dropped his guard or abandoned his wariness, things would be turned upside down, and woman would not remain inferior to him but become a superior being, no longer weak but infinitely powerful.

For the last five or six thousand years man has put all his capabilities and imagination into inventing a wide variety of bonds with which to encircle and pin down women. Yet, throughout, he has never been able to dispel this ingrained fear of the woman and the necessity he feels to watch her carefully. The inevitable conclusion is that this extreme wariness must be well-founded, built on sound reasoning, and motivated by basic natural factors. The first good reason which explains his attitude is the fact that man has violated nature and imposed an unnatural situation. For woman, from the very day she was made woman millions of years ago, has born children and affiliated them to herself as a natural consequence of a natural situation. Man only discovered the secrets of childbearing and childbirth recently. He remained buried in almost total ignorance for a long time and what one does not know one fears. He was therefore afraid of woman, afraid of the fact that she had this mysterious power to bear children and to give birth to them. It was not possible for him to rid his mind and his heart of a fear that he had carried within himself for millions of years. A few hundred years of light were not enough to dispel the heavy dark clouds of an unreasoning fear accumulated since the beginning of human life on earth.

Such a short span of time, if compared with the millions of years that have elapsed since the first forerunners of man peered anxiously through the gloom of high forest trees, could not eradicate from his memory the image of the woman mother, giver and creator of life, and ancient goddess of all time.

The myth of Adam and Eve is the story of man's fear of woman. Were it not for this fear, no one would have thought of attributing evil, sin and devilry to Eve. For the she devil is nothing but a living embodiment of man's innate fear. Woman who was able through her power and sorcery and seductive beauty to lead Adam into a trap, to make him drop in one fell blow from the high heavens to the menial earth, and to be the cause of his destruction, his downfall and his death, must indeed be an awesome and fearful creature, and no one today can swear that at the dawn of the human race, she really was not a terrifying being.

Psychology emphasizes the close link that exists in the psyche of the human being between fear and hatred. Fear indeed breeds hatred, and hatred in its turn is the sustenance of fear. They run together, and the continuity of one depends on the continuity of the other.

Freud admitted that man hates woman and that he envisages her as a source of danger. In his essay, *The Taboo of Virginity,* he maintains that man is in the habit of projecting his internal hatred on the external world, that is, relating it to something that he detests, or to anything with which he is not familiar.[1] Man also envisages woman as a source of peril, and the first sexual relation between him and a woman remains surrounded with the aura of danger. Thus Freud, the civilized, modernized man of science, does not differ essentially in his feelings towards woman from the tribal male who in some parts of Africa believes that if a woman steps over the leg of a man he becomes sexually impotent, or if he touches a woman during her menstrual period he is liable to drop dead.

If the fear of woman has left its imprint even on scientific thinking, the arts, and in particular literature, have also suffered from this deep-seated malady. The panic that Freud experienced when faced with woman has its almost exact counterpart in Bernard Shaw's emotional abhorrence for the female sex. In the area of literature, Shaw is not alone in his misogyny, and many are the kindred souls who share his feelings with enthusiasm. Among Arab writers I can cite the two prominent figures of Tewfik El Hakim and Abbas Mahmoud El Akkad. And Freud's ideas about the passivity of women are reflected in Tolstoy's works. Chekov, in turn, sang the praises of women's frailty and weakness in his story entitled *My Love,* just as Abbas Mahmoud El Akkad was enthralled with these 'female qualities' in his copious reflections on different aspects of Arab and Egyptian life:

> Women take refuge in sexual passivity and retreat, for nature has made of them a prize that is captured by the most powerful and competitive of males. A woman will wait until the most worthy of males succeeds in reaching her first, and then she will give signs of response, a response which is ambiguous in that it is composed of two contradictory but equal forces. On the one hand her freedom of choice, and on the other the logic of a situation forced upon her and in which she has no say. A perfect illustration is the behaviour of hens who patiently await the outcome of the struggle between cocks, or yield to the will of the male without appearing as though they really wish to resist.[2]

Singing the praises and virtues of passivity in woman as an expression of her fundamental nature inevitably leads to an attack on any positive traits or strength she may show, since these are considered as contradictory to her innate characteristics and to the very qualities which make of a woman what she is. A positive and strong woman is necessarily an abnormal person or a freak of nature, and merits vilification or hatred, or at least a measure of criticism and sarcasm.

Man's hatred towards strong and positive woman is so great that he projects on to her all the ancient fears that he has carried through the ages in the deepest recesses of his own self. Thus it is that strength and character in women were considered an irrefutable evidence of evil, deceit, hypocrisy, cunning, obscure designs, readiness to do harm, satanic attraction and seductiveness, sorcery and devilry.

If, as Abbas Mahmoud El Akkad says, woman is passive, waits upon man's will, and responds to him with equal measures of freedom of choice and absolute submission, how is it that another Egyptian author, Zaki Mobarak, sees in her the she-devil who leads him astray and causes him to fall from the high pedestal on which he proudly stands to the lowest depths of the pit, or that Ibn Mokafa'a, the Arab thinker, considers her capable of absconding with man's mind, his wealth, his poise and his majesty? How can her natural and innate passivity be transformed in the twinkling of an eye into a strong active and positive attitude, as happened in the case of Pharaoh's wife who tried to seduce Joseph? The beautiful woman offered herself to him upon which he cried out to God: 'My Refuge and Protector, God who hast chosen the best resting place for me.' Were it not for the fact that he was given the evidence of God's Almightiness, and that he was one of God's loyal servitors, he would no doubt have succumbed to her charms and fallen into evil doing and sin.[3]

Man had, in fact, put himself in a tight corner when he decided that woman was innately passive. From then on, any sign of being positive on her part had to be considered as some obscure machination, or desire to do harm, or sign of cunning, hypocrisy and deceit. Arab literature was therefore replete with women characters so full of cunning that man was in mortal danger if he approached them. They are depicted as adept at manipulating the arts of conspiracy, deceit and female seduction. El Akkad in person falls a victim to his own logic. He maintains that woman is a passive being, and then a few lines later passionately proclaims that she has particular capacities for doing harm and a natural leaning towards the worst kinds of deceit which are peculiar to the feminine self. 'Feminine deceit can be rightly considered a deceit characteristic to woman, for it is related to one of the traits of feminine nature which we find in all societies. It is neither imposed by custom nor by law, and it does not desert woman at any time, irrespective of what she herself wishes or wills.'[4]

El Akkad is intent on pursuing his logic so far, and with such fierceness, that he even wants to deprive women of the capacity to be *willingly* deceitful or cunning, and repeats what his forefathers among the thinkers and philosophers did when they stripped Eve of her positive role in evil and maintained that whatever evil deeds she was accused of were not the result of her own volition and choice, but a mere reflection of Adam's will or God's wishes and designs.

In Arab literature there have been many writers who were well-known for the deep-seated enmity and hatred they bore for women. Examples of these are El Ma'ari, El Akkad, and El Hakeem. El Akkad was described as the 'arch enemy of woman' and his hatred for the female sex was clearly reflected in many of his writings, and surpassed in its intensity the cold-blooded enmity evinced by his master Schopenhauer. El Akkad described woman as remaining an over grown child in all phases of her life, with many of the characteristics which in his opinion are usually associated with children such as rashness, immaturity of mind, a tendency to imitate others and to depend on them, to be fickle and capricious, and given to lies and hypocrisy. He believes that these characteristics are the vestiges of a natural savagery and primitiveness which the passage of thousands of years has not been able to mitigate or to refine.[5]

But El Akkad, almost in the same breath, upholds diametrically opposed ideas. Under his pen we see this creature that has not come of age, this immature child, this passive hen transformed suddenly into a force more power-ful than any other. It is in this light that he portrays woman in his novel *Sarah.* 'She is the force by which all living things in the universe and in the human being express themselves.'[6] To the author this force is so powerful, crushing and unjust that it differs in no way from that of a tyrannical state. In one of his poems he expresses his feelings as follows:

> My beloved, how cruelly unjust you are
> And how great is my woe
> Your empire is overpowering
> But you utter not one word to explain.
> The greatest tyranny a man can suffer
> Is the tyranny which he himself allows.
> You wound me to the depths
> And yet I kiss the hand that holds the cutting edge.
> The worst pain that a man can bear
> Is the pain in whose hurt he finds pleasure and joy.[7]

Here is an example of how hatred can turn into a love passion, into an un-healthy sentiment that finds pleasure in cruelty, injustice and pain, into masochistic love that accepts humiliation, and grovels and crawls, and even kisses the hand that inflicts punishment and plunges a dagger into the heart of the lover.

The masochistic Akkad, however, soon undergoes a metamorphosis and becomes a violent sadist, full of aggression against woman. A female for him must be harshly dominated by man. He must rule over her without mercy, and ensure that he does not fall captive to her *fitna* and her beauty. The beauty of a woman in his opinion is not a genuine beauty, it has no integrity of its own, and is not free in its flight, because it depends for its existence on being appreciated by man. A man alone is free because he is totally independent. His existence as an entity does not depend on anyone else, and therefore real beauty is the beauty of man. The beauty of woman is in fact only 'an ugliness.'[8]

Akkad's enmity and sadism towards woman goes so far that he not only gives himself the right to inflict pain and suffering on women, and to betray them, but also calls upon other men to do the same. His poems reflect very accurately the rather perverse feelings and designs he has on women with lines like: 'You are to blame if you desire for women, what was not even the intent of her creator.' And 'Betray her! And never be loyal or truthful to her. Only thus will you be really sincere to what is most important and essential in her.'[9]

Akkad means that it is only through betrayal that a man can reach a woman's heart and gain her love. For woman, according to him, is only loyal to a betrayer and only loves him who feels hatred towards her or abandons her. She never says yes unless she means no. Woman is slippery, cunning, lying, her fabric is woven of deceit and a desire to do harm.

The Koran in describing women says: 'Their treachery is indeed great.'

Akkad goes on to explain that to do harm to others, to weave conspiracies, and to deceive is part of the nature of woman and constitutes her weapons in the face of a man, irrespective of whether that particular man bears hatred or love for her in his heart: 'It is no use heaping blame and recriminations on her, for she will not deviate from her course. Love of deceit is her nature. It is her shield of protection, the coating of her make-up, and a mental exercise that gives her life and vitality. Deceit is the weapon of her conspiracies used against friend and foe alike.'[10]

Sadism and masochism are two faces of the same coin, and therefore it is not surprising to find substantial doses of both in Akkad's writings and poetry. However, he attempted to exaggerate the sadistic and aggressive aspects of his attitude towards women, probably as a compensatory mechanism born of a secret inferiority complex and as a tendency more in keeping with the outer form of an inflated, yet hollow masculinity. With him they become a tyrannical domination, a fierce though impotent desire to rule over women. For his purpose he drew widely from the Koran, and based himself on the passages that make men responsible for women and superior to them since with women it is not reason that controls their lives, nor a strength of will, and an incisiveness of opinion.[11]

Among the male authors I have read, both in the West and in the Arab world, irrespective of the language in which they have written, or of the region from which they have come, not one has been able to free himself from this age-old image of women handed down to us from an ancient past, no matter how famous many of them have been for their passionate defence of human rights, human values and justice, and their vigorous resistance to oppression and tyranny in any form. Tolstoy, with his towering literary talent and his denunciation of the evils of feudal and bourgeois Russian society, when speaking of women found nothing better to say than: 'Woman is the instrument of the devil. In most of her states she is stupid. But Satan lends her his head when she acts under his orders.'[13]

Arab literature is littered with the image of the she-devil, possessed of many faces:

> Sometimes when you look at her, you feel as though you are in the company of a playful child opening its innocent eyes with all the simplicity, astonishment and naivete of spontaneous nature, without artifice or deceit. Then, after a while, you look at her again, maybe on the same day, only to find yourself faced by an old and cunning creature who has exhausted her life in the daily practice of conspiracy hatched against other women and men. She laughs and presents to you a face that is meant for nothing else but passion. Then she laughs once more — maybe just a few moments later — and you are in the presence of a mind imbued with humour, and an intelligence sharp with sarcasm, a mind which is that of philosophers, and wits which belong only to those who have the experience of a long embattled life.[14]

In these 'thoughts' Akkad once more contradicts his contention that women are devoid of a brain with which to think, and that men should therefore lock them up in the home between four walls for being creatures without mind or religious piety or morals, 'idolators who have never known what it is to believe.'[15]

Akkad and other contemporary men of letters in the Arab world have not travelled very far from the positions held by their ancestors hundreds of years ago, nor does the image they paint of women differ much from the exotic curves of the slave women heroines in the 'classic' *A Thousand and One Nights.* Woman continues to appear on the scene as a capricious vamp, a playful and beautiful slave, a she-devil imbued with cunning and capable of a thousand artifices, an explosive danger versed in all the arts of deceit and conspiracy, a seductive mistress captivating in her passion. She is as positive and dynamic as Satan and his evil spirits, wherever matters of sex and love are concerned. Woman in all the aspects of the role she is made to play, whether it be that of a queen or a slave bought from the market, remains a slave. She may be the daughter of a king, fighting with courage, while her lover shivers in fear, yet she will always be made to call him master, and to serve him, just as Mariam El Zanaria placed herself at the service of Nour El Dine. In most of the stories she is bought and sold, and thus the characteristics and behaviour of the slave become a natural part of her milieu and of her apparel.[16]

A Thousand and One Nights, throbs with hundreds of these captivating women creatures who use magic and sorcery to reach their lovers. Women cast a spell on their husbands so that they cease to be obstacles blocking the path of their desires. It is interesting to note that in this book sorcery is the monopoly of these seductive beings versed in the secrets of conspiracy, intent on getting to where they wish to be, that is to their lovers' arms. Sleeping potions, drugs, anaesthetics are all used by these women to send their husbands into a deep sleep and then slip away to another man's bed. Thus the book has painted an image of women, with its own intrinsic logic and therefore its own peculiar system of rituals, that serves to maintain and reinforce the image handed down from the past. This phenomenon repeats itself throughout *A Thousand and One Nights,* right from the tale of Sultan Mahmoud, Ruler of the Black Islands, at the beginning of the first volume, through the almost endless nights to the story of Kamar El Zaman and his mistress in the fourth. Deceit, cunning and conspiracy in *A Thousand and One Nights* are invariably associated with women, love and sex.

Yet Shawahi and many of the other women mentioned in these tales in fact reflect the strong and positive Arab woman personality, who used to participate unhesitatingly in politics and war, carry her sword and put on her shield and fight in the front lines of the battle field. Such a woman was Hind Bint Rabia, mentioned earlier, who killed a number of Mahomet's followers in the Battle of Ahad. That is why in *A Thousand and One Nights* a woman who fights is not portrayed as a Muslim, but rather as an evil old witch or sorceress.

Just as some Arab women gained prominence in the fields of war, politics, and *fitna,* others became well known for their versatility, creativeness and understanding in literature, the arts and the sciences. There were free women, and also slave women, who reached a very high standing in these fields. Thus it was that El Rasheed was quite fond of marrying women who had sufficient culture and presence of mind to give a wise answer to some philosophical question, or to a problem of life that might arise, or who were sufficienctly versed in poetry to complete with grace and harmony an unfinished line or stanza, or to compose a poem which won his admiration. In the tales of *A Thousand and One Nights,* such occurrences find a place in the form of news items, stemming from literary writings.

Woman is at her best and most powerful when she takes on the form of a genie or spirit in *A Thousand and One Nights.* Men fall victims to her beauty and her spells, and go through great suffering and even torture to gain her favours.

The woman spirit or genie occupies a prominent place in these tales which indicates that the power and strength of women remained an idea and a feeling deeply ingrained in the mind and emotions of the Arab peoples, and continued to be linked with the supernatural powers of genies, devils, sorcery, *fitna* and sex. However, woman in modern Arab literature has not taken on both the form and the substance of these genies. She has discarded the form and kept the substance. She is therefore human on the outside like the others, but intrinsically she has remained a genie, imbued with the same fundamental nature that leads her to practise deceit, to betray, to conspire against others, and to seduce them into her traps. Thus she belongs much more to the world of genies and spirits than to the world of human beings. Zaki Mobarak describes what he considers as being her characteristics when he says that women have a greater power to destroy men than Satan and all his devils together. Akkad expresses the same view but attributes woman's capacity for destruction, betrayal and seduction to her innate weakness. Eve did not eat of the forbidden fruit and tempt Adam to do the same for any other reason than the fact that her nature makes her yearn for all that is not allowed. As a result of this fundamental weakness, she is given to seducing and to tempting others. For El Akkad the forbidden tree 'symbolizes and embodies all that lies within woman in the form of a desire to be subjugated, which breeds the pleasure she takes in rebellion, a capriciousness that gives birth to the pleasure of withholding herself, a suspiciousness and a tendency to doubt, a weak and inborn obstinacy, an ignorant curiosity, and an incapacity to resist and to overcome except by arousing passion, by exhibitionism and seduction.'[17]

Tewfik El Hakim has been given the title 'enemy of woman'. In this area he has contributed thoughts very similar to those of El Akkad although they might differ in points of detail. In his story *El Robat El Mokadass* (The Sacred Bond), El Hakim portrays a woman who rebels against her life. However this rebellion, according to the story, is not due to intellectual ambition, or to a desire to do something worthwhile in her life, but rather to fill the emotional vacuum with which circumstances have afflicted her. The intellectual in this story, who in fact represents the author, maintains that woman no longer has sufficient religious conviction or motives, and that his role is to awaken her conscience and to bring her to realize what is fundamentally wrong. Hakim in his turn describes woman as a creature who bears no loyalty or fidelity except to her 'baser instincts' and physical desires, and who behaves very much like Akkad's heroine, Sarah, taking not the slightest account of religious, intellectual or social values.

No one can help feeling that both El Akkad and El Hakim carry within themselves a conscious or unconscious fear, or even terror, of this feminine creature, endowed as she is with exceptional powers and sexual vitality, characteristics that are contained with difficulty inside the limits of conventional religious, moral and social values. For El Hakim, woman believes that pleasure and dissipation are her right and she speaks of this fact 'in terms that are full of the confidence and challenge, born of legitimate rights.'[18]

Arab literature also reflects the concept of honour as related to virginity discussed in the first part of this book. In fact this concept has not progressed much from its earliest, most primitive and absurd forms. In his novel, *Do'a El Karawan*, Taha Hussein describes this conventional attitude towards honour. The little girl, Hanadi, is slaughtered like a sheep by her maternal uncle, aided and abetted by the mother whom the author portrays as so weak that she is unable to protect her daughter and even participates with the uncle in the killing. The uncle goes scot free, and nowhere is he looked upon as a criminal but rather as a man worthy of respect for defending the honour of his family. (An oft repeated Arab proverb says: 'Shame can only be washed away by blood.') The young engineer who is responsible for having sullied Hanadi's honour also escapes punishment, and at the end of the novel is rewarded with the love of the victim's sister, Amna. At the beginning, the story revolves around Amna's desire to take revenge on the young man who was the cause of her sister's horrible death. In her words: 'there is now no way out of an inevitable struggle between us. The time will come sooner or later when we will know whether Hanadi's life has been taken without a price, or whether there still remains on earth somebody who is capable of avenging the blood that was spilt.'[19]

Amna does not for one moment envisage taking revenge on her uncle whose hand held the knife that ended the life of her sister. The author in his novel says of women that 'they are a stigma that should be concealed, a *horma* that needs to be protected, and an *ard*[20] that has to be kept intact.'

Taha Hussein, in this novel, sees woman as helpless once she has lost her virginity, impotent when she decides to take vengeance on those who have wronged her, and reduced to nothing the moment she falls in love.[21] She gravitates inertly within the orbit of man without weapons or power or strength or a will to do anything, even fending for herself. She is always a victim, destroyed, annihilated. She is annihilated by man, but also by a host of other things; love, hatred and vengeance, and a total subjugation to man that extends to all aspects of her life whether material, psychological, emotional or moral. On occasion Taha Hussein shows some sympathy towards woman, but his feeling is always that of the conventional Arab, the condescending mercy of the superior and powerful male who looks down from his heights on the weaker and inferior female. He describes the sexual struggle between Amna and the engineer, the male fighting with all the weapons and power at his disposal against the female who is conquered and subjugated and broken in advance, a struggle which illustrates almost to perfection all the overtones of a sado-masochistic relationship in both the hero and the heroine.

Woman in the literary works of Naguib Mahfouz, perhaps the most well-known of contemporary Egyptian writers, remains 'a woman' whether poor or rich, ignorant or cultured. Throughout, she is fundamentally the same since her honour does not go further than an intact hymen and a chaste sexual life. In most cases, her downfall and the loss of her honour are brought about by poverty. This is perhaps a step forward since, before Naguib Mahfouz, male authors always brought about the perdition of their heroines through their baser instincts, their passions (in the sense of sexual desire), their female weakness, or the fact that they lacked a mind or brain. In contrast, for Naguib Mahfouz the sins of women are attributed to economic reasons (poverty). Nevertheless, his conception of honour remains the same and its kingdom stays concentrated in the limited area of the external genital organs.

Although Naguib Mahfouz is progressive in so far as his views on social justice are concerned, his attitude and concepts in relation to woman do not differ much from those of his predecessors. He permitted her the right to education and work in support of the father or husband and as a contribution to the income of the family, on condition that she did not overstep the limits of morals and religion (morals in the sense of the patriarchal family), and the double standard prevalent in society where a man and a woman join in love or intercourse, but where it is only the woman who is considered as having fallen or been dishonoured. Mahfouz sometimes waxes enthusiastic and, in the words of one of his characters, calls for the construction of a socialist society and imagines a more humane and prosperous way of life: 'The hope of being able to fulfil what he had dreamt of in his imagination, without transgressing the precepts of religion, brought a feeling of happiness to his heart.'[22]

It was inevitable that Naguib Mahfouz should fall prey to insoluble contradictions. He allows a woman to work and earn in society, and at the same time denies her individual freedom. He permits her to love, yet stigmatizes her for being a fallen woman if she really does. He considers marriage as the only legitimate and permissible relation between a man and a woman, but when a woman thinks in terms of marriage he accuses her of conservatism, caution and an inability to love. One of his heroes, commenting on the desire of his girl to be betrothed to him, says: 'She wishes to marry me, not to love me. This is the secret of her caution and her coldness.'[23] He describes her on occasion as being an animal without brain or religious belief, and on others sees in her the source of all the power embodied in the things of this world. 'No movement emanates from a man unless behind it there stands a woman. The role played by woman in our lives is akin to that of the gravitational forces extending between the stars and the planets.'[24]

Separation between love and marriage was one of the results of a concept inherited from the distant past that glorified *el hob el ozri* or romantic love, and that considered marriage, of which sex is a part, as relatively sinful. This led to the division of women into two categories: the female characterized by seductiveness and sexual passion, and the mother pure, virtuous, virgin devoid of sex or passion.

Arab literature is threaded throughout with innumerable examples of these two opposing and contradictory categories of women. The mother symbolizes a great and noble love, whereas the female symbolizes a degraded kind of love. The sacred respect in which Arab men hold their mothers appears clearly in songs, poems, novels and culture.

Most heroines' hope in life is to legitimize their existence through marriage. The woman's world is limited to thinking of men and dreaming of a husband. After marriage, a woman is solely occupied with the art of keeping her husband. The mother trains her daughter to perfect this art and says to her: 'You must be a new woman to him every day, a woman who is challenging, tempting and seductive.'[25]

The man who marries a working woman, one with a strong personality and who is self-confident, is looked upon as being weak and dominated by his wife.[26] He is depicted as having opposed his mother who always warned him against allowing his wife to go out to work. Naguib Mahfouz describes this husband as being a failure because he is leading a life in which decisions rest with the wife who has the upper hand.

Naguib Mahfouz depicts the woman, Rabab, as bearing no real love for her husband and of nurturing a passion for another man. She betrays her husband with her lover and the author does not forgive her, but makes her die during an abortion.

For man, the feminine woman represents danger and an ancient fear, both related to sex. He therefore wishes her to be pure like his mother, in other words not a female, and as passive and weak as an angel child. At the same time he harbours a burning desire for the female. Her seductiveness and her charms captivate him, yet he is afraid of these qualities because when faced by them his resistance collapses.

Most contemporary Arab writers manifest an undisguised hatred towards bold and emancipated women. The hero of one of Abdel Hamid Gouda El Sahar's books feels disgust when he sees his beloved, Kawsar, wearing a bathing suit: 'His blood raced hotly through his head and he was seized with a feeling of impatience and disgust. She appeared to him shallow and abhorrent.'[27]

Most stories and novels depict the conservative type of man, overcome with repulsion when faced with an educated woman who mixes freely and dances with men. Yet, at the same time, he is overcome by an equal if not greater repulsion when in the presence of a woman whose face is hidden behind a veil or who comes from a poor family and is liable to be led astray because of her poverty. The educated emancipated woman, however, falls lower than any other in his eyes just because she is liberated. Torn on all sides by these conflicting forces, his defences completely collapse and he ends up

165

in a state of confusion: 'He felt as though everything had collapsed around him, and struck out blindly on to the road, like one who was lost. Deep down inside of him was the feeling of being surrounded by a strange and alien world.'[28]

Arab men are becoming more and more insecure and confused with the increasing number of women seeking, and finding, employment outside the home, and participating actively in the life of society. This movement away from domestic imprisonment has taken on momentum, especially after the spread of socialist ideas to the Arab countries. Arab literature has started to reflect this growing tendency and the conflicts and problems arising from it. Men tend to support the idea of women seeking a career or a job, and looking for work in order to earn money; but for them this remains simply a help in shouldering the financial responsibilities of the family, and ought to be only a secondary function for the wife whose main role is to look after her husband and children. The ideal woman in novels is still the beautiful, quietly angelic and obedient female, who does not show any particular boldness or ambition. The perfect woman is as pure, and as sweet, and as gently unassuming, as she ever was. A woman with courage or ambition, with eyes wide open, and who shows audacity and strength, is still considered ugly, repulsive, coarse and vulgar. In other words she symbolizes the prostitute, the fallen and degraded female.

The division of women into two separate categories is very clear in the works of Naguib Mahfouz and particularly in his famous *Thoulathia* (Trilogy) In this novel we have the character of the pure and virtuous Amina and her opposite pole, the prostitute Hania Om Yaseen. Other characters are the beautiful, shy and timid Aisha whose counterpart is the ugly, bold and brazen Khadiga. The novel also portrays two kinds of love, romantic love or *hob ozri* where sanctity and purity reign supreme, and on the other hand the passions of sex and sensuality, forbidden and sinful, as embodied in the lives of prostitutes and degraded sluts.

Arab writers have therefore borrowed from the categorization of women institutionalized by the patriarchal system. For, in this system, a woman belongs either to the category which is composed of sacred pure mothers and frigid, chaste, respectable wives, or to that which groups together the prostitute and the mistress, women who are warm, pulsating, seductive, but despised.

Naguib Mahfouz tried to use sexual aggression against women as a symbol of aggression against a nation or people. On the very same night that Yaseen chooses to violate his wife's black girl servant, the father forces their neighbour Om Mariam, to sleep with him, while the British troops march into the district of Cairo in which he lives. But despite this symbolism, at the individual level the honour and integrity of women remains for Naguib Mahfouz a totally different thing to that of men. The honour of women is preserved or lost depending upon the type of sexual relations which they have with men, rather than on the other aspects of their life.

It is ironic, then, that the woman prostitute plays a much more important role in Arabic literature than that which is accorded to the pure and virtuous woman. It is as though purity and virtue are not attractive enough to evoke interest, whether in real life or in the stories of men and women conjured up by an artist's imagination. The prostitute seems to symbolize real woman, woman without a veil or a mask. She is real woman for she has lifted the mask of deceit from her face and no longer feels a need to pretend that she is in love, or to simulate virtue and devotion.

Contemporary Arab literature is crowded with these prostitute figures. This is particularly the case in the novels of Naguib Mahfouz who is very fond of enveloping his prostitute characters in 'mists of humanity' which are the vapours of his superior soul, tempered with kindness and socialistic ideas. Circumstances for him are the cause of what befalls these women. However, his understanding of their situation has not moved from a superficial analysis of their social conditions to a deep and sensitive realization of the tragedy women are made to live, or a profound understanding of the real factors that have made them victims of unrelenting injustice.

Arab authors and men of letters, whether in the past or in the present, have not been able to penetrate the crucial area of sexual and moral tragedy in the life of women, and have therefore been incapable of expressing anything really worthwhile on the subject.

References

1. Sigmund Freud, *The Taboo of Virginity* (1918) in Standard Edition, Vol. 2, (Hogarth Press, 1957).
2. Abbas Mahmoud El Akkad, *El Mara'a Fil Koran*, (Dar El Hilal, Cairo) P.35.
3. *Tafseer El Tabri*, (El Matba'a El Maimania bi Mis), Vol.12, pp.98-103.
4. Abbas Mahmoud El Akkad, *Woman in the Koran*, (Dar El Hilal, Cairo) pp.17-18.
5. Abbas Mahmoud El Akkad, *Al Insan El Thani*, pp.7-8.
6. Abbas Mahmoud El Akkad, *Sarah*, Silsilit Ikra, No.108, p.129.
7. Abbas Mahmoud El Akkad, *Diywan El Akkad*, p.302.
8. Abbas Mahmoud El Akkad, *Hathihi Al Shagara*, pp.42-50; *Motala'at fil Kotoub wal Hayah*, p.67.
9. Abbas Mahmoud El Akkad, *A'asir Maghreb*, p.57.
10. *Ibid.*
11. Abbas Mahmoud El Akkad, *El Mar'a fil Koran El Kareem*, pp.22-3.
12. Abbas Mahmoud El Akkad, *Sa'at*, pp.20-1.
13. Tolstoy, *Memoirs*, 3rd August 1898, or quoted in Abbas El Akkad, *Hathibi El Shagara*, p.88.
14. Abbas Mahmoud El Akkad, *Sarah*, p.115.
15. *Ibid.*, p.84.
16. Soheir El Kalamawi, *A Thousand and One Nights*, (Dar El Maaref, Egypt, 1976), p.303.
17. Abbas Mahmoud El Akkad, *Hathihi Al Shagara*, p.15.
18. Tewfik El Hakim, *El Robat El Mokadas*.
19. Taha Hussein, *Doa'a El Karawan*, (Dar El Maaref Publishers, Cairo), p.135.
20. This word, *ard*, has a special sense in Arabic. It means the honour of a

man as embodied in his womenfolk. His duty is to keep his honour intact by preventing anyone (apart from the husband) from having any relations with one of the women. This is especially so with regard to protection of virginity.

21. Taha Hussein, *Doa'a El Karawan*, p.151.
22. Naguib Mahfouz, *Bidaya Wa Nihaya*, p.302.
23. *Ibid.*, p.298.
24. Naguib Mahfouz, *El Sarab*, (Maktabat Misr), p.310.
25. El Mazni, *Ibrahim El Thani*, p.52.
26. Naguib Mahfouz, *El Sarab*, p.249.
27. Abdel Hamid Gouda El Sahar, *Kafilat El Zaman*, (Maktabat Misr, Cairo,) p.325.
28. Abdel Hamid Gouda El Sahar, *El Nikab*, (Maktabat Misr), p.284.

PART 4
Breaking Through

18. Arab Pioneers of Women's Liberation

The eastern wing of the Arab world is characterized by its having been the birthplace of the most ancient civilizations known in history, namely those of Egypt, Babylon and Mesopotamia. These civilizations, and in particular Ancient Egypt, were the source of a cultural heritage which the currents of progress carried to Western Europe, and which became an inspiration and a source of knowledge to the further development of the arts and sciences by those Western men and women who took over the torch of human discovery and carried it further along the way. In turn, the Arabs were the initiators and the instruments of vast and dynamic changes which, after the establishement of the Islamic empire, were carried as far as Spain in the West and Indonesia in the East. Yet, despite all these profound and important contributions to the history and development of human civilization, the Arab countries and peoples are now classified among the backward or developing countries and are grouped with a major part of the earth's population under the term 'Third World'.

The forces of imperialism which hurled themselves in successive waves on the Egyptian river valley and the Arab countries were able to plunder many of their material and cultural riches, to conceal many historical truths and facts, and to distort or falsify the contributions that great Arab thinkers and savants have made to the cause of human progress and to laying the foundations of important areas in science and art. Thus it is that the contributions of men like Ibn Seena (Avicenna) and Ibn Khaldoun have remained almost unknown, not only in the West, but also in the East.

The Arab countries today are the arena of a continuing struggle carried on by neo-colonialism, a struggle waged with no respite on all fronts, be they economic, political, social or cultural, and in which all its forces and weapons

169

are utilized. The natural resources and riches of these countries are still mainly the preserve of imperialism and giant multinational corporations which pump out of these lands whatever they may have to offer. The vast majority still suffer from poverty, disease and ignorance, and little change has been brought to their lives. Every day they watch the riches of their land, of the earth upon which they walk and which is theirs, being drained away so that wealth can accumulate in almost unimaginable amounts in the hands of an infinitesimal minority who wield economic power in America and Europe, and the small number of Arab rulers who continue to co-operate with them.

The Arab peoples, whether men or women, have continued to resist the forces which deprive them of their right to a human and peaceful existence. Time and again they have risen up in revolt to overthrow reactionary rulers or fought to expel foreign invaders, whether from Persia, Turkey, France, Britain, or America.

Over the years Egypt has remained the heart of the Arab world due to its strategic position, the size of its population and its long history of resistance against colonialism and imperialism. Very often it has played a leading revolutionary role in the political struggles of the Arab countries, and also acted as a cultural centre of primary importance.

Egypt and the Arab world lived through many a dark decade, especially during the 19th century. The conditions of its people regressed visibly. The rulers of the country, in close co-operation with British and French imperialists imposed heavy burdens upon them in all areas of life whether economic, political or cultural. Woman's lot, as usual, was the worst since she had to support the double load of a patriarchal as well as autocratic class system.

However, extending through the second half of the 19th century, the people's resistance to foreign and local domination was mounting steadily, despite periods of retreat. This was accompanied by a vigorous reawakening and enlightenment in the areas of philosophy and political thought and knowledge. Gamal El Dine El Afghani was one of the notable pioneers and leaders of this awakening. Together with a group of his disciples, he played a prominent role in propagating progressive ideas on many important issues. One of his disciples, Ahmed Fares El Shidyak, published a book called *One Leg Crossed Over the Other* in 1855. This is considered one of the first books written in support of women's emancipation. Another leading thinker was Rifa'a Rafi'i El Tahtawi who insisted on the need to educate women and liberate them from the numerous injustices to which they were exposed. His two books, *A Guide to the Education of Girls and Boys* published in 1872 and *A Summary Framework on Paris* published in 1902, are considered milestones as far as the cause of women is concerned.

These pioneers campaigned widely for a popular Arab movement against imperialism, and called upon the Arab people to fight relentlessly against all the limitations imposed upon their independence and freedom. Their patriotic and enlightened ideas led them to realize that the cause of women's emancipation was one of the crucial fronts in the struggle against backwardness, foreign colonialism, and internal reactionary forces.

Among the well-known leaders in this intellectual and cultural awakening were Abdallah Nadeem and El Sheikh Mohammed Abdou, both of whom contributed in a very substantial manner to the progressive trends in Egypt and the Arab countries. Sheikh Mohammed Abdou wrote on numerous occasions criticizing the inferior position allotted to women and vigorously attacking the practice of marrying several women and divorcing them without restraint, both of which were considered the natural right of men. He also campaigned for the abolition of concubinage and women slaves, and upheld the principle of equality between women and men as being the essence of Islamic values.

As a result of these ideas, Sheikh Mohammed Abdou was exposed to virulent attacks launched against him by the religious authorities and thinkers of the time. But he did not retreat or hesitate to continue propagating his ideas. He maintained that one of the most important sources of the weakness and passivity which had assailed the Arab peoples was the backwardness of women, since they have been deprived of knowledge and assiduously kept away from its sources, in contradiction to what is required and necessitated both by life and religion. This has been done by constructing an almost impenetrable wall around them. In one of his speeches at the Islamic Charitable Association, he said: 'We wish that our daughters should be educated. For Allah the Almighty has explained "To them are due the same good deeds that we expect from them." There are many sacred verses that repeat the same idea, and clarify that both man and woman share in fulfilling the same duties towards life and towards religion. To leave our girls a prey to ignorance, and taken up with stupid pursuits, is indeed a great crime.'[1]

One of the most important books dealing with the question of women's emancipation is entitled *Tehrir El Mara'a* (Liberation of Women). It was published in the year 1900 and its author was Kassim Ameen. In 1911 he followed it by a second book entitled *El Mara'a El Guedida* (The New Woman). Kassim Ameen insisted on the need to educate woman so that she could protect the family and bring up her children in a better way. He based himself strictly on the teachings of Islam and in no way infringed upon them, yet he became the target of violent accusations levelled against him by the religious authorities and thinkers of El Azhar University. These men were important pillars supporting the rule of the Khedive Ismail, a rule that involved a barbaric exploitation of the Egyptian people and a tyranny supported by the colonial powers. Kassim Ameen was also exposed to the disapproval and anger of the Khedive himself, and was attacked by politicians of the time, including the national leader, Mostapha Kamal, who wrote an article in the newspaper *El Lewa* in 1901 opposing Kassem Amin's ideas about the emancipation of women. As a matter of fact, despite its rather ambiguous patriotic colours, *El Lewa* was very often the mouthpiece of orthodox reactionary leaders and thinkers. During the same period, Abdel Hameed Khairi published his book, *Solid Arguments in Answer to Kassim Ameen,* in which he resolutely opposed the idea of women's liberation. Similarly another author, Ahmed El Boulaki, wrote a treatise entitled *The Pleasant Companion Exposing the Dangers of*

Women's Liberation.

However, Ahmed Lotfi El Sayed and the group of men who co-operated with him expressed the progressive ideas of their generation in the newspaper, *El Gareeda*. He vigorously supported the campaign in favour of women, and was joined in this effort by Waley El Dine Yakan, Saad Zaghloul (later the national leader of Egypt after the First World War), Mohammed Hussein Heikal, Taha Hussein and Salama Moussa,[2] Mostapha Fahmy, Farag Antoun, Ahmed El Zayat and Mostapha El Manfalouti. The newspapers, *El Manar* (The Lighthouse) published by Rasheed Ali Rida', *Al Moktataf* and *Al Hilal*, opened their columns to articles on women's liberation.

Arab women participated right from the beginning in this struggle for the emancipation of women. Among these pioneers was Aisha El Taymouria who composed literary works and poems in Arabic, Turkish and Persian. She was followed by Zeinab Fawaz who built a reputation for poetry and eloquence. A third was Malak Hefni Nassef who became famous as *Bahissat El Badia* (the Searcher in the Desert) (1886-1918). She wielded her powerful pen in defence of women's rights. She was a contemporary of Kassim Ameen, but her writings were considered as a development of *Rifaa El Tahtawi's* ideas which she considered reformist, whereas Kassem Ameen supported them as being a call to women's liberation.[3] Malak Hefni Nassef was such a talented writer that Lotfi El Sayed described her works as being a true example of those women authors who have surpassed many of the men writers living during the same period.[4] She was a consistent fighter for the right of girls to education.

Another notable pioneer among women writers was May Ziada. She was able, despite the very strict and reactionary orthodoxy prevalent at the time, to establish a literary salon in Cairo during the years 1915 and 1916. Numerous Arab and Egyptian thinkers, men of letters and writers used to attend the literary debates she was accustomed to organize every Tuesday. She was only twenty years old, yet because of her mature and brilliant mind the old venerable generation of thinkers and writers in Egypt gathered around her salon.

May Ziada lived in Egypt, but her mother originated from Palestine and her father was Lebanese. Her young age and her parentage were both handicaps, but nevertheless she was able to impose her personality on literary circles in Egypt, to mix and talk freely with men, and to correspond regularly with them at a time when the veil still hung heavily over the faces of many Egyptian women in the same sector of society.

Her life ended in tragedy, a true reflection of the cruelty, loneliness and difficult problems that surround an intelligent, sensitive and gifted woman living in a man's society where females are looked upon as receptacles for the development of the embryo or as bodies designed for male pleasure. She was exposed to a severe emotional crisis as a result of her love for Abbas Mahmoud El Akkad, the Egyptian writer mentioned above. Their relationship was a failure and a severe shock to her, largely as a result of his backward, complicated and confuse attitude towards women. Once their relations were severed, she lived in terrible lonliness despite the fact that many men were courting her favours. She was looking for a man who could understand her as a human being, and as a a mind and heart, rather than as a body to be desired and used. But she was never to find such a man.

No one could understand her tragedy, her sadness, and the reason for her withdrawal into solitude. Her parents and relations accused her of madness, and insisted on her being admitted to the Asfouria Hospital for Mental Diseases in Lebanon. As she stepped over the threshold, she looked around her and then said quietly, 'Could they not find a more dignified prison for me than this one?'[5] She begged the hospital authorities to let her leave, and went on hunger strike time and again. This situation continued for several months until a committee of eminent doctors was commissioned to examine her. The report was written by Dr. Martin, a Frenchman, and it categorically affirmed that she was completely free of illness, whether physical or mental. But the hospital authorities still refused to discharge her, on the pretext that she was in need of care to improve her health before leaving.[6]

May Ziada's life ended in a small flat in Cairo where she died while still in the freshness of her youth, with no one by her side, abandoned, misunderstood. She left behind her writings, poems, paintings and the lectures she had delivered in Egypt and Lebanon about literature, art and the emancipation of women. An exceptional talent and a gifted artist, she was rewarded for her genius by loneliness, accusations of madness and an early death.

May Ziada's fate, in all its sadness and cruelty, is no different from the fate of any woman who is a pioneer and who tries to change the attitudes and behaviour of society towards women. It is no different from that of the intelligent and even brilliant women (wise witches or sorceresses) who were tortured and burnt in the Middle Ages, accused of madness or sin or witchcraft. Nor is it any different to the fate of many clever and gifted women, whose only reward for their outstanding qualities is terrible loneliness or accusations of abnormality, hysteria or madness.

In agricultural societies such as Egypt, the vast majority of women have toiled in the fields, side by side with men, for thousands of years. The economy of the country and its production therefore depend on the sweat of peasant men and women. Were it not for the fact that rural women leave their homes every day before sunrise, it would not be possible for the men who oppose women's emancipation to have their morning meal. Yet, in Arab societies, there are still a large number of men who do not agree to women going out to work or being educated. Their argument is that, if a woman leaves her house to engage in such activities, she will lose her femininity — and probably her chastity and honour too.

These arguments are always brandished whenever we come to the question of woman's work in a patriarchal and class society. Such societies do not permit woman to work outside the home except for the purpose of exploiting her even more atrociously, since in most cases she is an unpaid hand whose labour is forthcoming as a free part of the total family effort. This is the case of rural women who work in the fields as an appendage of the father, the husband or the brother, and under their control. Another example is that of female labour in the factories, where recourse is had to women if there is a scarcity of labour, as happens during wars, or in the early stages of industrialization, or when the capitalist or the State desires to have the same work done for a lower wage. Very often, especially in the so-called developing countries, child labour is also drawn upon as a part of the family effort in the fields, to do specific jobs like harvesting or fighting against pests, or in cities to increase family income by being engaged in a small workshop or trade. In all cases the woman or the child, whether at home or at work, is under the absolute authority of men.

Arab women first penetrated into the factories after the First World War when there was a rapid drop in the availability of male labour. The Arab countries, like other countries of the world, were obliged to engage female labour in order to ensure that the factories did not close down, and that the machines continued to turn at the required speed. A contributing factor to the need for female labour was that imported goods became scarce and had to be replaced by locally manufactured articles. This led to an expansion of industry in many countries and a subsequent demand for more labour.

These opportunities for employment naturally first attracted those who were poor and needy among the women and girls. For in the poorer classes of society, where people face a continuous struggle in order to obtain their daily bread, people cannot afford to be sensitive about traditions and social customs. The barriers of society and old values therefore collapse before the need for food. A man who belongs to the working or poor peasant class is forced to buy a loaf of bread to feed himself, rather than a veil with which to cover his wife or daughter's face. Poverty will force him into sending his wife, his daughter or his sister to work as a servant in a house where there may be many men, or as a factory hand where she stands side by side with men for long hours of the day. He cannot in these circumstances allow himself to think too deeply about the traditions and moral codes which prevent the sexes from mixing freely.

That is why it is only women belonging to the middle or upper classes who have known what it is to wear a veil or to be imprisoned in their homes. For the economic need to send women folk out to work does not arise in such families.

In Arab countries the poor classes represent the vast majority of the people. The feudal and capitalist classes, and the states which represent their interests, have exploited the situation of the hungry and deprived to offer them the most arduous and inferior of jobs for the lowest pay. Women and children, of course, had the worst of the bargain and the conditions of work, the pay and the types of labour offered to them were right at the bottom of the ladder, in the deepest of inhuman pits. The husband, after a day's work would return to his home and rest, whereas the working woman had no time to rest. Once back, she had to look after the needs of her husband and her children. She is therefore torn between her activities at the work place and her duties at home; constantly threatened with being discharged if she becomes pregnant, compelled to look after her child, once born and faced with divorce if at any time the husband feels that she is neglecting him and his home.

In Egypt the first census of women participating in the wage-earning labour force was taken in 1914. They were only 20,000 at the time, that is 5% of the total number of employees. In those days girls and women from poor families were seeking jobs in large numbers in the factories and ginning mills. The working day exceeded 14 hours, and the daily pay was around three piastres but sometimes dropped as low as 18 millimes.[7] However these few piastres were better than the hunger that threatened many families. There were no labour laws to enforce any health or safety standards to protect the women, and the sections in which they worked were always worse than those of the men. The value of women was considered socially lower than that of men. In addition they did not protest or struggle for better conditions, accustomed as they were to accepting humiliation and contempt. As a result of inhuman working conditions, long hours, exhaustion and inadequate nutrition a woman could not stand the pace at the factory for more than four or five years. after which she was no longer fit for anything. The owner of the establishment would discharge her just as he would get rid of a worn out part, and she would be thrown out onto the streets to be replaced immediately by a young woman eagerly waiting at the gates of the factory for her chance to earn a loaf of bread or a plate of lentils.

These poor unhappy women, exhausted in body and soul, whether at work or in their homes, were the first women to rebel in 20th Century Egypt, the first to strike and to occupy the premises of the factories, the first to demonstrate in the streets and demand that their human dignity be respected, the hours of work be shortened and determined by law, and maternal leave be accorded for pregnancy and childbirth. In those days no maternal leave whatsoever was allowed, and so a working woman, who had given birth to a child, would hasten to the factory on the following morning, lest she lose her job. Sometimes she would even hide the fact that she was married, since for the employer this would often be enough reason to discharge her. Women who were looking for jobs would never mention that they were married for young unmarried girls were always preferred by the management. If a woman should happen to become pregnant she would do everything to hide the signs as carefully as possible, as though she had committed some crime, or was bearing an illegitimate child. In most cases she would try some primitive rural method of abortion, such as introducting the stalk of a vegetable called *mouloukhia* into the cervix of the uterus. This very often ended up in her dying of haemorrhage or infection.

During the same period women of the upper classes had started to form the first women's organization. These efforts bore fruit in 1923. However in view of their wealth, and the fact that they were isolated from the poorer classes, they knew nothing about the conditions of working women, and the inhuman exploitation which was their lot. One of the demonstrations organized by working women ended in a gathering at the premises of the new Women's Federation, but the aristocratic leaders who were responsible for its activities paid no attention to the grievances of these poor women, and concentrated on the issue of abolishing the veil, which was unlikely to evoke much enthusiasm amongst them since in any case the working women in factories and fields had never known what it was to wear a veil.

Toiling women in the industrial areas and rural villages constituted the female force that participated vigorously and effectively in the national revolution of 1919. They went out onto the rural roads, side by side with the men, cut the telephone wires and disrupted the railway lines in order to paralyse the movements of the British troops. Some of them participated in storming the improvised camps and jails in which many of those who had led the uprisings or participated in them had been imprisoned. Women were killed or injured when British troops fired on them.

It was from the ranks of these toiling masses of women that the female martyrs of the 1919 national revolution came. Some of them are known, such as Shafika Mohammed who was killed by the British on the 14th of March 1919, Hamida Khalil from Kafr El Zaghari Gamalia,[8] Sayeda Hassan, Fahima Riad and Aisha Omar. But hundreds of poor women lost their lives without anybody being able to trace their names.

The industrial workers and peasants played an outstanding and powerful role in the national uprising of 1919, but history and historians have devoted their efforts and concentrated the limelight on the leaders who were drawn from the ranks of the upper classes. Similarly little has been said about the masses of poor women who rushed into the national struggle without counting the cost, and who lost their lives, whereas the lesser contributions of aristocratic women leaders have been noisily acclaimed and brought to the forefront.

The poorer classes of Egyptian men and women did not gain much out of the revolution of 1919. They were fuel to its flames, burnt in the conflagration, consumed. The fruits of their sacrifices, the benefits of their revolutionary struggle went to the upper classes, just as the credit had gone to them before.

What happened in the political struggle against the British was repeated in the movement for women's emancipation. The movement was not representative of the overwhelming majority of toiling women, and its leadership ended, just as the political leadership did, by seeking accommodations with the British, the Palace and the reactionary forces in the country. The women's movement therefore became a pawn utilized to serve the interests of the palace and the reactionary parties. It kept away from an active involvement in the national and political life of the country, and limited its activities to charitable and social welfare work.[9]

In 1923, as I mentioned briefly, Hoda Shaarawi founded the Women's Federation. This organization succeeded in raising the age of marriage for girls to 16 years in 1924, but failed to make any changes in the laws related to marriage, divorce etc or to win for women the right to vote, despite the persistent efforts made by it under the leadership of Hoda Shaarawi and Cesa Nabarawi. Although 53 years have elapsed since the birth of the Federation, nothing has been achieved since it did not have the backing and active involvement of women behind it. Marriage laws in Egypt until today still permit a man to divorce his wife whenever he wishes, and to marry several women. Some Arab countries, however, have moved ahead of Egypt and have developed their laws to ensure that they respond to the changing situation of Arab women. As regards the vote, Egyptian women did not gain this right until the constitution of 1956 was promulgated under Nasser's regime. This was one of the gains linked to the victory over the British, French, and Israeli invasion of Egypt, the nationalization of foreign capital and a series of social gains for the underprivileged classes.

Egypt was not the only Arab country in which women participated actively in the struggle against foreign imperialism and internal oppression. Women all over the Arab world fought side by side with men in the struggle for national liberation and social justice. In 1914 Syrian women joined the secret societies which were opposing an attempt to change the administration and the life of the country so as to conform with the Turkish pattern. In 1919 Damascus witnessed the first women's demonstration against French occupation, which was repeatedly fired upon by the troops. Once more, women participated in the revolutionary uprising of the Syrian people in 1925. Palestinian women in their turn have taken to arms side by side with men in the popular resistance against the Israeli occupation of Arab lands.

In Iraq, women played an important role against imperialism and the reactionary intrigues of the Royal Family, and have worked actively to accelerate the national and social transformation of the country. Iraqi women now enjoy equal political rights with men and an Iraqi woman is always included as a Minister in the different Cabinets.

In other countries, like Jordan, despite the severe curtailment of democratic liberties, and the constraints put on all political activity, at different periods women have organized their struggle on the various fronts of activity whether economic, political or social. Many demonstrations have brought out thousands of Jordanian women who have courageously faced the police and armed forces in defence both of political prisoners placed behind bars by King Hussein's regime and of Palestinian guerrillas rounded up by police and many forces.

Sudanese women have a fine tradition behind them. They were an important force in the Sudanese national liberation movement against the British, and were able to build up a strong and active Federation which had deep roots among urban and rural women and was known for its enlightened and advanced stand on the crucial issues which affect the future of the Sudan and of Sudanese women. Many Sudanese women have given their lives for the cause of their people and for the emancipation of their sisters in the towns and villages. Fatima Ibrahim is a woman whom many will remember.

In 1943 Lebanese women organized huge demonstrations in the streets of Beirut and other towns in protest against the arrest of the political leaders of their country by the French authorities. Algerian women, from all walks of life and in all spheres of activity, joined the ranks of the revolution against French occupation. The land of a million martyrs was also the land of hundreds of women martyrs and of female heroism even under the pain and humiliation of the most savage, inhuman and sophisticated torture which only Nazi-occupied countries and what was once South Vietnam have known. Gamila Abou Heraid and Gamila Abou Azza are only two amongst many others.

Palestinian women have maintained the same traditions and the same fighting spirit as their sisters in Algeria. The tribulations and misery of a people deprived of a home and a land for the last 30 years or so, and made to undergo untold oppression and injustice at the hands of the British even when their land had not yet been taken away, has produced generations of men and women steeled in the knowledge of sacrifice and the capacity to resist. Palestinian women have crept under cover of night into Israeli-occupied land in many an armed raid aimed at keeping the notion of an Arab Palestine alive. They have organized covert resistance against the military and administrative authorities, and participated by hundreds and thousands wherever it was possible to raise the banner of civil disobedience or to demonstrate in the cities and towns of Jerusalem, Nablis, Rafah, El Khalil and Bissan.

Every day women and young girls volunteer to join the ranks of the Palestine Liberation Army, either in the armed forces or in the medical and social auxiliary services. They have lost everything, so what do they have to fear? The long list of martyrs could fill the pages of a whole chapter, but among the most well known are Leila Khalid, Fatima Bernawi, Amina Dahbour, Shadia Abou Ghazala and others whose intrepid stories will one day be listened to with passion by the coming generations of young girls and women.

In every corner of the Arab world, women have protested, fought and resisted: in the Democratic Republic of Yemen and in Somalia where they have been given the same rights as men, and are working side by side with them to build a new society free of oppression and exploitation, and in Kuwait, Libya, Tunisia and Morocco where they have contributed with varying degrees of understanding, fortitude and self-sacrifice to the cause of human justice, freedom and peace for man and woman alike. In some of the Arab countries, women have gained new rights in society and within the family. New laws have been promulgated abolishing polygamy and according equal status to men and women as far as divorce is concerned.

Women have been accorded the vote in most Arab countries. But, in spite of their new opportunities, very few are in a position to take advantage of them and to participate in politics, or present themselves as candidates for elections. In Egypt the number of women who go to the polls does not exceed 0.53% of the total votes cast in the general elections!

As time goes by, it is becoming clearer that the recognition of women's right to vote, or to take an active part in political life, does not on its own make any fundamental change in the position of women who stand on the lowest rungs of society. Whether they throng to the voting booths or abstain, succeed in getting into parliament or fail, the position of a woman belonging to the poorer classes of society does not improve except in very minor ways. She remains a prey to exploitation and oppression, a vassal to her husband and a prisoner of the class to which she belongs. Even when there is a strong women's organization that can reap the benefits of new laws, and a sweeping movement towards social change, the progress that women can attain remains limited.

In no country in the world has it happened that women have achieved equal rights with men simply because they have been given their political rights. All the clamour of voices on radio, television and in public meetings, all the oral and written statements, all the clash of cymbals, the beating of drums and the floating of banners, all the throbbing speeches on democratic rights and the freedom of women cannot change the fact that, as long as feudalistic, capitalistic and paternalistic systems persist, the votes of women will very often be used against the real interests of women, in exactly the same way as the votes of the workers and peasants are very often used against their interests.

The Egyptian Revolution of 1952 accorded to workers and peasants 50% of the seats in the National Assembly. But not one seat has been reserved for women. And despite the fact that worker and peasant representatives enjoy the privilege of wielding half the parliamentary voting power, in fact it is almost never the genuine and authentic representatives of the toiling masses who have been able to get themselves elected. Most often it is representatives of the upper classes who have been able to occupy the seats that are not theirs by right, in the name of the workers and peasants. A thousand subterfuges have been used to operate this conjuror's trick. The definition of a worker or a peasant has itself been so elastic and fluid that it allowed those belonging to high income groups to come forward disguised as workers and peasants.

If a certain number of seats in the National Assembly were reserved for women, the result would probably be the same. Women of the upper classes who support the *status quo* would probably be elected, or perhaps some of the men might even disguise themselves as women and slink in to the female compound!

Only with a strong militant organization, progressive and truly democratic parties, and a society where movements for social change are gathering momentum, can such measures bear fruit. In this sense, legal and political rights for women can be of value only if backed by a popular revolutionary movement.

Despite the fact that in Egypt we have had a woman Cabinet Minister since 1962 and six women members of parliament, the vast majority of Egyptian women are still poor, ignorant, illiterate and riddled with disease, and spend long hours of the day and part of the night toiling in the factories, offices, fields and homes. They live a life of exhaustion, inhuman and pitiless, a prey to the autocratic domination of a father, a husband, a brother, or any other male member of the family. Even the small minority of women, usually from the middle class, who have had a higher or university education are still prisoners of old traditions, exposed to the vagaries of the man or men in the family, and to the weight of a new burden, that of a full-time or part-time job with all the extra effort it entails.

If the affairs of state or administrative power pass into the hands of women within the framework of a class society built on capitalism and of a patriarchal family system, men and women will still remain the victims of exploitation. If a woman President should replace Nixon or Ford or Carter in the United States, as long as the structure of society remains as it is, capitalism will impose its exploitation, its expansionist aims and its aggressive policies, and patriarchal values will dominate the life of women. When Golda Meir became Prime Minister of Israel, things remained the same for both men and women, and the policy of Israel continued to be that of aggressive imperialist Zionism. The fact that Bandaranaike was Prime Minister in Sri Lanka, or Indira Gandhi held the post in India has not abolished the patriarchal system or rescued women from the clutches of exploitation in society and in the home.

The complete and real liberation of women, whether in the Arab countries or the West or the Far East, can only become a fact when humanity does away with class society and exploitation for all time, and when the patriarchal system with its values, structures and vestiges has been erased from the life and mind of the people. In other words, women can only become truly liberated under a socialist system where classes have been abolished and where, furthermore, the systems and concepts and laws of patriarchalism have been completely eradicated.

These fundamental changes have not yet taken place in any of the countries of the world, including the Arab world or even the countries that have chosen the socialist path where, despite the fact that the situation of women has changed radically in many ways, the heritage of patriarchalism is fighting its last battles.

The liberation of women, however, is now on the order of the day, and in every part of the world this movement is gathering an unprecedented momentum.

Perhaps the most important steps taken by the Egyptian Revolution of 1952 are those related to the establishment of a ceiling on landholdings, the drastic limitations put on feudal land ownership and feudal exploitation, as well as the nationalization of the banks, insurance companies and big corporations. The National Charter promulgated on 21 May 1962 contains an extremely important provision of paramount significance not only for women, but for the whole of society: 'There is an urgent need to abolish the remaining chains and constraints that severely limit the free action of woman, so that she may be enabled to participate with dynamism and effectiveness in building up a new life.'

Throughout the past period, since the beginning of the Revolution, increasing numbers of girls and women have sought education in the schools and universities, and an increasing flow of female labour has entered many areas of productive, administrative and service activity. Nevertheless, the chains have not been lifted from the majority of Egyptian women.

The same situation prevails in other Arab countries where socialist slogans have been raised and socialist policies implemented, and where the national charters or laws underline the need to remove all obstacles that prevent women from participating freely in the life of society and that narrow down their chances of gainful and fruitful employment. This is true of the Sudan, Iraq, Algeria, Somalia, South Yemen and Syria. A consistent socialist policy would have required that all these countries' governments promulgate, in addition to economic legislation aiming at ensuring real social justice, a series of new laws and regulations governing the relationships between men and women, abolishing the dominion of men over women in all spheres of life, ensuring for women the exercise of all the economic, social, moral and personal rights enjoyed by men, and relieving women of the heavy burdens related to household chores and the bringing up of children.

None of the Arab countries, however, have taken such steps. Some of them have put limitations on a man's right to divorce or on his freedom to marry several wives. The laws related to marriage, divorce, parentage, inheritance and the charge of the children continue, however, to give the man a predominant position in almost all Arab countries.

Arab women have gained new rights in society and the family as a result of the more enlightened position taken by some rulers and thinkers, as a reflection of new economic and social necessities, and due to the increasing consciousness of women, their rising educational standards and increased participation in work and in earnings that are characteristic of new situations. But these changes have not affected the majority — the millions and millions of poor, toiling, illiterate women who continue to combine their arduous and exhausting tasks outside the home with the burdens associated with husbands and many children. Millions and millions continue to bow their heads in obedience to the laws of marriage and divorce. They continue subjected in the family and outside to the iron fetters of outworn traditions and double moral standards that outlaw the woman alone and punish her, and that cause girls and women to support alone the suffering of inhuman marriage relationships and the sexual anarchy and capriciousness of men. Millions of women go on enduring man's thirst for more than one wife or mistress, the threat of divorce that hangs over their heads like the Sword of Damocles, the tragedies related to virginity, chastity, honour and circumcision, the fear of pregnancy and child bearing whether inside or outside of marriage, the problems and risks of illegal abortion, and even the worries of birth control which the man usually refuses to share.

The problems of Arab women undoubtedly differ according to the class to which they belong. They become worse the lower the woman drops in the social scale. There is, however, an area of problems common to all women, namely that of marriage and divorce. The moment a woman marries she finds herself living under the shadow of what is known as the 'common law'. And we can say without hesitation that, at least in Egypt, this law has not received the attention and concern it deserves, from any man or group of men associated with the political leadership of ruling circles of the country, whether prior to or after the Revolution of 1952. It has always been, and to this day remains, the exclusive domain of government officials in the Ministry of Social Welfare, or of a limited number of upper class women in their various organizations or groups. Moreover, some of the women leaders who have become members of the people's assembly (the National Assembly or Parliament) have assiduously kept away from discussions and activities related to these laws. They thereby sought either to avoid the accusation of being narrow-minded and giving their attention to limited 'women's problems' or did not have the courage to face the orthodox religious and reactionary forces strongly entrenched in many sections of society. Politicians, even those who claimed to be socialist in orientation, continued to lack the necessary seriousness and understanding when faced with matters related to women's liberation, or to the common law. They consider that questions dealing with relations between men and women have nothing to do with 'higher politics' or the 'great issues of society'. Yet they participate with enthusiasm in any electoral meeting, or trivial discussion in the socialist union, or in the people's assembly, and throng eagerly to the receptions and parties so common in diplomatic life.

And yet the 'high politics' of a country and the 'great issues of society' are not related to, and are never really settled in the meeting halls, corridors and salons for which these men and women have such a great predilection. They rest, in fact, with the small events and details of the daily life of millions and millions of men and women. They depend, for example, on our capacity to ensure that the peasants leave for their fields in the morning after having passed urine which is free of blood, since bilharzia has been calculated to cause an economic loss to the country equivalent to 50% of the national income. They depend on our capacity to provide each worker with a breakfast of cheese and *foul* (a bean with a high protein content) every morning before he or she leaves for his work, so that they can stand in front of the machine without undue fatigue. They depend on the husband not beating his peasant wife every day before she leaves for the field and making her a cripple, on women employees riding on public transport without being trampled underfoot or physically assaulted, on a wife being able to refuse sex with her husband if she is tired or ill, on the man caring sufficiently for his children and not escaping into the arms of another wife or mistress.

These apparently small and trivial happenings of everyday life such as eating, urinating, having sexual intercourse, going out to work each morning and riding a bus or a tram, are the things that constitute society, a system and a State. They are the elements, the material of politics, of 'higher politics' of 'great issues', of important battles and ringing slogans of human progress and civilization. Those who are involved in 'politics' and yet neglect such matters do not even know what the word politics means. For peasants cannot work and produce effectively if they suffer pain and lose blood every time they go to the toilet. A male or a female worker will be unable to produce with calm and efficiency unless sexually satisfied. A wife cannot be constructive and participate in the life of society if she is oppressed sexually and emotionally. In other words, human beings in general cannot work and create and produce if they are not permitted to think freely and healthily about sex, experience it with depth, and practise it with understanding. When people think or feel or practise, there are always economic repercussions to the way in which they do these things. It is, therefore, not possible to separate the sexual and emotional life of people, and their economic life. Any separation is artificial and will lead to ideas that are incomplete, shallow and distorted. The history of the human race was not created by economic activity alone as some socialists seem to believe, nor by sexual instinct and sexual relations alone as the Freudians tend to uphold, but by an equal combination and interrelation of both, in which each of the two stands at the same level and possesses the same importance.

Taking an interest in the cause of women's liberation or in the common laws of marriage and divorce will not, therefore, reduce the prestige of the socialist politician or make out of him a person of minor value. On the contrary, one of the essential criteria by which a true socialist can be judged is his attitude towards women, and towards the cause of their liberation. The more socialist a person is, and the more human, the greater will be his or her preoccupation with the situation of women.

A change in the law is not sufficient to bring about real liberation. Any law can remain a few dead words unless the necessary cultural, political and organizational efforts are made among the people so as to ensure a radical change in the institutions which govern the life of men and women, and in particular the abolition of the patriarchal system and the traditions and values it has maintained.

References

1. Abbas El Akkad, *Mohammed Abdou*, (Tabet El Tarbiah wal Talim, Egypt), p.299.
2. Salama Moussa, *Mokadimet El Superman*, (Introduction to the Superman), (Tabat Salama Moussa, Cairo,) p.29.
3. Magdi Nassef, *Aathar Bahithat El Badia* (Tabat El Mo'assassa El Misria), p.35.
4. Ibrahim Abdou, *Tatawur El Nahda El Nissa' eya*, (El Aadab, Cairo, 1945), p.12.
5. Taher El Tanahi, *El Sa'at El Akhira* (The Last Moments), pp.111-2.
6. *Ibid.*
7. At the present rate of exchange one piastre would be around 1.3 cents; 18 millimes would be almost two cents.
8. Abdel Rahman El Rafi'i, *Fi Aakab El Sawra El Masria*, Vol.I, (Maktabat El Nahda El Masria, Cairo, 1959), p.211; Doria Shafik,1955, p.119.
9. Mohammed Anis, El Sayed Ragab Haraz, *El Tatawour El Siassi Lilmogtama El Masri El Hadith*, Cairo, pp.190-1.

19. Work and Women

For thousands of years, society has imprisoned woman within the four walls of the home and entrusted her with the function of serving the family, the husband and the children, free of charge except for her food, her clothes and a roof over her head. The exceptions to this rule have all along been women workers, peasants, servants and slaves. A woman who was constrained to live within the confines of the home never went out unless there was an overpowering reason to do so, such as a severe illness that had to be treated in hospital. She would then hide her face behind a heavy veil, and be accompanied by a man of the family. Sometimes a woman would be lying on her death bed, yet her husband would refuse to allow her to be examined by a male doctor.

The strict segregation between the sexes that was in vogue among certain classes of society led to the development of female occupations and vocations whose purpose was to cater and serve the cloistered women of the middle and upper classes. One of the first of these vocations was that of nursing, the members of which profession were almost exclusively drawn from the poorer classes since for a girl or woman to work outside the house was considered a shame and a dishonour to the family that was supposed to be capable of feeding and clothing its women folk.

Arab rulers established schools for midwifery and nursing so that those who were trained there could devote themselves to the service of upper class women. For example Mohammed Ali, the ruler of Egypt, in the mid 19th century, noticed that upper class families were in need of the services of nurses and midwives. For this purpose he bought some black Sudanese girl slaves and entrusted a Frenchman called Clot Bey with the task of training them in the art of medicine and surgery.[1] This was in addition to the eunuchs (castrated male slaves) who were the first students in the midwifery school attached to the School of Medicine in Abou Zaabal. In those days, for a woman to appear in the streets was considered a public affront to morality. It is not surprising, therefore, that when the school of nursing and midwifery taught its female students some elements of the anatomy of the human body, Egyptian men expressed their indignation against teaching girls a subject which was in complete variance with what was considered at the time to be the code of morality.[2]

In 1842 the first school of midwifery was established in Egypt. This was followed 31 years later by the first primary school for girls, El Seyoufia, opened in 1873. Its pupils were, to start with, the young white girl slaves destined to serve in the palaces of the ruling class. During the intervening period, no school for girls was established, apart from those destined for poor girls or orphans who were to be trained for domestic work in the houses of the aristocracy, or to cater for some of the needs of the army such as sewing clothes for the soldiers.

The authorities at the beginning strictly forbade the teachers and girls in these schools the right to marry, in order that they might devote themselves completely to the accomplishment of their tasks. A written commitment was taken from each one of them, and these poor girls, in view of their pressing need for the meagre income that would one day be theirs, were forced to accept this condition. As time went by, they constituted a group of lonely and miserable spinsters afflicted with a variety of neuroses and mental illnesses since sexual relations were only allowed within the framework of marriage, or with prostitutes who were considered as degraded and unworthy beings.

It was looked upon as a shame for a respectable family to send one of its daughters to such a school, and so better-off girls remained locked up in the home awaiting the day of marriage. Meanwhile they were assiduously taught the art of female seduction, as the only means to keep a husband once he had been captured. This was all the more necessary since a man was allowed to divorce for the most trifling reason, or indeed for no reason at all, and to marry several women at the same time, in addition to the women slaves whose number was only limited by the means at his disposal.[3]

Official secondary education for girls was only started at the dawn of the 20th Century with the establishment in 1900 of a women teachers section in the Sania School. Secondary education for boys, however, had already been launched in 1825, 75 years earlier. The Egyptian University opened its doors to girls in the year 1929, when it admitted a total of four female students.

The enrolment of girls at all levels of education subsequently gathered increasing momentum, especially after the Revolution of 1952. However, the number of technical and skilled women workers, as compared with the total number of female employees was only 18.9% in 1969. This means that the vast majority of Egyptian women (81.1%) were still occupied in agriculture, domestic service, or minor clerical jobs.

The majority of the women employed in services were doing domestic work as servants. Everyone knows the unspeakable economic, social and sexual exploitation to which female servants were, and still are to a great extent, exposed. Women in the active labour force, earning a salary or wage (i.e. not including peasant women and housewives) represented only 6% of the total female work force (those who belong to the age groups capable of working) and 6.5% of the total active work force in Egypt.[4] It increased to 9% by 1976.

The vast majority of toiling women in Egypt are peasants who work for their men folk and families without receiving any remuneration, or housewives who in essence are unpaid domestic servants. This applies to the great majority of women in all Arab countries. In Syria the active female work force represents only 16.1% of the total number of women. Of the working women, 88% are engaged in agricultural activities while the rest are employed in state administration and institutions, in social services, in industry and in commerce, especially as shop sellers and shop attendants.[5]

Women peasants constitute the bulk of the female work force in Arab countries. Since they are not paid for their work, statistics dealing with different aspects of the labour force often chose to neglect their existence. For example, in the labour force statistics of Egypt, working women are usually calculated as representing only 9% of the total active work force. However, if women peasants are added to the women who work for a wage or salary, the number of female working women would immediately jump to almost half the total active labour force, to become one of the highest proportions in the world.

Paid employment outside the home has no doubt played a role in the emancipation of some Egyptian women, and in particular of those who are educated. They have become economically independent or liberated and a number of them have been able to wrest new rights for themselves from the grasp of society and the family, despite the harshness and injustice of marriage laws in relation to women. Some of them refused to marry as the only way to avoid the risk of becoming victims of such marriage laws, and yet others married and then chose to divorce when they felt that their freedom and independence were being threatened by the husband, the family, or society.

There are no laws in Egypt at present that discriminate between the sexes, in so far as education or employment are concerned. Yet, in actual practice, discrimination is a frequent occurrence. One example of this discrimination is what happens in the appointment of judges. The men who dominate the judicial system in Egypt have been able to prevent women from becoming judges on the assumption that a woman, by her very nature, is unfit to shoulder the responsibilities related to a court of law. This assumption is built on the fact that Islam considers the testimony of one equivalent to that of two women. The argument, therefore, is that testimony only consists in witnessing to something that has or has not happened, and if a woman cannot be trusted to the same degree as a man in such matters, how can she be considered the equal of man when required to give a decision on a point over which two parties are in disagreement?

Although Egyptian women have been accorded ministerial responsibilities since 1962, to this very day they have not been allowed to become judges. Men are still discussing whether women are suited to enter the holy priesthood of the judicial body or not. The last thing I remember reading in relation to this question is an article published in the daily newspaper, *El Akhbar,* on 12 January 1976 where the author maintains that the post of a judge is forbidden to women by Islam: 'It is superfluous to explain, that according to

Islam, ten conditions must be fulfilled for a person to judge. Without these ten conditions, the very essence of "judging" is non-existent, and the right or even possibility to be accorded this high function is lost. These ten conditions are: Islamic belief, reason, *masculinity,* freedom, maturity, justice, knowledge and to be a complete individual with a normal capacity to hear, to see and to speak."[6]

In addition, women are not allowed to hold posts of an executive nature, such as that of a Governor, or the Mayor of a town, or the Head of a village.[7]

This reflects clearly the fundamental contradictions that continue to dominate modern Arab society. For although a woman is allowed to become a Minister, to have under her thousands of male and female employees, and to take decisions on matters of great importance and significance, she is not permitted to become a judge in a small and minor court of law which deals with traffic violations, or limited disputes and quarrels between individuals, or to become the head of a village with a few hundred or thousand inhabitants.

Those who oppose the right or need for women to become judges or heads of villages are inconsistent and afflicted with the same contradictions from which society suffers. None of them seems to have thought of criticizing or of opposing the appointment of a woman as Minister. Does this mean that in their view the functions of a Minister do not require that she should fulfil the same conditions that Islam has laid down for those of a judge, namely, a sound reason, masculinity, a sense of justice, knowledge, and a normal capacity for speech? Or is it that the appointment of a Minister is a decision by the Head of the State, and that to these people the decisions of the Head of the State are to be considered as more important than the sacred directives of Islam?

The Egyptian woman worker had no right to maternity leave until the year 1959, when the new labour laws included specific sections dealing with the rights of women workers, one of which was the right to 50 days maternity leave with pay equivalent to 70% of the wage. The same legislation excluded women from certain occupations which it considered injurious to their health, or inappropriate to their special situation as women. In many cases these stipulations did harm to women workers since a lot of employers used them as an excuse to refuse employment to women, or to force them to accept lower wages or types of employment that did not correspond to their skills. This was especially true of employers in the private sector.

Women who are employed in government administration or elsewhere in the public sector are paid equal wages as compared to men. However, they are not afforded the same opportunities for promotion, or for appointment to responsible jobs, or for training directed towards the preparation of employees for the higher posts.

In the laws and regulations related to the system of pensions, there was a marked discrimination between the sexes which has been only partly remedied. At one time a woman could not have the benefit of her own salary or pension as well as that of her deceased husband. However, since 1971 a woman is allowed to combine both, and to be paid a part of her husband's pension which must not exceed 25 pounds per month.[8]

Egyptian and Arab society still considers that women have been created to play the role of mothers and wives, whose function in life is to serve at home and bring up the children. Women have only been permitted to seek jobs outside the home as a response to economic necessities in society or within the family. A woman is permitted to leave her home every day and go to an office, a school, a hospital or a factory on condition that she returns after her day of work to shoulder the responsibilities related to her husband and children, which are considered more important than anything else she may have done. Although some Arab countries such as Egypt, Algeria, Syria, Sudan, South Yemen, Somalia and Iraq have, to different degrees, followed policies which they consider as socialist, in none of these countries have any real steps been taken to solve the problems of working women, and above all to provide facilities that could reduce the burdens of cooking, cleaning, serving in the home, and bringing up the children. The provision of appropriate institutions or facilities does not seem to be a matter of importance to the rulers of these countries. The working women in these Arab countries have not yet become a sufficiently strong and organized force that could exert pressure on the State and ruling classes, and so ensure a more rapid and radical response to their needs. Women's organizations are still either groups of women from the upper classes seeking an outlet for their charitable or social inclinations, or sections of the socialist political parties or federations that have no independent existence or initiative of their own and function as passive bureaucratic appendages only marginally concerned with the real problems of women in general, or of working women in particular.

Undoubtedly, the employment of women outside the home has helped them to attain a greater degree of freedom and independence from the husband or father. This is particularly so since Islam has clearly given women the right to control their own possessions and money, without any form of tutelage by the men.[9] Nevertheless, work and a job can be a new form of exploitation if it is within the context and social circumstances of a class society which is governed by unequal relations between people of different social strata or sexes, or of a patriarchal family where the man dominates the woman, body and mind, in accordance with law, customs and religious legislation. For if a woman's body and mind are enslaved, how can she be free to dispose of her money? Is it possible for a woman who is afraid that her husband might divorce her at any moment, to oppose him when he interferes with the way she handles her own earnings? The law can force a woman to return to her husband, and send her back under police escort, so how can she be free to dispose of her money, when she is not even free to dispose of her life?

That is why jobs and work for women outside the home have not yet led, in general, to the liberation of the Arab woman, and in most cases have only burdened her with new anxieties, problems and responsibilities.

Work for any human being, whether man or woman, can never liberate the body and the mind and become a really human experience unless it is linked to, and carried out within the framework of a just society which affords equal opportunities to all, based on their capacities and talents, and not on the class or sex to which they belong.

Despite the ever growing number of employed and educated women in the Arab countries, the great majority of them still do not know even how to read or write. The educational system so far has played almost no role in ridding society of the outmoded conventions and customs and conservative ideas that still hold sway over the minds of both men and women. Even educated people are still dominated by backward concepts, superstitions and fantasies that have been handed down to them by their mothers and fathers, and that are often taken up and repeated by Arab rulers, politicians and thinkers. Thus people continue to be misled and exploited.

Many of the regimes in the Arab countries are still very far from being socialist or progressive, and continue to co-operate either openly or surreptitiously with the imperialist and reactionary forces in the world. To serve their purposes, they have built up powerful cultural and informational systems that are busy spreading misleading and superficial concepts and ideas. The content of educational curricula has remained rigid, unimaginative and incapable of responding to the needs of children and adolescents growing up in a fast-changing society. Here again, the attempt is to breed conformist, confused and obedient citizens, to ensure that they will not become agents of change. Education remains far removed from the life of society and depends on cramming young heads with innumerable and irrevelevant details. The different branches of knowledge are taught in water-tight compartments and little is done to show how different phenomena are interrelated. There is no attempt to build up a comprehensive understanding of the world, of society and history, and no real effort to show the real causes that lie behind the problems faced in life. Independent thinking, broadmindedness, tolerance and initiative are not encouraged. On the contrary, the aim is to train an army of passive, mediocre citizens, well suited to become bureaucrats in an administrative system, punctual executors of decisions taken by others, and submissive to authority, rulers and leaders. In this well regimented effort, the place assigned to women is that of a continued subservient role, whether at work or in the family, in both of which she is supposed to bend herself to the will and dominion of men.

Among the most serious obstacles that confront Arab women in so far as their employment and work is concerned are the laws related to marriage and civil rights. These laws still give the husband an absolute right to prevent his wife from taking on a job, travelling abroad, or even going out of her home whenever she desires. Arab societies once more have adopted a contradictory attitude calculated to perpetuate the exploitation of women by allowing it to take on other forms. Women, especially in the poorer classes, are being encouraged or even pressurized to seek employment in factories, offices and fields, and yet at the same time they are left totally at the mercy of their husbands whose permission must be sought for this purpose. The husband is not restricted by any rules, and the decision is totally his, irrespective of how arbitrary it may be. The criterion will almost always be the way in which he conceives of his authority, his interests and his needs. Women are thus the subjects of a double exploitation. They are exploited by the State and the employers on the one hand, and by the husbands on the other. Their efforts in the factories, offices and fields are badly needed by the State. Therefore, in a few Arab countries, there has been some hesitation about giving the husband an absolute right to prevent his wife from seeking employment or going out to work. For, if the men should think of exercising such a right, it might have dire consequences for the economy of a country. Women's labour in many areas is crucial, especially in so far as agricultural activities, State administration, a number of specific areas of industrial production and certain professions are concerned. As a result, governments tend to adopt an ambiguous stand.

The labour laws in some countries like Egypt, Syria and Iraq allow women to be employed outside the home. Yet marriage regulations and common law give the husband an uncontested right to refuse his wife permission to leave the house, go to work, or travel. The position taken by such Arab governments is in flagrant contradiction with the Universal Declaration of Human Rights which considers the right to work as one of the essential and inviolable rights of men and women in any society. It is also in contradiction with the precepts and laws which govern human activities, whether these have been prescribed by the authority of men on earth or by the authority of God in heaven. These laws and precepts not only consider work as a right to be enjoyed by all human beings, but also impress upon all people the need to engage themselves in work for the good of society, and portray it as one of the virtues and human qualities which should be rewarded and encouraged. The position of Arab governments is again contradictory: while their representatives in international organizations and conferences declare that women have now been liberated and given their rights, how can they explain the fact that at the same time a special committee dealing with the status of Arab women has been set up under the Arab league. This Committee in one of its decisions has emphasized that 'women should be accorded the complete right to work unless the husband has insisted on including in the marriage contract a clause to the contrary. However, even if this is the case, a wife has the right to go before a court to obtain permission to work if a new situation has arisen which necessitates this change.'

Despite the limitations of this clause, the rules of marriage and common law have not been amended accordingly, and the husband still exercises an absolute authority to prevent his wife from working. This is true of most Arab countries including those that have declared their policies to be socialist-oriented. The Federation of Syrian Women, for example, continues to demand the right of women to work, and that no divorced woman should be deprived of the charge of her children if she seeks employment.[10]

The common law in Egypt gives the husband the right to prevent his wife from working if he so wishes. In the new draft law which has not been promulgated,[11] only a few minor changes have been made in the clauses which were previously in force, and these have not affected the essential authority of the man over his wife. One of the clauses is related to women's work, and stipulates that it is the husband's right to prevent his wife from working unless she insists on including her right to work in the marriage contract drawn up between them at the time of betrothal. In this case, the husband is not allowed to prevent his wife from working unless there arises a situation which would do harm to the interests of the family if she insists on applying the clause.

All this goes to show how Arab countries continue to take a very hesitant attitude insofar as the right of married women to work is concerned, despite the fact that this right has always been considered a fundamental human right in all international charters, legislation, committees and organizations including the Arab League. It is well known how husbands take advantage of their prerogatives, and how they manoeuvre under the guise of the higher interests of the family and the children to strip women of their rights. In actual fact most husbands in so doing are only thinking of their own narrow interests at the expense of society, the woman and even their children. According to where they feel the most benefit to themselves lies, they will either stand between their womenfolk and work, or encourage and even pressurize them to look for employment if the extra income will come in useful to them.

One of the most important motives for the opposition to women's work shown by many husbands is the fear that independent earnings will lead the wife to be more conscious of her personality, and her dignity, and that therefore she will refuse to accept the humiliations she was subjected to before, refuse to be beaten or insulted or maltreated, reject her husband's playing around with other women or marrying another woman or keeping a mistress, and reject an empty and indolent life at home which saps her of any self-respect or strength to defend herself as a human being.

It is very common to read in Arabic newspapers about husbands who have no qualms in upsetting the life of their women just to satisfy a desire to exploit or dominate them. To illustrate the callousness with which men often treat their wives, let us take one of the incidents published by the daily newspaper *El Akhbar* under the title 'A summons from the husband to his wife: Leave your job immediately'. The court decides: 'A woman who works without the permission of her husband should be considered an outcast.'[12]

If we come to the clause which permits the wife and husband to include in their marriage contract her right to work outside the home, we will find that such a stipulation has relevance only to a very small number of exceptional women who have fought sufficiently hard to stand up to society and the family, and to be independent economically, morally and psychologically. This is very difficult for a girl who is only on the verge of marriage and, therefore, usually still very young even though she may have a high school or university education, or have occupied a job for many years. The traditions and pressures of society and the family are usually too heavy for her to insist on including such a clause in her marriage contract. It is very much like one of the original clauses in the law of marriage which gave woman the right to divorce if originally included as a stipulation in the marriage contract. This did not in any way limit the man's almost absolute freedom to divorce his wife at any time, and only made her his equal in so far as divorce was concerned. But where was the girl or woman in a highly traditionalist society who would have the audacity to insist on such a clause? In addition, where was the man who would climb down from his male throne and accept the contempt of his family and friends by agreeing to his young wife's right to divorce, or even agreeing that she should dare impose on him any conditions at all before marriage? This would be tantamount to upsetting the established and almost eternal order of things, for the man who comes forward to marry a woman or girl is always in a superior position. He is the one that is desired, sought for eagerly, and even pursued, and therefore it is his natural prerogative, his right, and not that of the girl to impose conditions. The girl, in any case, has usually no say at all either in the choice of man, or in the marriage, for it is the father or the family who have decided everything.

For most Arab men, to even think of a wife working outside the home is nothing more nor less than a direct reflection on his position and prestige as a male, and an affront to him as a man. The maleness of a man or his manliness is still considered to reside mainly in his capacity to rule over his wife, to dominate her, to cater to her needs financially, and not to allow her to mix with other men in offices, on the streets, or in a public transport. This is especially so if he is a real 'he man', a man with a capital 'M'. Cultured Arab intellectuals, on the whole, have been able to overcome these complexes, but most other men are still captive to such ideas. An Arab man might be obliged to allow his wife to work outside the home for economic reasons, but deep down within himself he will always feel his inability to provide for his family alone as a weakness or something to be ashamed of. The working wife herself might even share his reactions and feel some contempt for him because he is obliged to make her work. A wife who does not work may, in turn, take pride in the fact that her man is sufficiently well off to take care of her needs. All these distorted ideas and feelings are due to the fact that woman's work outside the home does not of itself lead to the true liberation of the woman as long as it continues to operate within the framework of a class society and under the patriarchal system.

References

1. Ahmed Ezzat Abdel Kerim, *El Taaleem fi Ahd Mohammed Ali,* Maktabat El Nahda El Masria, 1938, p.297.

2. Ibrahim Abdou, Doria Shafik, *Tatawour El Nahda El Nissaiya min Ahd Mohammed Ali Ila Ahd Farouk,* Cairo, Al Aadab, 1945,p.41.

3. Zeinab Farid, *Tatawour Ta'aleem El Bint fi Masr fil Asr El Hadith,* Risalat Magisteir Gheir Manshoura, Koliyet El Tarbia, November 1961.

4. *El Mara'a El Misria fi Eishreena Aman (1952-1972),* Markaz El Abhath wal Dirasat El Soukaneya. Al Gihaz El Markazi Lilta'abia El Ama wal Ihsa'a, p.51-72.

5. Al Ittihad Al Aam El Nissa'i, Legnat El Dirassat Al Markazeya, *El Mara'a El Arabia fil Kotr El Souri* p.49.
6. *El Akhbar,* daily newspaper, 12 January 1976, under the title *Gawla fi Tareek El Tasheeh* by Ahmed Fathy El Kadi.
7. Nassar, *Houkkouk El Mara'a fil Tashre'e El Islmai Wal Dawli El Mokaran,* Dar El Nashr wal Sahafa Alexandria, 1957, p.147.
8. *Kanoun El Ma'ashet El Misri,* No. 62, 1977.
9. Ahmed Khairat, *Markaz El Mara'a fil Islam,* Dar El Maaref, Cairo, 1975, p.6.
10. Al Ittihad El Aam El Nissa'i, *El Mara'a El Arabia fil Koutr El Souri,* El Matba'a wal gareeda El Rasmia, 1974, p.28.
11. *Al Ahram,* Cairo daily newspaper, 29 February 1976.
12. *Akhbar El Yom,* Cairo, 26 July 1975, p.10. .

20. Marriage and Divorce

Laws of marriage and divorce in Arab countries are mainly based on Islamic legislation which in turn is drawn from the Koran, the sayings or *'Ahadith'* of the Prophet Mahomet, and the studies of Islamic thinkers and men of knowledge aimed at explaining and developing the ideas contained in these two sources.

The verses of the Koran and the sayings of the Prophet do not relate to a single period of time, but are spread over many years. Since each verse or saying was linked to a particular circumstance or incident, and to a particular setting in terms of place and time, they often tended to embody conflicting directives or instructions, or at least an orientation which was not always in conformity with a uniform line of thinking. This is especially true in relation to the life of women, and their problems.

Islamic legislation punishes the thief by ordering that his hand be cut off. However, the legal systems of Egypt and the Arab countries have not included this provision in their jurisprudence. Other laws have replaced this rather severe sentence. For, if we study the history of the Arab countries, it will not be difficult to observe that the political power of the State was never at a loss when it came to promulgating laws that were in contradiction with Islamic precepts and legislation. No religious institution was able to oppose these laws. On the contrary, religious authorities and institutions very often co-operated with the State and political leadership, and submitted religious teachings to the exigencies of politics by looking for, and finding new explanations for, old religious texts which corresponded to the wishes and needs of the rulers. Islamic institutions changed and developed the ideas and explanations of the religious authorities with the aim of adapting them to modern society just as the Christian Church did when the winds of change and modernization swept through Europe.

The political leaders and the State moved rapidly in the task of changing religious legislation so as to ensure that it remained in line with the economic structures that were under continuous remoulding as society moved from one stage to another, from feudalism to capitalism and then to socialism. The same political leaders and the same State apparatus, which acted so decisively and quickly in so far as religious legislation related to economic needs was concerned, reversed its attitude in the question of women's status and suddenly became as slow, lethargic and negative as it had been fast moving, dynamic and full of initiative. Changes in religious legislation related to marriage and women's life were kept in abeyance. The reason for these two diametrically opposed attitudes is obvious. Political power and the State throughout history have reflected the interests of the ruling class. The powers that dominated were not only the representatives of a class structure, but also the representatives of a patriarchal system where the man is king. In addition, many of the economic and social changes that took place did not reach deep into society and did not strike at the root of exploitation because they were not accompanied by a wide, truly democratic mass movement.

No wonder therefore, that the majority of women in America and Europe lose their names after marriage and take their husbands' name instead. Many of them also do not have the right to control their financial resources and dispose of them according to their own free will. Arab wives are better off than their American and European sisters as far as these two areas are concerned, since an Arab woman keeps her name after marriage and disposes of her money in full freedom and without requiring any form of permission from her husband. These are the only remaining and very minor vestiges of the matriarchal system that prevailed in Arab society before Islam, and of the broadmindedness and tolerance of Mahomet the Prophet of Allah, when compared with other prophets and religious leaders. However, despite the fact that Arab women keep their name (their father's name, of course) after marriage, and have the legal right to manage their own property, income and money, yet the laws bind them very tightly and the customs make the husband the arbiter and controller of a woman's destinies and therefore, obviously, of what is much less important, her money. So these vestigial rights lose most of their practical significance, and often do not come down from the realm of theoretical assumptions to that of solid reality.

The State and political leaders in some Islamic countries, such as South Yemen, Somalia and Tunisia, have been able to break away from the strict application of Islamic legislation in the legal provisions related to marriage, divorce, abortion, etc., and have promulgated new laws which have abolished polygamy, restricted man's right to divorce, legalized abortion and accorded women the same share of inheritance as men. The Somali State has gone even further, and allows government officials not to fast in the month of Ramadan so that production does not drop.

Religious thinkers and leaders all along have differed in the opinions that they uphold according to whether their interests are linked with the *status quo* and reactionary forces, or alternatively are an expression of their sympathy for the poor and oppressed people in the towns and villages. Many of them also change their opinion from time to time according to the political thinking and ideology of those who are in power.

Sheikh Mohammed Abdou was one of the Moslem religious pioneers of the late 19th and early 20th centuries who opposed polygamy and who said that, if it did have a rationale or responded to a need in the early stages of Islam, it was certainly harmful to the Islamic nation in the modern era. Sheikh

195

Ahmed Ibrahim in his turn insisted that:

> We must take the initiative to formulate a comprehensive common law regulating marriage and divorce and analyse the opinions of the different schools of thought and of the legislations in a new light, more in conformity with the scientific awakening and the fundamental changes that have occurred in recent times. We must build our laws on two religious cornerstones. The first cornerstone is that of Islamic legislation in all its original simplicity and purity, the second cornerstone is that of people's lives and the realities proved by scientific thought in different stages of our development and in different places.[1]

Islam is considered one of the most tolerant and least rigid of religions, rational in many of its aspects, adaptable and leaving scope for change. It, therefore, permits what is known as *igtihad,* or original interpretation (not copied, or repeated). The religious leaders of the different schools of Islamic thought always considered *igtihad* a necessity. Even Imam Ahmed Ibn Hanbal, who was the leader of that religious sect or school of Islam (out of four such schools) considered to be the most rigid and orthodox of all, always insisted that *igtihad* or original interpretation, was absolutely necessary and that the existence of independent thinkers with a capacity for original understanding and interpretation was a condition which could not be done away with in any period if 'competence' was to be attained. Ibn Toumaima insisted that the scope for original interpretation should be kept wide open to all people, and that they should be allowed to think freely and not be obliged to adhere strictly to the fixed ideas of a school or sect. Commenting on the freedom for *igtihad* and the independence which mogtahideen (original thinkers) should enjoy, he says: 'This is a difference in time, and not a difference in truth. If the leader had lived in our time, he would have said what we say.'

If we study the question of polygamy as dealt with in Islam, we will find that the opinions of religious thinkers differed widely. A group of them believe that Islam does not allow polygamy and base their position on what was mentioned in the Koran under 'Sourat El Nissa': 'Marry as many women as you wish, two or three or four. If you fear not to treat them equally, marry only one. Indeed you will not be able to be just between your wives even if you try.'[2]

This group of religious thinkers insists that Islam has forbidden polygamy, since a man is not permitted to marry more than one woman unless he can treat his wives equally and not differentiate in the slightest degree between them. And the Koran then goes on to say that this is impossible no matter how hard a man tries. Logic suggests that to marry several wives implies a preference, a preference for the new wife over the preceding one. This preference in itself is sufficient to make equality and justice impossible even if the man were to be the Prophet himself. As a matter of fact, the Prophet was not able to treat his wives with absolute equality. One of the conditions was to divide the nights he spent with them equally, so that they all enjoyed the same opportunities for companionship, love and pleasure. But Mahomet was human and was not always able to keep to such a rigidly just division of his nights. He used to prefer Aisha to his other wives and loved her more deeply. Aisha, in one of her stories, explains:

'Souda, the daughter of Zama'a (she was one of Mahomet's wives), grew old. The Prophet of Allah, Allah's blessings and peace be upon him, used not to visit her often. She had heard of the special place I held in his heart, and knew that he spent more nights with me. She feared that he might abandon her and that she might lose whatever place he had for her in his feelings. So she said to him, "Oh Prophet of Allah, the day that is meant for me you can take for Aisha, and you are relieved of your promise." And the Prophet of Allah, Allah's blessings and peace be upon him accepted her offer.'[13]

Furthermore, in the book *El Tabakat El Kobra,* it is said that Hafsa, the wife of the Prophet, went out one day. The Prophet of Allah sent for his woman slave who came to Hafsa's house. When Hafsa returned and entered through the door, she found the Prophet with the woman. She said to him, 'O Prophet of Allah, in my house, on my day and in my bed!' And the Prophet of Allah answered: 'Be silent, I swear to Allah that I will never touch her again. But say nothing about what happened.'[4]

Other religious thinkers believe that divorce in Islam is not the absolute right of the husband, and that he must consult a judge first, and not take a decision completely on his own, as happens in our day.

The common law governing marriage and divorce which is in force in Egypt can be considered, and justly so, one of the most backward in all the Arab countries, and one of the most unjust and arbitrary as far as women are concerned. This law was promulgated in 1929, which means that the destinies of Egyptian women living today are governed by a law almost half a century old, and which allows men to continue their shameful and inadmissible oppression and exploitation of women.

The Egyptian Federation of Women, together with other groups of women and enlightened men, made repeated and stubborn attempts to change the common law or at least modify some of its clauses, but hardly any results were attained.

Many people think that Islamic precepts and legislation are the main obstacle to change insofar as the common law is concerned. Yet the same Islamic precepts and the very same legislation have not prevented other Islamic countries from making the necessary modifications, or even promulgating entirely new laws. Furthermore, Islam has not prevented the profound legislative and judicial changes in other spheres that were made in Egypt after 1952. Examples of such laws are those related to a ceiling on land holdings, or the new clauses introduced into the penal code in relation to adultery and theft. In these last two areas, the new rulings are definitely not in line with

Islam in which the punishment for theft is cutting off the culprit's hands, and that for adultery stoning both the woman and the man to death.

The laws on marriage and divorce in Egypt still allow the man to divorce at will and to have several wives. A man with a wife and ten children can give them up in the twinkling of an eye if one day, while walking down the street, he happens to meet a woman who arouses his desire and agrees to marry him. Such happenings are not a figment of the imagination, but occur every day and bring with them untold misery and suffering to women and to children.

A new draft law aiming at modifying the common law legislation in existence was published recently. The newspapers announced that it had been widely discussed by the religious authorities over a period of years, and that as a final step it had been submitted to the highest religious body in the country, namely the Institute of Islamic Studies. The suggested amendments brought about by the new draft law were published in the issue of the daily, *Al Ahram,* dated 29 February 1976. Anyone familiar with the original legislation would immediately perceive that in essence the new draft has not changed anything, and that the almost absolute right of men to give free rein to their sexual whims and fantasies has not been touched, since they can still divorce with the same ease. The relevant clauses stipulate that it is the man who decides on divorce, on condition that he is in full possession of his reason, mentally balanced, sober, not under the effect of a sudden blow, or surprise, or anger. But it is the husband who decides whether all these conditions are fulfilled. In other words, he himself decides if his reason and mental balance are intact, if he is sober or not, angry or not, and under the effect of a sudden surprise. Thus he is his own judge, or to be more precise, both plaintiff and judge at one and the same time. One of the clauses in the new draft also stipulates that a husband can be divorced from his wife if he says three times in succession: 'You are divorced. You are divorced. You are divorced.' all in one breath, or at one go. This is considered one divorce just as was the case previously when a husband could say 'I divorce thee thrice' and be considered to have divorced his wife once. A husband has the right to three divorces. However, if after one of these divorces his ex-wife gets remarried, it is no longer counted and once she returns to his fold he regains his right to three divorces!

The woman in the new draft law has gained some minor rights which, however, remain illusory and even laughable. One of them is her freedom to refuse to live with her husband's other wife or wives under the same roof. The second is to seek a divorce if her husband marries another woman. Now if we examine the situation of women in Egypt, most of whom are poor peasant women, working as unpaid labourers in their husband's field and home, or poor city dwellers. We wonder where is the woman who will have the courage to ask for a divorce when she knows that her fate will be either to be thrown out on the street to fend for herself under very difficult circumstances, or to return to her family's house where she will be another unwanted or rather doubly unwanted female, since she will have become a permanent burden, with little or no chance of remarrying. The woman who decides to live alone is a prey to moral and economic vagrancy. She is shunned by all in a society which considers divorce for women as a shame, and yet which is accustomed to exploit their work in farm and home without paying them a wage.

Another 'right' accorded to women in this new draft law is to travel on pilgrimage without her husband's consent, on condition that she is accompanied by a man 'forbidden' to her (namely, her father or brother). She is, however, obliged to travel with her husband wherever he may be required or wishes to go. As reagrds the system of *Beit El Ta'a*, a court decision compelling a woman to return to her husband under police escort can no longer be enforced.

It is clear that all these minor changes have not affected in any way the essence of a backward and archaic attitude to women, embodied in *Beit El Ta'a*, and the injustice which is still the lot of a married woman in Egypt. Furthermore, the changes are in glaring contradiction to Islamic precepts and legislation, no matter what the responsible religious authorities may say, precepts which are built on the humane principle: 'Let man and woman live together in kindness and mutual help and, if they part, let them separate in the same way.'

Problems of divorce and polygamy in Egypt are not the problems of women alone, but also of men and children. Many a time do we learn of children who have been left without food or shelter after a divorce, or divorced women who have been driven to prostitution as their only means of livelihood, or young daughters abandoned by their fathers for the arms of a mistress or the bed of a new wife. Divorce for a woman can sometimes mean a salvation and an escape from the sufferings of her life, a salvation and an escape which is usually never within her reach, or only a gift thrown at her by her husband. No matter what the situation is, it is always the husband who makes the decision. One word from him can mean divorce; yet at other times he may obstinately refuse to divorce his wife, intent on proving his authority, on showing that he is the lord and master, or on keeping his wife as an enslaved domestic servant. He is supported in whatever position he takes by unjust and cruel laws. He can force his wife to come back to him by getting a court decision, only for her to find on her return that he now has another woman in the house.

But the most difficult situation is perhaps that of the divorcee who has no job, or no income from which she can live, and who has to make do with the miserable pittance she may get from her husband as allowance. In most cases, however, the wife never receives anything, for the man is able to sidetrack the law itself in a multitude of ways, or because the law itself is so deficient and indulgent towards men that he has no difficulty in escaping his obligations and may even be encouraged to do so.

One of the strangest stories I have read in this connection was once again published in the daily, *El Akhbar*, which has a keen smell for sensation. This was on the 21st of September 1975 under the title 'No allowance for a woman who goes on a pilgrimage without her husband's consent.'

It is not necessary to enter into the details of the farce entitled Alimony. Suffice it to say that it is only a temporary and meagre entitlement, that is soon discontinued at the slightest excuse, after which the divorced woman remains without an income and without anyone to look after her.

A paid job is of course a protection as far as a woman is concerned, and provides her with a steady source of income which caters to her vital needs. But an unemployed woman without a husband is most often left to the mercy of the streets — without work, and with no income; and alone she has to fend for herself, to literally get her loaf of bread from the jaws of an avid and pitiless society. She must learn the art of stealing if she decides to be a thief, or the tricks of man-baiting if she decides to make money out of her body. In both situations she is exposed to ending in prison. And for such women there is a women's prison in El Kanatir on the outskirts of Cairo — a yellow stone building with rows of narrow barred windows, squat and ugly and monstrous, in the midst of flowering gardens and wide expanses of green fields.

My footsteps took me to El Kanatir. I had always wanted to see a prison or even spend a few days in one if necessary. There I met a variety of women, the outcasts, the downtrodden suffering street walkers, the unrecognized, anonymous and pitiful victims of a class society and a patriarchal system. Women who had been deprived of a chance for education, or an opening for work because of blind tradition, or lack of material opportunities, or for a multitude of other reasons. Women who had lost their husbands through death or more often divorce. Women deprived of any form of legal justice, since the law will punish the prostitute but not the man who climbs up to her room.

No matter how unhappy these women may be, I realized that day on my way back home that they were perhaps more fortunate than others. At least they had a roof over their head, a meal to eat even if it smelt, a rough tunic to wear, a thin blanket for cover, and some companionship in the cell. Thousands of other women having lost all sources of income lead a humiliating life. The day comes when a divorced woman no longer receives her allowance. Often she is left without shelter, constrained to move from one relative's house to another, begging for her meals or seeking a few feet on which to spread her tired body. In many cases she ends up as a domestic servant, a prey to blows, insults and harrowing work that starts at the break of day and extends late into the night, a victim of sexual aggression which she will accept to keep her job and a roof over her head.

Following divorce, and despite her difficult position, it is the mother who most often assumes the responsibility and burden for bringing up and educating her children after separation from the husband. Once again her inferior position, her feeling of maternal responsibility imposed upon her by society, her fear of being criticized by those that are around her, since people are much more severe with a woman who neglects her children than with a man, her love for her children as a human being and as a mother, the unlikelihood of her getting married again (marrying a divorced woman is like having a stale meal), the constraints that surround a woman's personal and social freedom, the irresponsibility of the father with regard to his children (which makes the woman who has been separated from her husband even more bound to her children), all these factors together make a divorced woman much more conscious of her responsibility towards her children, much more attached and linked to them, and much more determined to give herself completely to serving them and bringing them up. The man on the other hand, who never loses his freedom to indulge in sexual licence, pleasure, marriage or love, can afford to forget about his children, or at least not be too much taken up with them. We rarely hear of a father who divorced his wife and then devoted himself totally to the care and upbringing of his children. In addition, most men divorce their wives in order to marry another. He therefore tries to get rid of his children so that he can give himself fully to the enjoyments in store for him with his new wife. If this is not possible, it is the children who are made to suffer at the hands of the stepmother, with whom the father will usually side against his own children.

Despite all these facts, the new draft of the common law wrests from the mother the charge of her children after the age of seven for boys, and after the age of nine for girls. The girl over the age of nine is obliged to live with her father whether she likes it or not. The boy at the age of seven can choose between living with the father or with the mother. Where is the attempt to think of the welfare and future of the girl in this law? Where is the justice, the humanity, the commonsense in forcing a young girl of nine to go and live with her father and stepmother when she yearns to remain with her mother?

Why this violation of mothers' rights to the advantage of the father? How do the responsible authorities who are legislators so easily forget that young girls who have been led astray and made to become prostitutes, are very often the neglected children of a father who has remarried, or has taken a mistress on whom he spends all his money and showers all his affection and care? Most of these girls are the victims of poor families torn and disrupted by divorce or a father with several wives.

One of the strangest and most unimaginable provisions in the laws of marriage and divorce in Arab countries relates to what is commonly known in our language as *Beit El Ta'a* or the 'House of Obedience' and the description which is sometimes applied to wives *El Neshouz* (the 'Freak', the 'discordant one', or the outcast). The word *Nashiz* is a common word in the Arabic language and is used to describe a wife who disobeys her husband's orders even if that husband should be a drunkard, a debauche, a pimp, a thief, or a drug trafficker.

If a husband beats his wife, with reason or without reason, and drives her to run away from him to her family's house, he can if he wishes by force of law, under what is called the *Beit El Ta'a*, send a police escort to drag her back to him. If she refuses to obey and come back, then she becomes in the eyes of the law, *Nashiz*.

Many Arab Islamic countries have already abolished this abhorrent and outrageous institution of *Beit El Ta'a* and have considerably modified the laws related to marriage and divorce. Yet Egypt, which in many ways has been a

201

pioneer of progress in the Arab region and which at one time led the whole world as far as civilization goes, still maintains the system of *Beit El Ta'a*.

People who say that *Beit El Ta'a* is based on Islam are either ignorant or dishonest. The Prophet of the Muslims frequently said that a woman should not be forced to live with a man she does not want, or whom she hates, and explained on several occasions that, to start with, a woman should be allowed to choose the man she is going to marry.

According to Islam also, a woman is allowed to tear up the marriage contract if she has been forced to conclude it, or was cheated when she entered into the marriage agreement. The Prophet himself broke up the marriage of Khansa'a, the daughter of Khozam El Ansaria, because she was forced into it by her father.[5]

The laws regulating marriage and divorce in Arab societies are in fact one of the legal remnants of feudalism and the patriarchal system where the woman becomes like a piece of land owned by the man, who is permitted to do as he wishes, to exploit her, to beat her, to sell her at any time via divorce, or to buy over her head, a second, third, or fourth wife. As regards the rights of the wife, they consist of equality of treatment with the other wives of her husband. Whether it is possible for a man to give the same treatment, care and affection to an old wife as he gives to a young one, or to a semi-used one as he gives to a new one, is of course another question, which is further complicated by the fact that he is the sole judge of his own behaviour.

When we come to the clauses that give the judge the right to divorce a woman from her husband, then we suddenly discover how strict the law can be. These clauses stipulate that such a divorce is allowed in only a certain number of situations or cases.[6] If a husband is imprisoned for a period exceeding three years, the divorce is not granted to the woman until the judge assures himself that the sentence passed on the husband in effect exceeds three years, that it is being executed, that more than a year has passed since the date of initial imprisonment and finally that the sentence is final (passed through all stages of appeal etc.). A woman can also ask for divorce if the husband is not providing her with the means of livelihood, or if he is certified insane, or is afflicted with leprosy, or has beaten her so often that she has been harmed (this implies that beating that has not led to harm is permissible), or if the husband has been absent for a long time. (All these cases necessitate the judge assuring himself that sufficient evidence of their *de facto* existence is available). The law, however, puts severe restrictions even if proof is forthcoming. For example, the wife will not be allowed to divorce the husband if she knew before marrying him that he was afflicted with the ill for which she wishes to divorce him, or if the affliction came on after marriage and she accepted the situation without immediately asking for a divorce.

Even in those Arab countries where there has been an attempt to limit the man's right to divorce, the matter has not been left completely to the judge as is the case with the wife, and the restrictions placed on his right to divorce have been nowhere nearly as severe as they are in the case of the woman. We should also not forget who the judge is. Is he not himself a man living within the relations of a feudalistic or capitalistic class society, afflicted with all the concepts and structures of a patriarchal system? Is not the judicial system and the police system a part of the State apparatus which decrees and governs and rules in the name of the dominant class in society, serving its interests and implementing its one-sided view of justice?

It will never be possible for an Arab woman to enjoy the same rights in marriage and divorce as the Arab man does, as long as the society remains divided into classes and dominated by the patriarchal system. The institutions of marriage and divorce, of prostitution and of illegitimate children are essential for the existence and continuity of the class and patriarchal society. Divorce was invented in order that the man may be able to be rid of the wife he does not any longer want, at the lowest possible price (the alimony or allowance, or delayed payment of dowry). The systems of divorce also permit him to ensure his ownership of any child that may be born after divorce provided the woman became pregnant when they were still married. Moreover he has the right to supervise and control her for a period of three months called *El Idda* to ensure that no child belonging to another man should possibly be allowed to slip in under his name and share the inheritance with his other children.

In all the social systems that the world has known since the birth of the patriarchal family, class society and slavery, the right to divorce has always in fact been the exclusive prerogative of man. Class society has made of woman a commodity to be bought and sold under different systems of dowry, alimony etc. Capitalist society liberated the peasants from the heavy chains of feudalism not for reasons of humanity but because the new capitalist class, the new productive forces were in need of the free unfettered labour of the 'liberated peasant' to work in the new factories springing up rapidly. Thus it was that labour itself became a commodity, sold on the market. The capitalist was assured of buying it at the cheapest possible price, just as women are bought cheaply by their husbands, and of being able to throw it back on to the market whenever his need for labour diminished, just as the husband does with a wife he no longer wishes to keep.

An Arab man can take back his wife during the first three months after divorce (*El Idda*) even against her wish, since she remains his property for that period of time before being finally and irrevocably separated from him. During these months she is in a transitional, floating, amorphous stage. She is his wife, and yet not his wife. She is not permitted to marry until the *Idda* is over, and she has to wait passively at the beck and call of her former husband who may ask her to return to his home at any time. Only once the *Idda* is completed, can she think of remarrying again.

The capitalist system instigated other far-reaching changes in which again the situation of the worker and the woman have much in common. It freed the serf as we have said and made of him a freed labourer to be employed at will in exchange for a wage, with the aim of ensuring an elastic supply and demand situation as far as labour was concerned. Similarly capitalism freed the woman from the serfdom of the home, again not for humane reasons, but in response to the need for women's labour in the factories. If, in addition, the capitalist system has accorded to women the same freedom of divorce as men in the advanced industrial countries, the aim has been to carry this process to its logical end, to ensure that female labour is rid of all constraints, floating, available on the market, and ready to respond to the employers' need when required. This necessitated that the woman be given a greater degree of freedom from the yoke of the man. New laws on marriage and divorce were promulgated under what came to be known as the Civil Marriage Laws. Modern capitalist society, in its never ending thirst for production and profit, continued to uproot vestiges of the feudal system and religious practices that no longer corresponded with its interests. The link between marriage and religion was severed just as religion was separated from the State, not for reasons related to human progress, nor out of a humane attitude towards women but so that the wheels of economic exploitation could turn more rapidly and more smoothly. Capitalism was undoubtedly the midwife to a tremendous and hitherto unknown progress, mainly by releasing tremendous productive forces and material possibilities. However, insofar as the 'soul' and humanity of men and women were concerned, it was a monster without pity.

These changes can perhaps explain why divorce rates are much higher in developed capitalist countries than they are in semi-feudal societies, why divorce is more frequent in cities and towns than it is in rural areas, and why these rates are rising rapidly among employed working women as compared with unemployed housewives living at their husbands' mercy, or peasant women working free of charge for their menfolk.

A study of divorce rates in Egypt[7] shows that they are around 2.9% in Cairo and Alexandria which are the two biggest cities with a heavy concentration of large and medium industry, big corporations and government establishments, and with the highest percentages of paid working women. These rates however drop to 1.2% in Kafr El Sheikh, 1.3% in Sohag, 1.4% in Menoufiah, 1.9% in Dakahlia etc. (these are different provinces in North and South Egypt).

The same picture with some minor variations can be found in all Arab countries. In Syria, for example, divorce rates are also higher among paid working women than they are among housewives.[8] For the first category it is 2.2%, whereas among the latter it is only 0.6%. Similarly, the marriage rates among working women are lower than they are among non-working women. The percentage of married women among employed women is only 46.7% whereas for housewives the corresponding figure rises to 78.2%.

These trends are understandable. A woman who can feed herself does not need to submit to the humiliation and oppression which are very often the destiny of married women who depend on their husbands to feed them and who fear to divorce because in divorce lies the threat of hunger.

If we leave aside the question of food, and come to sex, or to the need of women for sexual satisfaction, we find that marriage is the only available and possible relationship within which an Arab woman can practise sex. Premarital relations are severely forbidden to girls in Arab societies. This even applies to masturbation which also is considered as sinful. An unmarried or divorced woman, or a widow, cannot have sexual relations unless she marries. Such women, if they find no husband, will remain virgins or spinsters or widowers throughout their life. A woman may sometimes risk her reputation to build up a free relation with a man, but in that case she risks the scorn and contempt of society which will often consider her no better than a prostitute.

Nevertheless, in recent years, Arab countries have witnessed a growing number of paid working women, professionals, career women etc. who have to a large extent developed a spirit of independence both morally and mentally, and who refuse to be pressurized or obliged to submit to the patriarchal institution of marriage and divorce, who have chosen their own way of life, and obliged society to respect their free personality and recognize their work.

The great majority of Arab women, however, are still forced into marriage as their only way to satisfy essential bodily needs, and are still terrorized by the mere word 'divorce' which means hunger, no home, and the unrelenting remarks of those around them. They therefore accept any treatment at the hands of their husbands, no matter how bad, without rebelling or even complaining. A woman may even serve the second, third, or fourth wife of her husband, as often happens in Egyptian villages. Moreover things may go further, and a peasant woman sometimes goes in search of another wife for her husband in order to keep him happy, or to mitigate the degree of his cruelty towards her, or to ensure that he has a male child by this new wife, if she herself has been unlucky enough to give him only female children. For who is more unhappy or unfortunate than a peasant woman from an Egyptian village, who has not been able to have a son? Her lightest punishment is a blow on the face every now and then delivered by her husband with all the heavy weight of his hand, or his coarse and deafening voice shouting out for the slightest reason 'thou art thrice divorced'.

Sometimes a woman may prefer hunger, destitution and homelessness, to living with her husband. But in that case she will find all the doors to divorce securely locked. For the law is severe, very severe, and the judge also is severe, even more severe than the law. But severest of all will be the family, especially in an Arab rural setting. In this setting the family is not composed of father, mother and children only, it is not a nuclear family as it is in the cities and the developed industrial countries. It is an extended family composed of numerous members, a grandfather and grandmother, fathers and mothers, uncles both paternal and maternal, brothers and sisters, and children. These extended families are still the dominant pattern in Arab rural society, and they are the authority in all matters related to marriage and divorce for women. The decision is always taken in conformity with the interests of the family, and not those of the woman. She may be forced into divorcing a poor man in order to marry a rich one. Or she may never be allowed to divorce, and even if she runs away, she may be returned to her husband accompanied by a stream of insults, blows and humiliations of all sorts, especially if her family is poor and cannot afford to keep either her or her children. She is thus exposed to all the pressures and punishments of a veritable clan, cruel, exacting and insensitive to anything else but the exigencies of material gain or loss, and the laws of tradition.

Time and again, day in and day out, such crimes are perpetrated under the thick cloak of religious, moral and human values, and amidst a clutter of high sounding words about Islamic legislation, the duty of woman, the need to obey her husband and to respect him, the integrity of the family and the future of the children, and a host of other well worn phrases which women are so accustomed to hear.

The Arab man, on the other hand, is not supposed to take into consideration the integrity of his family and children, despite the fact that it is he who owns them, and not his wife. The law, religious legislation, and customs all permit men to deal in the most irresponsible way with their womenfolk and children. The law and religious legislation permit men to have four wives at the same time. The man can, however, outwit even this very liberal law and have more than four. This he does through the system which we have already examined called *Idda* which allows him to divorce a woman for three months and then ask her to return. In the meanwhile, she can be replaced by another wife. This means that the man can have four wives legally married to him at one time, and four others on *Idda,* that is women who were his wives until very recently but are now on a temporary divorce. This game of musical chairs can go on indefinitely and is another form of the old pre-Islamic *Zawag El Muta'a,* or marriage of pleasure, only made possible because of the extreme ease with which a man can divorce. Through *El Idda* a man can therefore have any number of wives, and can go on changing from one to another. This practice was very common among the richer people in the Islamic society of Somalia, especially after the abolition of concubinage and women slaves. Under the new regime, attempts are being made since 1969 to abolish it by changes in legislation and re-education, but old habits die hard especially where modernization processes are slow.

There are other forms of what may be called transitional marriages where the situation lies somewhere between marriage and non-marriage, and which are permitted by Islamic religious law to Islamic men. One of them is called *Mahr Sharti* in which the marriage lasts for a specified period of time. This period is usually short and the situation here again resembles *Zawag El Muta'a* or *El Zawag El Moakat* (temporary marriage). Another form is *Al Khotba El Siriya* where the man marries in secret so that his wife should not be angry or offended. These complicated arrangements sometimes lead to strange situations when the two wives meet by accident, or when the children of two different women meet a man when he is on a visit to their school, only to discover that they have the same father.

In Egypt, there is also a form of marriage known as *El Zawag El Orfi* in which no written marriage contract binds the two partners. This permits the man to lay his hands on the pension paid to his wife by the government if she happens to be the beneficiary of such a pension. The law deprives women of their government pension if they get married, and a written contract is evidence which cannot be denied. Many of my neighbours and friends had recourse to this contractless marriage. A woman in this situation would often be a hidden second wife, for ever threatened by insecurity and living in fear of the government, in fear of society, and in fear of her husband; driven to a fate over which she has no control, she remains alone and unprotected.

Statistics gathered in Tunisia, ten years after the promulgation of the new legislation which accords equal rights to men and women in divorce before a court of law, have shown that cases of divorce are becoming more numerous.[9] In addition, the percentage of divorce cases among working women is higher than it is among housewives. Many Arab commentators and writers have proffered repeated warnings against such tendencies which they consider to be symptomatic of the dissolution of the family, and of marriage ties, which poses a severe threat to the stability of Arab societies just as it has led in recent years to the break up of Western society. To their mind modern industrial relations carry with them a transformation of the old pattern of male dominance over women into a new phase of so-called equality between women and men. This leads to a rupture of the old solid marriage ties which existed previously between men and women, since the men no longer feel superior to women and therefore morally bound to shelter and protect them, a feeling which at one time made them hesitate to divorce easily.[10]

Some Arab intellectuals and thinkers consider that the rise in divorce cases is due to the economic independence enjoyed by an increasing number of Arab women, which permits them to escape from the stranglehold of men, since they can now fend for themselves even if alone.[11] This explanation is probably the correct one. For, indeed, why should a woman who can earn her own living submit to the humiliations of an unhappy marriage governed by the norms of a patriarchal autocracy?

Many Arab men resist these social changes and oppose the economic developments and needs which are drawing more and more women into seeking employment in commercial enterprises, industry, government departments and various professions. But the forces that are driving women out of their homes are so powerful that nothing can any longer stand up against them and oblige women to relinquish their new positions in life.

It is very clear nowadays that the extended patriarchal family has now relinquished many of the functions it originally used to fulfil in favour of the various bodies and institutions of the modern state. Arab societies are no longer composed of patriarchal tribes, and the state has usurped much of the authority and rights previously exercised by the father or husband. It is not difficult to foresee that this trend will continue and that the functions of the family will steadily shrink, and with them the authority once exercised by the male head of the family.

The Arab man used to be responsible for the protection of the family and its security. But at present the state has its own security and police forces that have replaced the man in the fulfilment of such functions, and which undertakes to ensure the security of the family and to punish all aggressors against it.

One of the areas of struggle between man and the state apparatus is that of family vengeance or vendettas, a practice which is still common in Upper or South Egypt. If a male member of a family is killed, the unwritten laws of custom dictate that his murderer must be killed in turn or, if this is not possible, a man from the family of the murderer. However, such acts of vengeance or vendettas have nothing to do with women which shows that they are considered objects of little value, and not human beings. A woman may be the cause of a vendetta but she never becomes the 'blood' which must be avenged.

The Arab man from Upper Egypt still believes that it is a subject of shame if the police or any of the security forces of the state replace him in taking revenge for his family. Honour implies that he must take vengeance for himself, without recourse to the state which is considered an admission of weakness.

Another field of struggle between the authority of man and that of the state is that of women's employment or paid work. Here too, the patriarchal family is fighting a losing battle, and is gradually giving up its prerogatives one after another in the areas of production, legislation, education, punishment, family planning etc.[12]

In Arab societies it is a fact that religion plays an important part in preserving the family structure. Nevertheless religion has been incapable of preventing the state and its institutions from usurping many of the functions, and thus much of the authority, once exercised by men within the family.

Religion has been separated from the state in Western industrial societies, and the powers of the Church have retreated in the face of the capitalist and technological offensive that has torn down many of the sacred values related to Christianity and the feudal system.

However, religion has not been separated from the state in most Arab Muslim countries. This is one of the factors that prevents many Arab thinkers from undertaking an objective critical analysis of the family as an institution, and of the changes it has been undergoing with time. Free thinking where religion is concerned is still a forbidden and dangerous pastime in most Arab countries in the same way as the exercise of freedom of thought is fraught with risks if exercised in the realm of politics and systems of government, especially if it extends to questions of class struggle. This is also true of sex and its related problems.

Three topics, a 'sacred trilogy'[13] are to be approached with care, or preferably not at all. They are religion, sex and the class struggle. Arab intellectuals and thinkers are afraid to deal with them in their writings, or at least to study them in depth. Most of the Arab or Islamic social reform movements, therefore, are characterized by the fact that they are limited to making superficial changes that do not affect the essence of the problems in society.

This weapon is brandished and used by many people, and in particular those who are busy plundering the riches of the Arab peoples, whether they sit in the board rooms of international companies or rule the destinies of these peoples from the Western and some of the Arab capitals.

Nevertheless, Arab thinkers and intellectuals are becoming much more bold and outspoken in their criticism of the injustices and oppression to which Arab women and men are exposed. Arab women also have gained a new courage in facing their societies and the problems that beset their lives. For they know that with liberation they stand to lose nothing else but their chains.

Freedom has a price, a price which a free woman pays out of her tranquility, her peace, her health, when facing the opposition and aggression of society against her. Be that as it may, a woman always pays a heavy price, in any case, even if she chooses to submit. She pays it out of her health, her happiness, her personality and her future. Therefore, since a price she has to pay, why not the price of freedom than that of slavery?

I believe that the price paid in slavery even if accompanied by some security, and the peace of mind that comes from acceptance, is much higher than the price paid for freedom, even if it includes the menaces and aggression of society. For a woman to be able to regain her personality, her humanity, her intrinsic and real self is much more worthwhile than all the approbation of a male dominated society.

References

1. *Magalat Kouliet El Houkouk Lil Mababith El Kanouneya Wal Iktisadeya*, First Year No. 1, Cairo, 1945.
2. *Koran, Sourat El Nissa:* Verse 3.
3. Mohammed Ibn Saad, *El Tabakat El Kobra*, Dar El Tahrir, Cairo, 1970, p.36.
4. *Ibid.*, p.134-5.
5. See *Saheeh El Bokhari*, Vol. 7, p.18 and *Al Isaba*, Vol. 8, p.65 and Abdallah Afifi *El Mara'a El Arabia fi Gaheleyatiha wa Islamiha*, Vol.2, p.60.
6. See *Ahkam El Ahwal El Shakhsia fil Shari'a El Islameya*, Abdel Wahab Khallaf. Matba'at Dar El Koutoub El Masria (Second Edition), 1938, p.165.
7. *El Mara'a El Masria fi Eishreen Aman (1952-1972)*, Markaz Fl Abhath Wal Dirasat El Soukania, El Gihaz El Markazi Lilta'abia El Aama wal Ihsa'a.
8. El Maktab El Markazi Lil Ihsa'a (Damascus), *Al Mara'a El Amila biloghat El Arkam*, Silsilit El Dirasat 20, pp.11-29.
9. El Sheikh Abdel Hamid El Sayeh, *Al Islam wa Tanzeem El Ousra*, I.P.P.F. Regional Office for the Middle East and North Africa, 1971, Vol. I, p.175.
10. Quoted from the Jordanian newspaper *El Destour* dated 8/9/1971: El Sheikh Abdel Hameed El Sayeh, *Al Islam Wa Tanzeem El Ousra*. IPPF Regional Committee for the Middle East and North Africa, 1971, Vol. I, pp.175-6.
11. *Ibid.*, p.218, Sayed Mohamed Zaffar.

12. See Salah Kansouah, *Ihtimalat Zawal Moussasat El Ousra fil Mougtama'a wal Dawla*, (Workshop on Family and Kinship), Kuwait University, November 1976.
13. See Bou Ali Yaseen, *El Thalouth El Moharram*, Dar El Talia, Beirut, 1973.

An Afterword

I have maintained that:

1. Islamic, Arab or Eastern cultures are not exceptional in having transformed woman into a commodity or a slave. Western culture and Christianity have subjected women to exactly the same fate. As a matter of fact, the oppression of woman exercised by the Christian Church and those who upheld its teachings has been even more ferocious.

2. The oppression of women is not essentially due to religious ideologies, or to whether she is born in a Western or Eastern society, but derives its roots from the class and patriarchal system that has ruled over human beings ever since slavery started to hold sway.

3. Women are not mentally inferior to men as many people would like to believe. On the contrary, history shows that women started to exercise the powers of their mind before men, and were the first to embark on the quest for knowledge. The first goddes of knowledge was Eve, later to be succeeded by the Pharaonic Isis.

4. The great religions of the world uphold similar principles in so far as the submission of women to men is concerned. They also agree in the attribution of masculine characteristics to their God. Islam and Christianity have both constituted important stages in the progress and evolution of humanity. Nevertheless, where the cause of women was concerned, they added a new load to their already heavy chains.

5. The emancipation of Arab women can only result from the struggle of the Arab women themselves, once they become an effective political force. This necessitates the formation of politically conscious, disciplined and well organized women's movements, and a clear definition of their objectives and methods of struggle as well as of the rights for which women must fight.

6. History has proved that revolutionary changes, wars of liberation and the radical transformation associated with the establishment of socialist systems, accelerate the pace of womens' emancipation. The Algerian war of liberation brought with it greater freedom for women, and the same process is taking place in the national struggle of the Palestinian people. The socialist revolutions in Europe, Asia, Africa and Latin America have succeeded in destroying many of the age-old chains that held women prisoners of oppression. This relationship is at the heart of the fundamental links that bind the

emancipation of women to the cause of people's liberation from imperialism, capitalism and class exploitation.

7. Arab women preceded the women of the world in resisting the patriarchal system based on male domination. Fourteen centuries ago, Arab women succeeded in opposing the unilateral use of the male gender in the Koran when its passages referred to both men and women. Their outspoken objection was couched in terms that have remained famous: 'We have proclaimed our belief in Islam, and done as you have done. How is it then that you men should be mentioned in the Koran while we are ignored!' At the time both men and women were referred to as Moslems, but, in response to the objections voiced by women, Allah henceforward said in the Koran: 'Al Mouslimeena Wal Mouslimat, wal Mou'mineena wal Mou'minat.' ('The Muslims, men and women, and the believers, men and women.')

8. In the traditions and culture of the Arabs and Islam, there are positive aspects which must be sought for and emphasized. Negative aspects should be exposed and discarded without hesitation. Women at the time of the Prophet obtained rights of which today they are deprived in most Arab countries.

9. The portrayal of Arab woman in past and contemporary Arab literature does not reflect a genuine image of her. It is Arab woman as seen through the eyes of Arab men, and therefore tends to be incomplete, distorted and devoid of a clear understanding and consciousness.